The Future of the Occupation of the Palestinian
Territories after Gaza

Erwin van Veen
Editor

The Future of the Occupation of the Palestinian Territories after Gaza

Scenarios, Stakeholders and 'Solutions'

Editor
Erwin van Veen
Clingendael Institute
The Hague, The Netherlands

ISBN 978-3-031-93797-2   ISBN 978-3-031-93798-9 (eBook)
https://doi.org/10.1007/978-3-031-93798-9

© The Editor(s) (if applicable) and The Author(s) 2025. This book is an open access publication.

Open Access This book is licensed under the terms of the Creative Commons Attribution 4.0 International License (http://creativecommons.org/licenses/by/4.0/), which permits use, sharing, adaptation, distribution and reproduction in any medium or format, as long as you give appropriate credit to the original author(s) and the source, provide a link to the Creative Commons license and indicate if changes were made.
The images or other third party material in this book are included in the book's Creative Commons license, unless indicated otherwise in a credit line to the material. If material is not included in the book's Creative Commons license and your intended use is not permitted by statutory regulation or exceeds the permitted use, you will need to obtain permission directly from the copyright holder.
The use of general descriptive names, registered names, trademarks, service marks, etc. in this publication does not imply, even in the absence of a specific statement, that such names are exempt from the relevant protective laws and regulations and therefore free for general use.
The publisher, the authors and the editors are safe to assume that the advice and information in this book are believed to be true and accurate at the date of publication. Neither the publisher nor the authors or the editors give a warranty, expressed or implied, with respect to the material contained herein or for any errors or omissions that may have been made. The publisher remains neutral with regard to jurisdictional claims in published maps and institutional affiliations.

Cover illustration: © Melisa Hasan

This Palgrave Macmillan imprint is published by the registered company Springer Nature Switzerland AG
The registered company address is: Gewerbestrasse 11, 6330 Cham, Switzerland

If disposing of this product, please recycle the paper.

Preface

The cease fire in Gaza of 19 January 2025 brought a belated, limited and yet welcome end to fifteen gruesome months of destruction. It was the beginning of an end in the sense that it could have closed out the most recent episode of violence in the history of Israel's occupation of the Palestinian Territories that started on 7 October 2023. Yet, this was not to be as the slaughter in Gaza turned into overt genocide. Hence, it was also the end of a beginning as the future of the Israeli occupation of the Palestinian territories faces major uncertainties such as widespread repression and insecurity, the grievances and destruction of Gaza, profound moral failure, the pro-Israel leanings of the Trump presidency, a weakened Iran, the support of most Israeli political parties for annexation, a Levant that lies in ruins and the rise of the Arab states on the Persian Gulf.

One thing is certain, however. Israeli's and Palestinians will mostly remain where they are and the question about the nature of their co-existence will persist. The poet Rumi remarked: 'don't try to put out a fire by throwing on more fire'. It is remarkable, then, that Israeli governments have for decades sought to bring safety and wholeness about by methods more likely to achieve the opposite. The creation of the contemporary state of Israel might be understood through the lens of the suffering of Jewish people throughout the centuries and the evil of the Holocaust, but it also commenced a road of pitiless violence, large-scale forced displacement and the dehumanization of another people, which is now winding its way through Gaza where Israeli atrocities have become too numerous to count. Yet, the brutal murders of 7 October 2023, the wholesale destruction of Gaza and the mass killing of its people suggest that worse might be to come, bearing in mind the words of Yousef after the loss of his wife and children in the massacre at the Sabra and Shatila refugee camps in 1982: 'I seek vengeance, nothing more. And nothing less. And I shall have it. And you shall see no mercy' (in Abulhawa's 'Mornings in Jenin').

We need to understand what the violence that results from occupation can look like after Gaza and, especially, to consider how it can be prevented from spiraling yet further. All of us have this duty as human beings capable of moral judgement and acting upon it. With this in mind, the bundle outlines scenarios for the future of occupation, provides a series of essays analyzing the interests and objectives of the main stakeholders of occupation, and offers reflections on how to create conditions that can enable new conversations about ending occupation as peacefully as possible.

The bundle is written in the language of geopolitics—analytical and somewhat distant. It does not do justice to the many stories, experiences and emotions that have been so powerfully rendered in works like Abulhawa's 'Mornings in Jenin', McCann's 'Apeirogon' or Smilansky's 'Khirbet Khizeh'. It aims to enrich the thinking and the acting of diplomats, intellectuals and activists all the same.

Brussels   Erwin van Veen
January 2025

Bibliography

Abulhawa, Susan. 2011. *Mornings in Jenin*. Paperback edition. London: Bloomsbury.

Ǧalāl-ad-Dīn Rūmī. 2004. *The Essential Rumi*. Translated by Coleman Barks. New expanded edition. New York: HarperOne.

Acknowledgement

During a gap year between secondary school and university, I spent four months working in a kibbutz on the shores of the lake of Galilee, one month earning pocket money by means of odd jobs in Eilat and six more months travelling the Levant, Egypt, Turkey and Iran. I suspect that this book is one of the subliminal culminations of a period in which hitchhiking through the West Bank was still possible and the hope of the Oslo Accords were fresh. I am deeply grateful to all those at the time that hosted me, spoke with me, accompanied me and helped me to marvel at the wonders of the region.

I have also been privileged over the years to talk, discuss, agree and disagree with remarkable Israeli's and Palestinians to whom I owe a debt of gratitude for sharing their experiences and perspectives.

I feel just as privileged to be in the company of the authors of this volume. We have put it together with the intent to shake up complacent policies and debates about the occupation of the Palestinian territories by providing more realistic avenues for reflection and action that are as evidence-based as possible. The point of an edited volume is to gather a variety of perspectives that, together, enrich our understanding of the matter at hand. It is therefore by no means a given that the authors contributing to this volume agree with all its different arguments and perspectives. They do agree I think, however, on the view that the current situation of occupation is a moral failure and requires profound change in respect of human dignity, life and rights.

Contents

1	Who Sows the Wind Will Reap the Storm Erwin van Veen	1
2	Scenarios for the Israeli Occupation of Palestine Erwin van Veen	19

Part I Direct Conflict Stakeholders

3	Hamas Walking the Path of Thorns Abdalhadi Alijla	43
4	The Palestinian Authority Watches Gaza Burn Mouin Rabbani	57
5	Israel: From Creeping to Decisive Annexation Gil Murciano	71
6	America's Enabling of Occupation Brian Katulis	87

Part II Neighbors

7	Hezbollah: Shaken to the Core Joseph Daher	101
8	Egypt as Israel's New Ally Maged Mandour	115

9   Jordan Between a Rock and a Hard Place   129
    Hasan M. Jaber

Part III   Regional Powers

10 Enduring Resistance from Tehran   147
    Hamidreza Azizi

11 The Rocky Road of Israeli-Saudi Normalization   163
    Paul Aarts

12 Let's Talk About Peace   179
    Omar Dweik and Erwin van Veen

Index   191

List of Contributors

Paul Aarts University of Amsterdam, Amsterdam, Netherlands

Abdalhadi Alijla Arab Reform Initiative (ARI), Paris, France

Hamidreza Azizi German Institute for International and Security Affairs (SWP), Berlin, Germany

Joseph Daher Bonn International Centre for Conflict Studies, Bonn, Germany

Omar Dweik University of Tilburg, Tilburg, Netherlands

Hasan M. Jaber University of Jordan, Amman, Jordan; Politics and Society Institute, Amman, Jordan

Brian Katulis Middle East Institute, Washington, DC, USA

Maged Mandour Political analyst, Zurich, Switzerland

Gil Murciano Mitvim Institute, Petah Tikva, Israel

Mouin Rabbani Jadaliyya, Fairfax, Virginia, USA

Erwin van Veen Clingendael Institute, The Hague, The Netherlands

LIST OF FIGURES

Fig. 2.1 Scenarios for the Israeli occupation of the Palestinian territories in the next 5–10 years 26
Fig. 2.2 Factors influencing the scenario driving forces 26

CHAPTER 1

Who Sows the Wind Will Reap the Storm

Erwin van Veen

Abstract The tragedy of 7 October 2023 left a searing scar on Israeli society, underlined the explosive state of fifty-eight years of occupation of the Palestinian territories and, paradoxically, accelerated Israeli annexation. A day of slaughter by Hamas, followed by months of forced displacement, starvation, destruction and mass killings of civilians by Israel—with genocidal intent if not results—put paid to existing ideas about conflict resolution. On the one hand, there may be no way back after the unspeakable atrocities that have occurred in Gaza. On the other hand, Israel has suffered huge moral and international damage by several legal judgments and a wave of global popular anger. It is also unlikely to become any safer. The complicating factor has been the growing involvement of Iran and the axis of resistance in the problem of occupation, both in supporting Hamas before 7 October 2023 and in launching a multi-front pressure campaign on Israel afterwards. This did not end well for Iran, but the risk is diminished, not gone. The challenge today is to understand how occupation can evolve given Israeli annexationist designs, weak Palestinian leadership and a mix of international neglect and

E. van Veen (✉)
Clingendael Institute, The Hague, The Netherlands
e-mail: eveen@clingendael.org

© The Author(s) 2025
E. van Veen (ed.), *The Future of the Occupation of the Palestinian Territories after Gaza*,
https://doi.org/10.1007/978-3-031-93798-9_1

negative involvement, especially from Iran and the US. The essay bundle undertakes this task by means of scenario planning and stakeholder analysis. It seeks to serve as an intellectual resource for conversation that can bring occupation to a peaceful end.

Keywords Occupation · Settlements · Oslo Accords · Hamas · Iran · Axis of resistance · West Bank · Gaza · Al-Aqsa

Setting the Scene

7 October 2023 brought home the message that the Israeli occupation of the Palestinian territories has produced an unstable situation ready to explode in unexpected ways with a concomitant risk of engulfing the Levant and even the Gulf. Hamas and a few other militant groups dragged the problem of occupation back to the center of Middle Eastern politics with a vengeance. In all likelihood, they succeeded beyond their wildest imagination. Yet, their massacre of over 700 Israeli and foreign civilians, as well as their abduction of over 250 hostages, were acts of infamy that call for justice (Independent International Commission of Inquiry on the Occupied Palestinian Territory, including East-Jerusalem, and Israel 2024). But these acts did not occur in isolation as they are backgrounded by decades of violent Israeli repression to maintain its occupation of the Palestinian territories since 1967.[1] In fact, Israeli occupation forces mete out a daily dose of death and humiliation to Palestinian civilians in the name of self-defense and combatting terrorism that, cumulatively, has produced far more casualties than those of 7 October 2023. The Israeli government also intentionally created 'hunger games'-type conditions in Gaza between 2007 and 2023 through a blockade, at times supported by Egypt (Baconi 2022). Israel portrayed its policy as a necessary response to the Hamas takeover of Gaza in 2007, but this itself was the result

---

[1] One can go back to the late nineteenth century for analysis of the Israeli-Arab/Palestinian conflict, including the writings of Theodor Herzl and the Hussain-McMahon correspondence (see e.g. Saʿīd et al. 2013). However, 1967 is a useful analytical starting point for the purpose of contemporary conflict analysis as it marks the start of Israel's occupation of the Palestinian territories which, in contrast to the foundation of the Israeli state in 1948, was not accepted by the international community.

of Israel, Fatah, the US and a number of European countries blocking Hamas from reaping the fruits of its legitimate electoral victory over Fatah in 2006 (Wagemakers 2024).

In light of Israel's—and at times Egypt's—blockade, it is no surprise that the 2012 UN Country Team's report on living conditions in Gaza made for grim reading even back then. The report also projected that the entire Gaza area would be unlivable by 2020 (United Nations Country Team in the occupied Palestinian territory 2012). Reality proved worse than the prognosis, in no small part due to violent confrontations between Israel and Hamas in 2014 and 2021 (Al-Shawaf 2023). In 1956, the Israeli general Moshe Dayan had already assessed violence originating from Gaza as follows:

> "Let us not cast the blame on the murderers today. Why should we declare their burning hatred for us? For eight years they have been sitting in the refugee camps in Gaza, and before their eyes we have been transforming the lands and the villages, where they and their fathers dwelt, into our estate." (Jewish Virtual Library, undated)[2]

Dayan went on to say that the only solution was to wield 'the steel helmet and the canon's maw' with iron determination. His words resonate in the present as Israel's military campaign in Gaza that followed the tragedy of October 7 has been brutal and included forced displacement, starvation tactics, indiscriminate mass killings of civilians and the deliberate destruction of civilian infrastructure (Levy 2023; Hage 2024; Hass 2024; Murphy 2024; UNRWA 2024; Van Veen 2024a). According to a growing number of experts, Israeli crimes include genocide (Bartov 2024; Mordechai 2025; Amnesty International 2024). In turn, Israeli politicians have justified their military tactics by equating the inhabitants of Gaza with Hamas militants (Republic of South Africa 2023), dehumanizing Palestinians (Mordechai 2025) and pointing to the interwovenness of militant and civilian infrastructure in Gaza's 365 km2 of dense and overpopulated urban terrain that its own policies and actions created (ICJ 2024, ICC 2024).[3]

---

[2] These lines are part of an eulogy for Roi Rotberg, a young security officer at the Nahal Oz kibbutz who died at the hand of Palestinian militants from Gaza in 1956.

[3] Note that the majority of the population of Gaza consists of Palestinian refugees displaced by the war of 1948 (and to some extent 1967), which Israel did not permit to

Perspectives on 7 October 2023 and Thereafter

Frames that contextualize 7 October 2023 and its aftermath diverge substantially. The Israeli government labeled the Hamas attack as a major act of terrorism against which it had to defend itself. It made the elimination of Hamas and the rescue of the hostages its primary war aims.[4] The tool it chose to accomplish these objectives was a massive military operation entitled 'Swords of Iron,' which started with bombardment and a ground invasion of Gaza City, gradually working its way down south to the town of Rafah bordering Egypt. Problematic aspects of Israel's framing and practices have included its intentional neglect of the preexisting condition of occupation, its dehumanization of Palestinians, a refusal to acknowledge the difficulty of eliminating an ideology of resistance, the tension between its war goals and the use of massive military force in a densely inhabited urban area.

The view of the Israeli public on October 7 and the war in Gaza offers a paradox. On the one hand, a Pew Research Center opinion poll of 30 May 2024 indicated that over two-thirds of Israeli's considered the government's military response against Hamas 'about right' or 'not going far enough' (Silver and Smerkovich 2024) with a poll of the Israel Democracy Institute (IDI) of February 2024 recording 68% of Israeli Jews being opposed to the provision of humanitarian aid to Gaza as long as Hamas had not released the hostages (Hermann and Kaplan 2024), even though Israel as occupying power is obliged to provide adequate humanitarian conditions under the Geneva conventions. On the other hand, many Israeli's have demonstrated against their government for failing to bring the hostages home via a cease fire in Gaza. For

---

return home in contravention of international law (Morris 2011). Some have argued that Israel ended its occupation of Gaza in 2005 when Ariel Sharon ordered a unilateral withdrawal of Israeli forces and settlers. However, the international legal criterion to determine a state of occupation is not physical military presence, but control. Israel kept control of Gaza's air and sea borders as well as most of its land border (together with Egypt) and hence control over the entry/exit of goods, people and services; plus telecommunications, Gaza's population register, water and the electricity supply. In this sense, Gaza's occupation continued after 2005 despite its internal governance being assured by Hamas (Independent International Commission of Inquiry on the Occupied Palestinian Territory 2024; Gross 2024; ICRC 2024).

[4] To which it added a third war aim eleven months later in September 2024, namely the return of its citizens to their homes in the north. More or less in parallel, the IDF switched its offensive focus from Gaza to Lebanon.

instance, a rally in September 2024 brought c. 750,000 Israeli's to the streets across the country (Lehmann et al. 2024) while a June 2024 IDI poll indicated that a slight majority of Israeli's favored a cease fire deal (Hermann et al. 2024). Another somewhat confusing indicator is that trust in Prime Minister Netanyahu among Israeli Jews was at rock-bottom in March 2024 even though support for his policies remained stable (Svetlova 2024). One way to understand these paradoxes is that the majority of Israeli's do not care about Palestinian casualties or the policies and actions that produce them, but are concerned about the well-being of their fellow citizens, their own liberties and the quality of their leaders.

On the opposite side of the spectrum, speeches by Abu Obaida in his capacity as spokesperson of Hamas' Al-Qassam brigades have framed 7 October 2023 as an heroic act of violent resistance by the underdog against the occupier who got what he deserved after decades of abuse of Palestinians and violations of the Islamic sanctities in Jerusalem. Abu Obaida portrays 7 October as the start of a longer campaign of violent resistance entitled 'Al-Aqsa flood,' which is ultimately expected to result in the liberation of Palestine. However, his discourse makes it clear that there is a long and bloody road ahead before the Palestinians can defeat the expansionist Zionist project that Hamas views as posing an existential threat to the Palestinian people (Agathocleous and Van Veen 2024). Despite the destruction of Gaza and the mounting death toll, the Palestinian Center for Policy and Survey Research noted that roughly 30–40% of Palestinians in the occupied territories, including Gaza, continued to support Hamas between June and September 2024, and that about 50% of Palestinians view armed resistance as the best way of ending occupation (PSR 2024a, 2024b). Although causality and survey validity are difficult to establish in times of war, and subject to change in light of later events, the narrative of the Al-Qassam brigades does appear to resonate among Palestinian, perhaps because rather than despite the destruction of Gaza.

Much of the world's citizenry has watched 7 October 2023, but especially the unfolding of 'Slaugtherhouse Gaza' (cf. Vonnegut 2000), with mounting horror. Israel's international reputation dropped by an average of 20% across a sample of 43 countries between September and December 2023, which were only the early days of its destruction of Gaza. The US remains the only Western country with favorable levels of support toward Israel and this, in turn, carries a cost for Washington in the form of declining positive views of the US across the world (Gordon 2024).

Countries like Ireland, Spain and Norway recognized the state of Palestine in response to the carnage while Turkey enacted sanctions and South Africa brought a genocide case at the International Court of Justice.[5] Nevertheless, Israel retains a number of Western allies in addition to the US, such as the UK, the Netherlands, Germany, Hungary and Czech Republic.

A Context of Occupation

The Israeli-Palestinian/Arab conflict of 1947/1948 became the Israeli occupation of the Palestinian territories in 1967 when Israeli forces conquered the Golan Heights, West Bank, Gaza, East Jerusalem and the Sinai. Gaza was already a refugee camp at the time, populated by Palestinians that Israel had prohibited from returning to their homes in the wake of the 1948 war. Whereas the international community accepted the creation of the state of Israel in 1948 within the boundaries of the armistice line (the 'green line'),[6] it neither accepted nor legitimized Israel's occupation of the aforementioned areas in 1967. In fact, hundreds of resolutions by the UN Security Council and UN General Assembly have since called on Israel to withdraw from these areas and end its occupation. Moreover, an advisory opinion of the International Court of Justice in 2004 rendered both the Israeli separation barrier and Israeli settlements illegal from the point of view of international law. Another ICJ advisory opinion of July 2024 assessed the entire Israeli occupation as unlawful. The Court found that Israel has no legal claim to the land, judged its occupation as violating the political, social and economic rights of the Palestinian population on a flagrant, daily and often deadly basis, and obliged Israel to end its occupation as well as to repair the damages its unlawful actions have caused (ICJ 2004, 2024).

It stands in stark contrast to these international summons that successive Israeli governments have authorized, funded, encouraged and protected settlement of Gaza (until 2005), the West Bank and East Jerusalem since 1967, regardless of their political orientation (Sasson

---

[5] By October 2024, nine further countries had requested to join South Africa's case against Israel, including Turkey, Mexico and Spain. See: https://www.icj-cij.org/case/192/intervention (accessed 7 October 2024).

[6] Official Israeli maps do not show the green line, as per an Israeli cabinet decision from 1967 (Kashti, 2022).

Report 2005; Pedahzur 2012). While precise numbers vary, there are around 140 settlements on the West Bank today that range in size from small villages to small towns, as well as around 160 outposts that range from small and primitive pioneer-style dwellings to emerging hamlets. They are inhabited by about 465,000 Israeli settlers. Another 230,000 settlers live in and around East Jerusalem (ICG 2024, UN OHCHR 2024). New outposts are regularly established by 'hilltop youth' which, although often portrayed as stand-alone extremists, merely represent the tip of the spear of larger and politically savvy settler advocacy networks that include the likes of the Yesha Council and the Moskovitz Foundation (Pedahzur 2012). Settlements and outposts are not 'scattered throughout the West Bank,' but built on west–east axes, along a north–south axis that runs through the heart of the West Bank or along a north–south axis that follows the Jordan River.[7] The aim is to create a grid that divides the West Bank in disconnected Palestinian zones with limited mobility between them (Weizman 2012). Settler networks have long wielded substantial political influence in Israel through political parties, loyal voting blocs and charismatic leaders. They have also infiltrated every level of the Israeli administration relevant to the settlement enterprise, which gives them administrative sabotage capabilities in political lean years and allows them to exploit legal loopholes to advance their project in years of political plenty (Pedahzur 2012). Supported by leading politicians like Ariel Sharon and Benjamin Netanyahu, their decade's long effort to settle 'Judea and Samaria' is enjoying a significant boost under the current government (Wilder and Heras 2023).

The Israeli settlement project is propelled by a mix of Zionist ideology, biblical claims and security considerations. It almost came to a halt because of the Oslo Accords, which were concluded between the Israeli government and the Palestinian Liberation Orientation (PLO) in 1993–1995.[8] These accords created a semi-autonomous Palestinian state that, subject to good behavior and good neighborliness, might ultimately gain full sovereignty even though the accords did not stipulate this. In essence, they made the Palestinian right of self-determination, specifically established by the UN General Assembly in 1974, conditional on Israeli and

---

[7] For a good geographical overview see: https://peacenow.org.il/wp-content/upl oads/2023/01/settlements_map_En_2023_.pdf; For a more detailed map with a zoom function: https://www.btselem.org/map (both accessed 14 October 2024).

[8] For an overview of the countless efforts to make peace: Saʿīd et al. (2013).

international assessment of its competence to govern with Israel's (security) interests as paramount criterion. Scholars like Edward Said (2001) saw these accords as subjugation. Nevertheless, Oslo's 'two-state solution' remained the international community's dominant mantra long after they had become obsolete by the election of Benjamin Netanyahu (1996), the second Intifada (2000–2005), and the accelerating shift to the political right in Israel in the early to mid-2000s. The split between Hamas and Fatah after the 2006 elections and 2007 Hamas takeover of Gaza also divided the Palestinian political leadership and made it easier for Israel to claim that there was 'no partner for peace.' Among other things, this ignored Mahmoud Abbas' faithful implementation of Palestinian-Israeli security coordination, which substantially reduced lethal incidents against Israel (Israel Policy Forum 2021, see also Chapter 4).[9]

Before 7 October 2023, the radical extremist parts of Prime Minister Netanyahu's coalition were already turbocharging the settlement enterprise. This resulted in rampages through Palestinian villages like Huwara on 26 February 2023, rapid settlement growth as well as an uptick in the rate of violent acts against Palestinians by Israeli settlers in complicity with the IDF (ICG 2024).[10] After 7 October, these trends accelerated. Consider, for example, Minister Ben Gvir issuing thousands of gun licenses to settlers without meaningful background checks. In response, the US and EU imposed sanctions on a handful of individual settlers and a couple of settler organizations (US sanctions were withdrawn on President Trump's inauguration day). Israeli military incursions in the West Bank also increased, especially in and around the refugee camps at Jenin and Tulkarm. The 'new' cycle of violence consists of aggressive settler behavior in a context of accelerating Israeli annexation, which triggers Palestinian resistance that is subsequently repressed by Israeli forces (see Chapter 5 for analysis of more structural developments regarding settlements). Palestinians living on the West Bank only have to look at Gaza to know what might come their way should they resist with violence. And yet, taking recourse to violence is becoming more popular due to a lack of alternatives (PSR 2024a, 2024b). However, the West Bank is not Gaza. It is not run by Hamas and it lies next to Jordan. Palestinians and

---

[9] The 'knife intifada' of 2015–2016 was largely the work of unconnected individuals.
[10] See also: https://www.btselem.org/settler_violence_updates_list (accessed 14 October 2024).

Israeli settlers live in checkered patterns. The West Bank also abuts East Jerusalem and the holy site of Al-Aqsa. In other words, an explosion of violence on the West Bank will be more dangerous and different from the destruction of Gaza. More dangerous because it may ultimately force the Arab and Islamic worlds into action. Different, because Israeli forces will likely struggle with a continuous stream of low-intensity violent incidents enabled by proximity.

Enter Iran

Although Iran's involvement with Hezbollah goes back to the early 1980s (Daher 2016), the Iran-linked 'axis of resistance' as a network and tool of Iranian coercive diplomacy emerged between 2003 and 2015.[11] Events like the US invasion of Iraq (2003), the Syrian civil war (2011–2024) and the Yemeni civil war (2013–) created opportunities for Iran to expand its influence by developing—or strengthening—ideological, material and personal ties with armed groups in Iraq and Yemen, and by expediting a number of armed groups to Syria. Today, the 'axis of resistance' is a decentralized network that brings a number of armed groups together that have different orientations and capabilities. The axis operates under Iranian patronage even though Tehran's influence varies by group (Azizi and Van Veen 2024).

The initial purpose of the network was to serve as a forward defense mechanism against US assault of Iran in the context of the US invasions of Afghanistan (2001), Iraq (2003) and President Bush adding Iran to the 'axis of evil.' In other words, the axis represented an insurance policy against US attack with Hezbollah's ability to strike Israel serving as key deterrent. The axis is also underpinned by shared anti-imperialist and antizionist ideology that is in part grounded in Iran's revolutionary Shi'a doctrine of 'standing up for the downtrodden and dispossessed.' This put the axis on the side of the Palestinians in their resistance against Israeli occupation. As the axis grew in strength, it also became a tool for political violence and diplomatic pressure to project Iranian power and resist US efforts to isolate Tehran after Washington's withdrawal from the nuclear deal in 2018. For example, the 2019 attacks on Abqaiq and Khurais

---

[11] This was largely after Jordan's King Hussain's warning of a 'Shia crescent' in 2004, which at the time existed mostly in demographic terms and with a solid dose of imagination.

(ascribed to Iran), as well as the 2022 attacks on the UAE (ascribed to the Houthi), sought to pressure Saudi Arabia and the Emirates to defect from the US/Israeli coalition, which duly happened.

Iranian ties with Hamas date back to 1987–1992. Despite Hamas being a Sunni movement grounded in the thinking of the Muslim Brotherhood, which contrasts with Iran's revolutionary Shi'a doctrine, shared political Islamism and resistance against Israel proved sufficient to develop a relationship. Iranian support increased with time and enabled both production of better missiles and greater precision, as can be inferred from the leap in the volume and accuracy of Hamas rocket fire on Israel during the 2021 evictions in Sheikh Jarrah (Samaan 2021; Skare 2023). Hamas military planning capabilities and tactical combat skills also benefited from Iranian support via Hezbollah. Their blossoming relation notwithstanding, Tehran appears to have been taken by surprise by 7 October 2023. Both the US and Israel went on the record to deny Iranian involvement (Skare 2023).

7 October 2023 nevertheless represented a sea-change in the involvement of the axis of resistance in the occupation of the Palestinian territories. Before this date, the main theater of conflict between Israel and the axis had been Syria. Here, a relentless Israeli bombing campaign against Iran-linked military sites and logistical facilities alternated with a persistent Iranian-cum-axis military built-up (Van Veen and Azizi 2024). After 7 October 2023, the axis engaged in a multi-front harassment campaign of Israel. This was largely executed by means of rocket fire and drone launches based on Nasrallah's 'unity of the fronts' strategy. Practically, it rested on several operation rooms that coordinated the militant activity of various axis members (Van Veen and Azizi 2024). One could argue that Hamas had successfully leveraged the political ideology of the axis to force it into conflict with Israel despite Tehran's reluctance. After having claimed to stand with the occupied for decades, the axis could not stay quiet once the Israeli campaign in Gaza started. But its involvement was halfhearted. Israel nevertheless absorbed serious damage for months on end, including the displacement of 60,000–100,000 citizens, de facto closure of the port of Eilat and occasional rocket and drone strikes on the Israeli heartland. But the axis itself suffered tremendously in what came next. Once Israel had decimated Hamas, it turned its intelligence and military might on Hezbollah, the Houthi and Iran itself. In short order, this brought Hezbollah to its knees ('down, but not out') and forced Iran to stand down, as well as agreeing to a cease fire in Lebanon. When

Hayat Tahrir al-Sham, an armed Syrian Islamist opposition group with Al Qaeda antecedents, captured Aleppo, Hama, Homs and Damascus in short order in December 2024, Iran was unable to mobilize sufficient forces with adequate speed to prevent the collapse of the Assad regime. This was due in part to the military punishment Israel had meted out to the axis in the months prior. In other words, the security threat that the axis of resistance poses to Israel has substantially diminished in the short- to medium-term, but it has not gone. Without change in any of the underlying conditions, it may yet reconstitute itself. For example by tapping into the grievances and anger that Israeli military action has produced in Gaza, the West Bank, Syria and Lebanon.

Why the Book Matters

7 October 2023 and its aftermath have highlighted the long-term tendency of the cycle of occupation, militant resistance and violent repression to deepen and escalate. The destruction of Gaza and accelerating Israeli annexation on the West Bank will ensure that violence and radicalization increase if the international community does not intervene. The conflict parties will not do so themselves: Hamas is decapitated (see Chapter 3), the PA is powerless (see Chapter 4) and the Israeli government pursues annexation with US support (see Chapters 5 and 6). Millions of Palestinians will suffer in particular as Israel commands far greater capabilities to wield violence than any Palestinian resistance group. Yet, Israel will also suffer. Morally, due to being responsible for the brutal repression, forced displacement and destruction of another society in a cruel twist of history. But also mentally and materially due to the permanent threat of violent Palestinian resistance that might be amplified by the Iran-linked axis of resistance, or other external actors, in the course of time.

Regional stability will moreover remain elusive as long as the Palestinian issue is unresolved. Annexation and resistance on the West Bank are likely to destabilize Jordan, for example. Moreover, it can prevent normalization of relations between Saudi Arabia and Israel, trigger another round of conflict with Iran in the future and cause new flows of refugees. Further afield, some European countries may become targets of violent extremism due to their support of Israel's military campaigns, including Germany, the Netherlands and the UK, and are certain to face further polarization in their own societies due to the gap between popular and elite opinion with regard to the appropriate policies and actions vis-à-vis Gaza. Perhaps most importantly, Europe and the US will at some point be faced with the consequences of having dismantled the international legal order regarding the conduct of war by their uncritical and unconditional support for Israel's disproportionate number of war crimes (International Criminal Court 2024). It should not be ignored that this order was painstakingly put together over the last century, in part in response to WWII Nazi atrocities.

If one accepts that Israel's unrelenting occupation of the Palestinian territories is the root cause of the tragedy of 7 October 2023 and the terrible events thereafter, one must ask how its acceleration will influence prospects for violence, as well as prospects for conflict resolution. This essay bundle does exactly that. It explores what the future of occupation can look like. Such an inquiry intends to raise awareness of the cost of non-intervention and help develop realistic ideas about how occupation can be ended.

Structure and Method of the Book

Much analysis of the occupation of the Palestinian territories focuses either on the history of the conflict or on the five main conceptual solutions available: a one-state solution based on displacement, subjugation and annexation; a one-state solution based on equal rights for all; a two-state solution based on mutually recognized sovereignty; a two-state solution based on Israeli sovereignty and Palestinian autonomy; and a confederal solution. Events after 7 October 2023 have pushed solutions two to five further out of sight than ever. Hence, consideration of the future of occupation requires a different approach. With this in mind, the essay bundle combines scenario planning with an analysis of the interests, objectives and actions of the main stakeholders involved in, or affected by, occupation to establish its likely features over the next years. On this basis, it develops a set of broad principles and proposes tangible actions that can help bring occupation to an end in as peaceful a manner as possible without presuming any particular solution.

Chapter 2 outlines four plausible scenarios for the future of occupation that range from tragic to catastrophic on the basis of factors such as political trends in Israel, the historic evolution of the conflict and the grievances that are being generated at present. It uses an established scenario planning methodology, the details of which are discussed in the

Chapter itself. Even if one of these scenarios comes to pass in the near future, the scenario set will continue to offer a mental map that can inspire diplomatic engagement intending to bring shifts between scenarios about. Subsequently, Chapters 3–11 analyze the perceptions, objectives, interests and actions of three sets of stakeholders engaged in, or affected by, occupation. Namely the direct conflict parties: Hamas, the Palestinian Authority/Fatah, Israel and the US; neighbors: Egypt, Jordan and Hezbollah; and influential regional powers: Saudi Arabia and Iran. Each stakeholder essay is written by a well-known researcher with a long experience of his subject matter. Finally, Chapter 12 re-visits the scenarios of Chapter 2 on the basis of the stakeholder analyses of Chapters 3–11 to sketch key principles and outline tangible actions that can help bring a peaceful end of occupation closer. Chapter 12 benefited from two research visits to Israel by its authors in September and November 2024.

On the whole, the essay bundle aims to provide an intellectual resource in support of meaningful conversation among diplomats, politicians, activists and civil servants whose work relates to the occupation of the Palestinian territories. Transforming the future begins with its re-imagination.

Conflict of Interest The author has no conflict of interests to declare that are relevant to the content of this chapter.

Bibliography

Abraham, Yuval. 2024. "'Lavender': The AI Machine Directing Israel's Bombing Spree in Gaza." *+972 Magazine*, April 3, 2024. https://www.972mag.com/lavender-ai-israeli-army-gaza/.

Al-Shawaf, Rayyan. 2023. "Making Gaza Unlivable." *Carnegie Endowment for International Peace "Diwan"* (blog). December 14, 2023. https://carnegieendowment.org/middle-east/diwan/2023/12/making-gaza-unlivable?lang=en.

Agathocleous, Sophia, and Erwin Van Veen. 2024. "Hamas 'From the Heart of Battle': Analyzing Abu Obaida's Discourse." *The Cairo Review of Global Affairs*, no. Summer 2024. https://www.thecairoreview.com/essays/hamas-from-the-heart-of-battle-analyzing-abu-obaidas-discourse/.

Amnesty International. 2024. "'You Feel Like You Are Subhuman': Israel's Genocide Against Palestinians in Gaza." MDE 15/8668/2024. London:

Amnesty International. https://www.amnesty.org/en/latest/news/2024/12/amnesty-international-concludes-israel-is-committing-genocide-against-palestinians-in-gaza/.

Azizi, Hamidreza, and Erwin Van Veen. 2024. "Iran and Gaza in Regional Perspective: Winning the Battle, but Losing the War?" *Iran in Transition* (blog). March 5, 2024. https://www.clingendael.org/publication/iran-and-gaza-regional-perspective-winning-battle-losing-war.

Baconi, Tareq. 2022. *Hamas Contained: The Rise and Pacification of Palestinian Resistance.* First paperback printing. Stanford, California: Stanford University Press.

Banco, Erin, and Nahal Toosi. 2024. "US Officials Quietly Backed Israel's Military Push against Hezbollah." *Politico*, September 30, 2024. https://www.politico.com/news/2024/09/30/us-israel-military-hezbollah-00181797.

Bartov, Omer. 2024. *Holocaust Scholar Says Israel Has Committed Genocide in Gaza*. WBUR Podcast. Online: Here and Now Newsroom. https://www.wbur.org/hereandnow/2024/11/22/holocaust-scholar-israel.

Daher, Joseph. 2016. *Hezbollah: The Political Economy of Lebanon's Party of God*. London: Pluto Press.

Dayan, Moshe. 1956. "Moshe Dayan's Eulogy for Roi Rutenberg - April 19, 1956." Eulogy, Nahal Oz, April 19. https://www.jewishvirtuallibrary.org/moshe-dayan-s-eulogy-for-roi-rutenberg-april-19-1956.

Foer, Franklin. 2024. "The War That Would Not End." *The Atlantic*, September 25, 2024. https://www.theatlantic.com/international/archive/2024/09/israel-gaza-war-biden-netanyahu-peace-negotiations/679581/.

Gordon, Anna. 2024. "New Polling Shows How Much Global Support Israel Has Lost." *TIME*, January 17, 2024. https://time.com/6559293/morning-consult-israel-global-opinion/.

Gross, Aeyal. 2024. "The Functional Approach as Lex Lata: The ICJ Advisory Opinion and the Status of Gaza." *Verfassungsblog* (blog). Verfassungsblog. October 12, 2024. https://verfassungsblog.de/the-functional-approach-as-lex-lata/.

Hage, Clare. 2024. "Tsav-9, the Israeli Extremists Stationed at the Borders of Gaza." *L'Orient Today*, February 27, 2024, Online edition, sec. Region. https://today.lorientlejour.com/article/1369557/tsav-9-the-israeli-extremists-stationed-at-the-borders-of-gaza.html.

Hareuveni, Eyal. 2021. "State Business: Israel's Misappropriation of Land in the West Bank through Settler Violence." Jerusalem: BTselem.

Hass, Amira. 2024. "Numbers That Stagger the Imagination: There's No Way to Quantify the Suffering in Gaza." *Haaretz*, April 10, 2024. https://www.haaretz.com/israel-news/2024-04-10/ty-article-magazine/.premium/numbers-that-stagger-the-imagination-theres-no-way-to-quantify-the-suffering-in-gaza/0000018e-c1db-d480-a99e-cfdf01240000.

Hermann, Tamar, and Yaron Kaplan. 2024."Most Israelis Support Deal to Release All Hostages and End the War in Gaza; Israelis Divided on How to Handle the Northern Front." *The Israel Democray Institute Israeli Voice Index June 2024* (blog). July 10, 2024. https://en.idi.org.il/articles/55018.

Hermann, Tamar, Lior Yohanani, and Yaron Kaplan. 2024. "Most Israelis Support Deal to Release All Hostages and End the War in Gaza; Israelis Divided on How to Handle the Northern Front." *The Israel Democray Institute Israeli Voice Index June 2024* (blog). July 10, 2024. https://en.idi.org.il/articles/55018.

Independent International Commission of Inquiry on the Occupied Palestinian Territory, including East-Jerusalem, and Israel. 2024. "Detailed Findings on Attacks Carried out on and after 7 October 2023 in Israel." Fifty-sixth session A/HRC/56/CRP.3. Geneva: Human Rights Council. https://www.ohchr.org/sites/default/files/documents/hrbodies/hrcouncil/sessions-regular/session56/a-hrc-56-crp-3.pdf.

International Committee of the Red Cross. 2024. "What Does the Law Say about the Responsibilities of the Occupying Power in the Occupied Palestinian Territory?" July 26, 2024. https://www.icrc.org/en/document/ihl-occupying-power-responsibilities-occupied-palestinian-territories.

International Court of Justice. 2004. "Legal Consequences of the Construction of a Wall in the Occupied Palestinian Territory." Advisory Opinion. The Hague: International Court of Justice.

International Court of Justice. 2024. "Legal Consequences Arising from the Policies and Practices of Israel in the Occupied Palestinian Territory, Including East Jerusalem." Advisory Opinion General List No. 186. The Hague: International Court of Justice. https://www.icj-cij.org/sites/default/files/case-related/186/186-20240719-adv-01-00-en.pdf.

International Criminal Court. 2024. "Situation in the State of Palestine: ICC Pre-Trial Chamber I Rejects the State of Israel's Challenges to Jurisdiction and Issues Warrants of Arrest for Benjamin Netanyahu and Yoav Gallant." November 21, 2024. https://www.icc-cpi.int/news/situation-state-palestine-icc-pre-trial-chamber-i-rejects-state-israels-challenges.

International Crisis Group. 2024. "Stemming Israeli Settler Violence at Its Root." Middle East Report N°246. Brussels: ICG.

Israel Policy Forum. 2021. "For West Bank Stability, Israeli-PA Security Cooperation Is a Necessity." *Israel Policy Forum* (blog). December 13, 2021. https://israelpolicyforum.org/2021/12/13/for-west-bank-stability-israeli-pa-security-cooperation-is-a-necessity/.

Kashti, Or. 2022. "Tel Aviv and the Israeli Government Spar over School Maps Showing 1967 Borders." *Haaretz*, August 23, 2022, sec. Israel News.

https://www.haaretz.com/israel-news/2022-08-23/ty-article/.highlight/ tel-aviv-schools-barred-from-using-map-of-israel-showing-green-line/000 00182-c71f-dae5-a58e-d79fc42e0000.

Khatib, Lina. 2024. "Interview: Hezbollah After Nasrallah." *Middle East Council on Global Affairs* (blog). September 29, 2024. https://mecouncil.org/blog_posts/interview-hezbollah-after-nasrallah/.

Konrad, Edo. 2024. "What Israelis Don't Want to Hear about Iran and Hezbollah." *+972 Magazine*, September 20, 2024. https://www.972mag.com/iran-israel-hezbollah-ori-goldberg/.

Lehmann, Noam, Iddo Schejter, Elana Kirsh, and ToI Staff. 2024. "Organizers Claim Largest-Ever Rally in Tel Aviv as Calls for Hostage Deal Intensify." *The Times of Israel*, September 8, 2024, Israel at war-day 381 edition. https://www.timesofisrael.com/organizers-claim-largest-ever-rally-in-tel-aviv-as-calls-for-hostage-deal-intensify/.

Levy, Yagil. 2023. "The Israeli Army Has Dropped the Restraint in Gaza, and the Data Shows Unprecedented Killing." *Haaretz*, December 9, 2023. https://www.haaretz.com/israel-news/2023-12-09/ty-article-magazine/.highlight/the-israeli-army-has-dropped-the-restraint-in-gaza-and-data-shows-unprecedented-killing/0000018c-4cca-db23-ad9f-6cdae8ad0000.

Mordechai, Lee. 2025. "Bearing Witness to the Israel-Gaza War." 2023–2025. https://witnessing-the-gaza-war.com/.

Morris, Benny. 2011. *Righteous Victims: A History of the Zionist-Arab Conflict, 1881–2001*. Westminster: Knopf Doubleday Publishing Group.

Murphy, Brett. 2024. "Israel Deliberately Blocked Humanitarian Aid to Gaza, Two Government Bodies Concluded. Antony Blinken Rejected Them." *ProPublica* (blog). September 24, 2024. https://www.propublica.org/article/gaza-palestine-israel-blocked-humanitarian-aid-blinken.

Pedahzur, Ami. 2012. *The Triumph of Israel's Radical Right*. Cary: Oxford University Press USA - OSO.

PSR Survey research unit. 2024a. "Public Opinion Poll No. 92." Ramallah: Palestinian Center for Policy and Survey Research. https://www.pcpsr.org/sites/default/files/Poll%2092%20English%20full%20text%20July2024.pdf.

———. 2024b. "Public Opinion Poll No. 93." Ramallah: Palestinian Center for Policy and Survey Research. https://www.pcpsr.org/sites/default/files/Poll%2093%20English%20press%20release%2017_Sept2024.pdf.

Republic of South Africa. 2023. "Application of the Convention on the Prevention and Punishment of the Crime of Genocide in the Gaza Strip (South Africa v. Israel)." Application institution proceedings containing a request for the indication of provisional measures. The Hague: International Court of Justice. https://www.icj-cij.org/sites/default/files/case-related/192/192-20231228-app-01-00-en.pdf.

Said, Edward W. 2001. *The End of the Peace Process: Oslo and After.* 1st Vintage Books ed. New York: Vintage Books.
Samaan, Jean-Loup. 2021. "The Military Lessons of the Gaza War of May 2021." *Trends Research & Advisory* (blog). July 1, 2021. https://trendsresearch.org/insight/the-military-lessons-of-the-gaza-war-of-may-2021/.
Sasson Report. 2005. "Settlement Outposts." Jerusalem: Prime Minister's Office - Communication Department. https://www.un.org/unispal/document/auto-insert-203215/.
Saʿīd, ʿAbd al-Munʿim, Shai Feldman, and Halīl al-Šiqāqī. 2013. *Arabs and Israelis: Conflict and Peacemaking in the Middle East.* New York: Palgrave Macmillan.
Silver, Laura, and Maria Smerkovich. 2024. "Israeli Views of the Israel-Hamas War." *Pew Research Center* (blog). May 30, 2024. https://www.pewresearch.org/global/2024/05/30/israeli-views-of-the-israel-hamas-war/.
Skare, Erik. 2023. "Iran, Hamas, and Islamic Jihad: A Marriage of Convenience." *ECFR* (blog). December 18, 2023. https://ecfr.eu/article/iran-hamas-and-islamic-jihad-a-marriage-of-convenience/.
Svetlova, Ksenia. 2024. "Netanyahu Might Be Losing Ground, but His Politics Still Resonate with Most Israelis." *Atlantic Council MENASource* (blog). March 6, 2024. https://www.atlanticcouncil.org/blogs/menasource/israel-gaza-war-netanyahu-polling/.
UN OHCHR. 2024. "STATE OF PALESTINE: Israeli Settlements in the Occupied Palestinian Territory, Including East Jerusalem, and in the Occupied Syrian Golan." Jerusalem: OHCHR. https://www.ohchr.org/sites/default/files/2024-03/Palestine-March2024.pdf.
United Nations Country Team in the occupied Palestinian territory. 2012. "Gaza in 2020: A Liveable Place?" Jerusalem: UNSCO.
UNRWA. 2024. "Gaza Supplies and Dispatch Tracking." October 18, 2024. https://app.powerbi.com/view?r=eyJrIjoiZTVkYmEwNmMtZWYxNy00ODhlLWI2ZjctNjIzMzQ5OGQxNzY5IiwidCI6IjI2MmY2YTQxLTIwZTktNDE0MC04ZDNlLWZkZjVlZWNiNDE1NyIsImMiOjl9&pageName=ReportSection3306863add46319dc574.
Van Veen, Erwin. 2024a. "In Darkness All Is Black: Exploring the Realities of Violence by the Israeli State and Hamas." *The Cairo Review of Global Affairs*, March. https://www.thecairoreview.com/essays/in-darkness-all-is-black-exploring-the-realities-of-violence-by-the-israeli-state-and-hamas/.
———. 2024b. "The Elusive Israeli Quest for Strategic Victory." *The MENA Chronicle | Fanack* (blog). October 7, 2024. https://fanack.com/politics/features-insights/the-elusive-israeli-quest-for-strategic-victory~269050/.
Van Veen, Erwin, and Hamidreza Azizi. 2024. "Playing with Fire: Patterns of Iranian-Israeli Military Confrontation." *War on the Rocks* (blog). June

25, 2024. https://warontherocks.com/2024/06/playing-with-fire-patterns-of-iranian-israeli-military-confrontation/.

Vonnegut, Kurt. 2000. *Slaughterhouse-Five or The Children's Crusade: A Duty-Dance with Death*. Repr. Vintage Classics. London: Vintage.

Wagemakers, Joas. 2024. *Hamas: Palestijns Nationalisme en Militant Pragmatisme [Palestinian Nationalism and militant pragmatism]*. Amsterdam: Amsterdam University Press.

Weizman, Eyal. 2012. *Hollow Land: Israel's Architecture of Occupation*. 1. paperback ed. London: Verso Books.

Wilder, Calvin, and Nicholas Heras. 2023. "The Looming Challenge in U.S.-Israel Security Cooperation." *New Lines Institute*, August 22, 2023. https://newlinesinstitute.org/strategic-competition/u-s-foreign-policy/the-looming-challenge-in-u-s-israel-security-cooperation/.

Open Access This chapter is licensed under the terms of the Creative Commons Attribution 4.0 International License (http://creativecommons.org/licenses/by/4.0/), which permits use, sharing, adaptation, distribution and reproduction in any medium or format, as long as you give appropriate credit to the original author(s) and the source, provide a link to the Creative Commons license and indicate if changes were made.

The images or other third party material in this chapter are included in the chapter's Creative Commons license, unless indicated otherwise in a credit line to the material. If material is not included in the chapter's Creative Commons license and your intended use is not permitted by statutory regulation or exceeds the permitted use, you will need to obtain permission directly from the copyright holder.

CHAPTER 2

Scenarios for the Israeli Occupation of Palestine

Erwin van Veen

Abstract The Hamas attack on Israel of 7 October and the subsequent Israeli destruction of Gaza have caused several shifts in the dynamics of Israel's occupation of the Palestinian territories, just as important continuities have remained. This mix makes scenario planning an appropriate method for analyzing the future of occupation. Scenario planning aims to unlock our mental imagination and invites us to consider different possible futures simultaneously. This helps develop a better understanding of how such futures should affect today's decisions and improve preparedness. With this in mind, the Chapter outlines four scenarios for the future of occupation. First, a 'Revisionist Zionism comes true' scenario, which amounts to a fast expansion of Israeli annexation that meets only low levels of Palestinian resistance. Second, 'Gaza on the Jordan River' that features a similarly fast expansion of occupation but which runs into stiff Palestinian resistance. Third, 'colonial-style suffering' that sees a return to occupation modalities and practices from before 7 October 2023. Finally,

E. van Veen (✉)
Clingendael Institute, The Hague, The Netherlands
e-mail: eveen@clingendael.org

© The Author(s) 2025
E. van Veen (ed.), *The Future of the Occupation of the Palestinian Territories after Gaza*,
https://doi.org/10.1007/978-3-031-93798-9_2

a 'squid game' scenario where gradual occupation meets heavy Palestinian resistance. Even if one of these scenarios comes to pass soon, the scenario set continues to offer a mental map to inspire diplomatic engagement that intends to bring shifts between scenarios about. While the scenarios are all bleak, they are amenable to international intervention.

Keywords Occupation · Scenarios · Settlements · Smotrich · Hamas · Fatah · Iran · Axis of resistance · West Bank · Gaza · Palestinian Authority · Annexation

INTRODUCTION

The Hamas attack on Israel of 7 October 2023 and the subsequent Israeli destruction of Gaza caused several shifts in the dynamics of Israel's occupation of the Palestinian territories. To begin with, the attack re-awakened a deep sense of insecurity among Israel's Jewish population, as well as creating a forceful socio-political drive for revenge. This has resulted in further dehumanization of Palestinians as a population group, both in Gaza and outside. It has also created a perception in some quarters, however incorrect it is, that the survival of the Israeli state and its people are at risk (Hermann and Kaplan 2024; Bartov 2024; Mishra 2024).[1] The uncertain fate of the c. 250 Israeli hostages that Hamas captured and the continuous barrage of rockets on Israel, primarily from Hezbollah and the Houthi, kept fear and revenge alive in many long months following 7 October. Another shift has been the steep decline in Israel's global and moral reputation due to the immense devastation its military campaign has wrought in Gaza and greater international attention for the structural violence caused by its occupation. This reputational freefall has caused protests around the world, divisions among Jewish diaspora communities and legal cases at both the International Criminal Court and the International Court of Justice. Yet another shift is that the events of 7 October and beyond brought greater interwovenness about between occupation and the regional conflict between Israel/the US and Iran/ the 'axis of

---

[1] A movement like Hamas with around 30,000 poorly equipped fighters and a supply of second-rate rockets cannot conceivably be considered a threat to Israel's existence as a country before or after October 7.

resistance,' however weakened the latter currently is as a result of Israeli and American military action (Van Veen and Azizi 2024).[2] It is uncertain how these shifts will work out in the long-term with regard to the future of Israel's occupation.

In the short-term, however, these shifts have already reinforced pre-existing views from before 7 October among nearly all key segments of Israel's political elites as well as important sections of Israel's population, namely that extended occupation of Palestinian lands is an Israeli right, that Palestinians can neither be negotiated nor lived with, that making Israel secure justifies all means necessary and that Israel ultimately stands alone in the world (Mishra 2024; Young 2024). The political instrumentalization of such convictions has, together with the (tacit) support of much of the international community, enabled Israel to destroy more than 60% of Gaza's built-up area (World Bank, European Union and United Nations 2024), kill an estimated 75,000 Palestinians by traumatic injury by January 2025 (Jamaluddine et al. 2025),[3] kill another estimated 112,500 Palestinians by indirect means like disease and starvation around the same date (Khatib et al. 2024; Jamaluddine et al. 2025)[4] and accelerate the annexation of East Jerusalem as well as the West Bank through Israeli state and settler paramilitary violence (Shir 2024).

At the same time, there are a number of continuities in the Israeli occupation of the Palestinian territories that pre-date 7 October 2023,

---

[2] None of these shifts involve Hamas since the movement has historically oscillated between more political and more militant postures, did not always rule Gaza and has been subjected to Israeli military action and targeted assassinations in the past (see Baconi 2022). Hence, from a strategic perspective, not much of the events of 2023–2024 are new insofar as they concern the organization, except for their scale. It is too early to assess how the movement will adapt to its current losses in Gaza.

[3] Jamaluddine et al. (2025) estimate 65,000 deaths for the period 7 October 2023 until June 2024. While the number of deaths due to traumatic injury likely tapers off after this period due to a decrease in combat operations, it seems a conservative guestimate to add 10,000 further deaths for the six remaining months of 2024, making for a total of 75,000 deaths by traumatic injury around 31 December 2024.

[4] Indirect deaths are hard to estimate. If one extrapolates data from Jamaluddine et al. (2025, p. 7), around 40,000 indirect deaths are likely between 7 October 2023 and December 2024 even though indirect deaths—in contrast with deaths from traumatic injury—are likely to increase regardless of the intensity of military operations. Using the 3–15 multiplication factor from kinetic to indirect deaths that Khatib et al. (2024) suggest in a conservative fashion, which takes account of the counterargument of Jamaluddine et al. (2025), by applying a modest factor of 1,5, to the estimate of 75,000 kinetic deaths suggests around 112,500 indirect deaths. This is likely an underestimate.

which include an ongoing political shift to the (far) right among Israeli voters since at least the mid-1990s (Pedahzur 2012; Keller-Lynn 2022), the subjugating governance and repressive modalities of Israeli occupation (Weizman 2012), unconditional US (military) assistance for Israel paired with firm political support for the country in about half a dozen European countries (Masters and Merrow 2024), the probable survival and revival of Hamas (or a similar movement), the persistence of peaceful as well as militant Palestinian resistance, an absence of serious international efforts to resolve the conflict (in part due to US cover for Israel), division among Palestinian political factions, as well as the authoritarian policies and underperformance of both the Palestinian Authority and Hamas.

An Increase in Uncertainty Points to Scenario Planning

This mix of change and continuity makes scenario planning an appropriate method for analyzing the future of the Israeli occupation of the Palestinian territories. It is also necessary because 7 October 2023 relayed a number of frames and approaches to conflict resolution to the archives of history. These include the Oslo agreements, the notion that occupation can be maintained indefinitely at low costs and the assumption that international pressure to undo occupation will remain insignificant. More to the point, the events of 7 October 2023 and thereafter have brought the international community to a major tipping point at which its members need to decide how to re-relate to the Israeli occupation of the Palestinian territories in terms of their political and diplomatic relations with the main actors: Hamas, Israel, Fatah and the US. If the bloodshed in Gaza was not enough to trigger such policy reflection, the advisory opinion of the International Court of Justice (ICJ) of 19 July 2014 on the unlawfulness of Israel's occupation of the Palestinian territories obliges all UN member states to consider how they can contribute to a swift end to occupation and to help repair some of the damage it has caused (Salam and Gautier 2024). A set of scenarios helps to think through the impact and consequences of policy decisions regarding the Israeli occupation of the Palestinian territories, which will be required in the years to come in the interest of international peace and security as per the stipulation of Article 1 of the UN Charter.

About the Science and Art of Scenario Planning

Before going into scenario content, a few pointers on the nature of scenario planning are necessary to situate the insights offered by this bundle of essays correctly. Scenario planning emerged from the military during World War II after which it was picked up by large companies such as the Anglo American Cooperation, AT&T and Shell in the 1960s (Schwartz 1996).[5] It has had its political applications, in particular in the form of the Mont Fleur scenarios that helped South Africa's political elites think through the democratic transition in 1991–1992 (Leroux and Maphai 1992). Today, scenario planning is widely used by all manner of private, public and international entities (Wilkinson and Kupers 2013). This is in part because the world of the late twentieth and early twenty-first century has become more complex due to, among other things, the shift from bi- to uni- and then multipolarity in geopolitics, easier and faster communication and transportation, as well as the gradual replacement of the universal WTO trading system by bilateral and regional arrangements (Huwart and Verdier 2013; Khanna 2016; Bekkers et al. 2023). Unforeseen consequences and unpredictable changes with substantial impact—what Taleb (2010) calls 'black swan events'—have become more likely. The Hamas attack on Israel of 7 October 2023 arguably was such a black swan event, at least in terms of its impact.[6]

Scenario planning is a way to think through the many uncertainties that the future holds by organizing and exploring key forces that are considered to influence the different ways in which the future can manifest itself in respect of a particular issue—such as the Israeli occupation of the Palestinian territories. Otherwise put, if the future emerges from a multidimensional array of intersecting cause-effect relationships that can dampen, neutralize and/or amplify one another, scenario planning aims to identify the most important cause-effect relationships and turn these into plausibly articulated narratives of what alternative futures can look like (Schwartz 1996; Van der Heijden 2005). Scenario planning accepts

---

[5] See for example: Shell Global. 2024. "Shell Scenarios." August 22, 2024. https://www.shell.com/news-and-insights/scenarios.html; Sunter (1987).

[6] The Yom Kippur War is often put on par with 7 October as representing a similar strategic surprise that was due to intelligence failures, military arrogance and political hubris. See: Bar-Joseph (2005). Yet, the consequences of these event have already diverged substantially.

irreducible uncertainty as an inevitable feature of the future that can to some extent be mapped and imagined, but not predicted. In this regard, scenario planning is different from forecasting, which attaches probabilities to specific events that are more narrowly defined and occur in a shorter timeline (e.g., less than a year). In the medium term, most issues are driven by a broader array of cause-effect factors, which increase variability and randomness. An extended time horizon also turns short-term risks into long-term uncertainties as trends are faced with a growing risk of disruption due to tipping points and black swan events (Van der Heijden 2005; Taleb 2010; Tetlock and Gardner 2016). This makes forecasting less effective. Scenario planning, instead, departs from the premise that the future exists in the plural until it happens, that this plurality can be mapped to an extent despite its complexity and that shifts between scenarios are possible (Schwartz 1996; also: Johnson 2012). Scenario planning is not prediction. It merely aims to unlock our mental imagination and invites us to consider different possible futures simultaneously. This helps develop a better understanding of how such futures may affect today's decisions and can improve preparedness.

In the process of mapping the future, scenario planning as methodology combines elements of science with elements of craft. On the one hand, scenario planning requires a correct identification of critical forces that drive the development of a particular issue in the future (Schwartz 1996; Van der Heijden 2005). This demands an understanding of the factors that influence these driving forces, which in turn requires deep analysis using qualitative and quantitative methods. Consider semi-structured, in-depth interviews with key decision-makers and conflict stakeholders to understand their views, frames and objectives; surveys to understand the perceptions of particular population groups; as well as longitudinal trend analyses of more predetermined elements like demography or even climate change impact. On the other hand, scenarios are not just a collection of facts and figures. They offer plausible stories about the future that may or may not come true. As such, they have an important storytelling component and can even be transformative in their interaction with social reality (Kahane 2012).

Four Scenarios for the Israeli Occupation of the Palestinian Territories

With this in mind, the Chapter outlines four scenarios for the future of the Israeli occupation of the Palestinian territories in Fig. 2.1.[7] They are, without exception, bleak. In fact, the least negative among them is an approximate return to the status quo from before 7 October, i.e., the gradual expansion of occupation by means of daily Israeli violence to repress and subjugate any resistance against it, but with the added element that the ruins of Gaza mean that just short of two million Palestinians will suffer even more than they already did. Such bleakness results from a number of factors that underlie the critical driving forces of the scenarios, such as the bellicose and expansionist intentions of most of Israel's political elites that have been laid bare by the events after 7 October 2023—confirming the shift to the ultra-nationalist and extreme right in Israel over the past decades (Pedahzur 2012; Anabi 2022)—the near-total unwillingness of both the West (especially the US) and the Arab world to take measures against Israel that would raise the cost of occupation, divided Palestinian leadership and the unresolved nature of the regional conflict between the US and Iran (see Fig. 2.2). Bleakness does not imply that the different scenarios are not amenable to international conflict resolution efforts—the concluding Chapter offers building blocks for such initiatives—but it does indicate that greater violence and suffering lie in store before such efforts can bear fruit. The scenarios also suggest that a possibility exists that the Palestinian issue will be 'solved' by brute violence.

The scenarios are based on expert conversations that preceded this book, extensive monitoring of the political and military situation in Israel and the Palestinian territories since 7 October 2023 (Clingendael 2023–2024) and existing research that is too extensive to enumerate here, but includes Morris (1999), Said (2001), Nusseibeh (2009), Yizhar (2011), Pedahzur 2012; Said Aly et al. (2013), Shavit (2015), Thrall (2017), Baconi (2022), Asseburg (2023) and Wagemakers (2024). Even if one of these scenarios comes to pass in the near future, the scenario set continues

---

[7] In the methodology of scenario planning, these four scenarios are based on a variant of the deductive approach in which a limited number of structural variables ('main driving forces') can be clearly identified on the basis of analysis of the underlying data (Van der Heijden 2005).

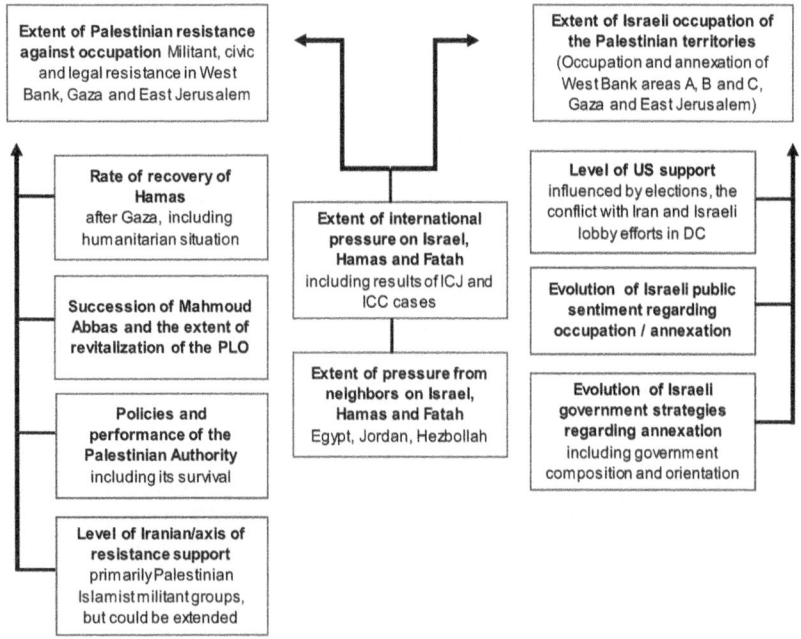

Fig. 2.1 Scenarios for the Israeli occupation of the Palestinian territories in the next 5–10 years

Fig. 2.2 Factors influencing the scenario driving forces

2 SCENARIOS FOR THE ISRAELI OCCUPATION OF PALESTINE   27

to offer a useful mental map that can inspire diplomatic engagement intending to bring shifts *between* scenarios about.

The main driving forces of future scenarios are the rate of expansion of Israeli occupation and the extent of Palestinian resistance because both have a high level of uncertainty and a high level of impact. Moreover, despite external dynamics and support, occupier and occupied retain sufficient agency and autonomy to determine primary conflict dynamics despite the fact that conflict dynamics are structurally tilted in favor of Israel. Issues such as the role of the US as political and military protector of Israel, Western European countries as its passive diplomatic supporters and Iran's support for Hamas and Palestinian Islamic Jihad are factors that influence these two driving forces. Important, but not decisive in themselves. They are naturally part of each scenario, however, and formally articulated in Fig. 2.2.

Due to the limitations of this essay bundle, the scenario narratives below are best seen as headline stories that can be deepened and revised by means of a deliberative scenario planning process that involves actual conflict stakeholders. Their purpose here is analytical, namely to provide a mental map of what the future of occupation can look like. Bear in mind that the scenarios are not entirely mutually exclusive, i.e., certain events could occur in several scenarios, and that shifts between scenarios remain possible even after one of them has to come to pass.

Revisionist Zionism Comes True

In this scenario, the Israeli government annexes the entire West Bank, de factor or de jure, in a few decisive actions.[8] This necessarily goes hand in hand with increased repression by means of greater spatial delineation between Israeli settlers and Palestinians (e.g., no-go areas, checkpoints and Israeli-only roads); tighter regulation of Palestinian mobility, residence and work options; as well as both targeted and structural forms of violence to eliminate any militant Palestinian resistance and to pressure Palestinian residents to submit or leave. Israeli settlements expand rapidly

---

[8] Revisionist Zionism is understood here as a political ideology that envisages the establishment of a Jewish-dominated state within the boundaries of Mandatory Palestine. The notion of 'Greater Israel' goes beyond the territorial aspirations of revisionist Zionism and can extend to the Litani, Nile and Euphrates rivers as furthest boundaries of the Israeli state, incorporating parts of Lebanon, Egypt and Jordan as well as Iraq.

in this scenario, including in north Gaza. South Gaza effectively becomes a prisoner camp under high surveillance and in permanent humanitarian crisis. Palestinian displacement and Israeli resettlement also accelerates in East Jerusalem. A successful judicial reform 2.0 removes the minimal legal constraints that had so far mostly prevented the rapid seizure of private Palestinian land and gives the Israeli government carte blanche to advance occupation in practical terms. In this scenario, what remains of the Palestinian Authority is reduced to providing municipal governance and auxiliary policing in the urban areas of Nablus, Jenin, Jericho, Ramallah and Hebron. In Israel itself, ultra-nationalist and extreme right factions dominate politics. The 'hilltop youth' and extremist settler organizations that use violence to fast-track Israeli annexation of the West Bank, like 'Nachala' and 'Tsav 9,' professionalize and become paramilitary forces to be reckoned with. Among Israel's population, there is a strong sense that security is best guaranteed by annexation and controlling or expelling as many Palestinians as possible. Palestinian resistance in this scenario is minimal due to the slow recovery of Hamas' armed capabilities as a result of recurrent Israeli operations and strict controls, especially along the border between Egypt and Gaza; low levels of Iranian support due to its domestic weakness, or even implosion after the Israeli/US war of aggression of June 2025, and blows suffered by the axis of resistance; as well as Israeli disarmament of most of the Palestinian Authority's security forces with US support via its office of the United States Security Coordinator (USSC). US military aid remains in the order of several billions per year (USD 3.8 billion/year today) (Masters and Merrow 2024). Washington also keeps providing cover for Israel in the UN Security Council and puts bilateral pressure on allies to follow US policy. For example, Washington compels Egypt and Jordan to maintain strict border controls, using financial support packages for their cash-strapped governments as leverage.

There are several roads leading to this scenario. For example, Prime Minister Netanyahu completes his term, manages to shift the conflict frame from Gaza to Iran on a permanent basis after Tehran decides to weaponize its nuclear program following US strikes on its Fordow facility (thus leveraging and reinforcing the existential insecurity of Israeli society, and garnering global sympathy) and successfully blames 7 October 2023 on the military and intelligence establishment while aggressive West Bank annexation helps his extreme right-wing partners to surge in the polls. Rule by the conservative, ultra-nationalist and/or extreme right continues in a next term, underpinned by divisions and fundamental insecurities among many Israelis, as well as an extremist and highly dedicated settler vanguard movement. Alternatively, Netanyahu is forced to step down at some point and loses the next elections, but Israel's ultra-nationalist and extremist parties return to government within a few years aided by a few high-profile violent incidents of Palestinian resistance on the West Bank in which dozens of settlers perish.

One major consequence of this scenario is that the Israeli government can finish what it started in 1948, namely the conquest of territories it views as belonging to the Jewish state of Israel ('Eretz Yisrael') and the expulsion or marginalization of their Palestinian population that started with the 'Nakba' (i.e., catastrophe). The combination of full annexation, the 2018 nation state law and judicial 'reform' 2.0 ensures the entrenchment of an apartheid system that is enforced by an ever more sophisticated system of laws, surveillance as well as (para-) military repression. Another major consequence of this scenario is the further deterioration of the universality of the global rules-based order as the international community watches without acting how the Israeli state completes its conquest of territories that do not belong to it. This sets a major precedent for Russian designs on Ukraine, Chinese designs on Taiwan and those of any other country with a poorly substantiated claim on someone else's territory. A final consequence of the scenario is the continued suffering of the Palestinian people in ever worsening circumstances. At some point in the future, these are likely to give rise to forms of violent extremism that can link up with a revival of Islamic State-style organizations.

Gaza on the Jordan River

In terms of annexation, this scenario is similar to the previous one with the major differences that the Palestinian Authority is dissolved or abandoned, Palestinian urban centers on the West Bank are walled off and turned into humanitarian slums while Israeli military repression acquires an intensity that is reminiscent of the IDF's campaign in Gaza in 2023–2025. It includes daily assassinations, collective punishment by destroying entire villages and forced displacement across the West Bank. In large part, this is due to far greater Palestinian resistance. Which, in turn, is the result of the Palestinian Authority's security apparatus successfully evading disarmament, going underground and forming the core of resistance cells throughout the West Bank together with Hamas armed elements. The latter enjoys a recovery in Gaza as well as abroad. Egypt and Jordan informally relax their border controls out of anger with Israeli destruction, enduring occupation and arrogance in its bilateral relations, acting on the belief that their own stability is more important to the US than toeing the line on its pro-Israel policies. In an act of subtle subversion of US and Israeli annexation policy, Gulf States like Qatar and the Kingdom of Saudi Arabia provide undercover financial support to Egypt and Jordan to reduce their vulnerability to US financial pressure. Palestinian armed resistance is further buoyed by high levels of Iranian support, or from other foreign sources, as Tehran's domestic politics and economy stabilize after the Israeli-US war of aggression of June 2025, and in the wake of Khamenei's succession. Such support goes in particular to Islamist resistance groups, but increasingly also benefits other armed Palestinian groups. Logistics run via smuggling networks in southwestern Syria and northern Jordan where high levels of poverty create an enabling environment, as well as via the Islamic Resistance in Iraq and Jordan. The latter has become vulnerable to both foreign infiltration and domestic upheaval due to the monarchy's alignment with the US. Iran ultimately outlasts Israel and the US during the long 2023–2025 confrontation that started after 7 October. This is due to Tehran's ability to absorb Israeli and American blows while Israel faces mounting international isolation because of the carnage it wrought in Gaza (see Van Veen 2024).

Pathways to this scenario include growing antipathy toward Israel in the Levant despite US efforts to contrary. This is mainly the result of Israel purposefully maintaining a 'hunger games' situation in Gaza, for example by 'thinning' its Palestinian population by neglect, starvation and continuous but random violence, and refusing to develop realistic plans for reconstruction. Gaza turns into a low-level insurgency as a result, and becomes a prisoner camp where slow death due to starvation and disease is as common as a quick death by sniper bullet or drone strike. Palestinians in the West Bank realize the full length to which Israel is willing to go in order to establish its dominance, which reinforces Abu Obaida's call to arms of 2023–2024 as the only possible response to the existential threat Zionism poses to the Palestinians (he is the spokesperson of the Al-Qassam brigades) (Agathocleous and Van Veen 2024). The succession of Mahmoud Abbas provides the tipping point after which the Palestinian Authority starts preparing its security forces for underground resistance under cover of maintaining security cooperation with Israel. Fear of annihilation of the Palestinian presence on the West Bank acts as a powerful stimulant for Hamas, large parts of Fatah, Hezbollah, (militant) activists in Jordan and Iran to work together.

The main consequence of this scenario is a protracted urban guerilla war against Israeli paramilitary settlers and the Israeli army that the IDF cannot win without indiscriminately targeting the Palestinian civilian population at large (see Abraham (2024) for the Gaza version). Israeli forces nevertheless seek to break Palestinian resistance by brute force, applying the Dahiya doctrine to Palestinian urban centers in the West Bank (see Van Veen and Azizi 2024). Other than further isolating Israel internationally, West-Jerusalem suffers few negative material consequences as long as US support remains steadfast. The revival of Hamas and foreign support-especially, but not exclusively from Iran-enable Israel and the US to frame the bloodletting as a fight against terrorism and external interference.

Colonial-style Suffering

In this scenario, Israel's occupation continues to advance hilltop by hilltop, outpost by outpost and street by street in both gradual steps and sudden bursts. It is concentrated in area C of the West Bank and East Jerusalem. Gaza remains under direct Israeli military rule in whole or in part, but features limited to no new settlement. Due to the ICJ judgment of 19 July 2024, ICC arrest warrants against Messrs. Netanyahu and Gallant, and a refusal to countenance a two-state solution as exemplified by the Knesset vote of 18 July 2024 (68 in favor, 43 abstentions, 9 against; see Magid 2024), Israel is viewed as an apartheid state in most of the world except for parts of the West where Judeo-Christian linkages, Holocaust guilt and business as well as military interests remain strong, and where far-right parties view Israel's ethno-centric policies as an example to follow (see Mishra 2024). Occupation is expanded only gradually because Israel's extremist political parties do not return to office after Prime Minister Netanyahu's tenure comes to an end, even though they remain a force to be reckoned with. As a judicial reform 2.0 remains stalled or off the table, political power shifts back to the center-right that favors a more gradual approach to annexation. In this, it is assisted by a pliant Palestinian Authority that does not reform. President Abbas' successor is cut from the same collaborative cloth as he is. The Palestinian Authority continues to act as auxiliary police force to the IDF and increasingly as humanitarian safety net. It remains corrupt and at the financial mercy of Israel. In this scenario, Palestinian Authority security forces are neither disarmed nor do they rebel, while Hamas fails to recover in the military sense due to Israel patrolling the borders of Gaza in strength. Furthermore, Iranian military support to Palestinian resistance factions remains low due to the Israeli/American war of aggression of June 2025, domestic protests and/or a deepening economic crisis that necessitates an accommodation with both the Gulf and the US. Saudi financial support incentivizes cooperation between the PA and Israel as part of an informal deal between Riyadh, Israel and the US.

The roads to this scenario run through early or regular elections that relegate Netanyahu to political history as they amount to a vote against extremist political parties and are followed by an inquiry into the political failures leading up to 7 October 2023. Iran and Hezbollah largely remain impotent and seek to recover from the deep wounds Israel and the US have inflicted on their leadership, military capabilities and social prestige, which prevents the Israeli prime minister from playing up external threats. As power shifts from the extreme right to the center-right, some of Israel's excesses in Gaza and the West Bank are curbed. The Israeli government enables structurally better humanitarian access to Gaza and reigns in some of the armed extremist settlers to forestall greater Palestinian resistance and international censure. Yet, the business of occupation continues and no Israeli political leader even pays lip service to a two-state solution. A return to Menachim Begin's proposal of 1977 that offered Palestinian autonomy and self-rule over a set of enclaves is all that is on offer.[9]

A major consequence of this scenario is that it forces a stark choice on the international community. After all, the internationally sanctioned solution to occupation, a situation that the ICJ rendered unlawful in its advisory opinion of 19 July 2024, is officially rejected by the occupying power while it expands occupation. Hence, realization of the ICJ's ruling requires imposing pressure on Israel, and yet the US as well as key European and Arab countries prefer to prioritize good bilateral relations. It is not clear whether this is sustainable in a multi-polar geopolitical ordering since Palestine can become a leading cause for anti-Western countries to

---

[9] Interestingly, this proposal originally included granting all Palestinians Israeli citizenship (Thrall 2017).

unite behind. In the long run, the failure of Palestinian resistance to bring change about by legal means also increases incentives to take up arms again, which can cause a shift to one of the other scenarios and even create linkages to reviving extremist movements across the Levant. However, in the shorter to medium term, this scenario signals a return to the dynamics of occupation before 7 October 2023.

Squid Game

In terms of annexation, this scenario is similar to the previous one with the differences that the succession of Abbas, revitalization of the PLO, international condemnation and modest Iranian support (or support from other foreign sources) enable greater armed Palestinian resistance. The succession of Abbas by someone like Marwan Barghouti opens the door to incorporating Hamas and potentially Palestinian Islamic Jihad in the PLO to revive the organization (see Pelham 2024). Using the Palestinian Authority as a front, the PLO once more becomes the center of civic and legal resistance against occupation in this scenario, in addition to running a network of underground armed resistance cells manned by the Palestinian Authority's security forces. The resistance operates from urban areas that are difficult for Israel to penetrate without massive collateral damage. While it is tempted to replicate its approach for dealing with Hamas in Gaza, more and more Israeli politicians and commanders face ICC arrest warrants in a context in which the ICJ already rendered Israel's occupation as unlawful and in which a genocide case hangs over Israel as the sword of Damocles. It has come to be viewed as an apartheid state *tout court* and even Western politicians no longer ignore paramilitary settler violence or IDF complicity in the repression of Palestinian armed resistance with the exception of the United States. Even so, the Israeli government uses collective punishment, targeted assassinations and regular military operations to take out resistance cells and leaders. As Palestinian resistance stiffens, the influence of Israeli extremist political parties and movements grows even though they were booted out of office when Netanyahu's tenure came to an end. Judicial reform 2.0 is put back on the table based on the justification that it is necessary to counter Palestinian terrorism. Hamas makes a recovery in the West Bank while its situation in Gaza remains dire as Israel keeps up stringent border controls and delays reconstruction efforts as part of its efforts to cleanse the area of Palestinians. Iranian support is limited as neither the

Palestinian Authority nor the revived PLO wishes to be closely associated with Tehran or elements of the axis of resistance. The Palestinian Authority does benefit from political and material support of Turkey, as well as financial support from Qatar, Kuwait and Saudi Arabia.

It is not so much the gradual expansion of occupation that triggers this scenario, which has after all been business as usual over the past decades, but rather the precedent that the destruction of Gaza sets for Israeli designs on the West Bank—i.e., its intention to establish total control and its willingness to resort to total destruction in case of serious resistance. From this perspective, there is little to lose and armed resistance paradoxically becomes the Palestinian default response. In this scenario, resistance is enabled by factors like a shift in coercive profile of the Palestinian security forces, a partial revival of Hamas and modest foreign support (such as from Iran), but also by greater constraints on Israel that prevent it from repeating its modus operandi of Gaza in 2023–2025. Palestinian resolve is constantly strengthened by a daily live broadcast of Gaza as permanent prison camp on the brink of starvation, plagued by contagious diseases and under strict Israeli military surveillance. There is little alleviation, no reconstruction and what limited order there is emerges from the barrel of a gun. The objective of eliminating Hamas is pursued by collective punishment, which many Israelis continue to condone.[10]

One important consequence of this scenario is that both international and Palestinian pressure on Israel grow while West-Jerusalem seeks to pursue gradual expansion, especially in West Bank Area C, and tries to avoid using indiscriminate force. Palestinian armed resistance under these conditions throws occupation in sharper relief, especially as militants avoid targeting Israeli civilians under a new leader like Barghouti. This sets the door ajar for stronger international intervention. In the meantime, the Palestinian death toll spirals as its armed resistance is no match for the Israeli military. Targeted killings and collective punishment abound. The low-intensity but steady bloodletting puts increasing pressure on Arab states like Jordan, Egypt and Saudi Arabia to intervene.

---

[10] In line with the widely held public sentiment in Israel of early 2024 that humanitarian aid to Gaza should be blocked as long as Israeli hostages remain in Hamas captivity (Hermann and Kaplan 2024).

Factors Influencing the Scenario Driving Forces

Each of the main driving forces of the scenarios is in turn influenced by several factors. These have been woven through the scenario narratives discussed above. Figure 2.2 summarizes them to present an analytically comprehensive picture. Naturally, each factor can be discussed in greater detail and this is precisely what subsequent Chapters do as they assess the evolution of the objectives, interests and actions of key stakeholders in the Israeli occupation of the Palestinian territories: the Israeli government, the Palestinian Authority (Fatah), Hamas and the United States (the four main conflict parties); Hezbollah, Egypt and Jordan (key neighbors); as well as Saudi Arabia and Iran (key regional powers). In this manner, the Chapters that follow expand the evidence base for the scenarios and offer ingredients for reflections in the final Chapter about how conditions can be created that enable new conversations about ending occupation.

Conflict of Interest The author has no conflict of interests to declare that are relevant to the content of this chapter.

Bibliography

Abraham, Yuval. 2024. "'Lavender': The AI Machine Directing Israel's Bombing Spree in Gaza." *+972 Magazine* (blog). April 3, 2024. https://www.972mag.com/lavender-ai-israeli-army-gaza/.

Agathocleous, Sophia, and Erwin Van Veen. 2024. "Hamas 'From the Heart of Battle': Analyzing Abu Obaida's Discourse." *The Cairo Review of Global Affairs*, no. Summer 2024. https://www.thecairoreview.com/essays/hamas-from-the-heart-of-battle-analyzing-abu-obaidas-discourse/.

Anabi, Or. 2022. "Jewish Israeli Voters Moving Right." *The Israel Democracy Institute* (blog). August 30, 2022. https://en.idi.org.il/articles/45854.

Asseburg, Muriel. 2023. *Palästina und die Palästinenser: eine Geschichte von der Nakba bis zur Gegenwart* [Palestine and the Palestinians: A history from the Nakba until the present]. 5. Auflage, Originalausgabe. C.H. Beck Paperback 6062. München: C.H. Beck.

Baconi, Tareq. 2022. *Hamas Contained: The Rise and Pacification of Palestinian Resistance*. First paperback printing, 2022. Stanford, California: Stanford University Press.

Bar-Joseph, Uri. 2005. *The Watchman Fell Asleep: The Surprise of Yom Kippur and Its Sources*. SUNY Series in Israeli Studies. Albany: State University of New York Press.

Bartov, Omer. 2024. "As a Former IDF Soldier and Historian of Genocide, I Was Deeply Disturbed by My Recent Visit to Israel." *The Guardian*, August 13, 2024, The long read edition, sec. World news. https://www.theguardian.com/world/article/2024/aug/13/israel-gaza-historian-omer-bartov.

Bekkers, Frank, Koen Aartsma, and Tim Sweijs. 2023. "Barsten En Blokken: Confrontatie En Samenwerking in Een Wereld van Wisselende Coalities." Strategische Monitor. Den Haag: Clingendael and HCSS. https://www.clingendael.org/sites/default/files/2024-02/Barsten_en_Blokken_Strategische_Monitor_2023_final.pdf.

Clingendael. 2023–2024. "Expert Insights: Israel-Hamas War." Clingendael. Accessed August 24, 2024. https://www.clingendael.org/publication/expert-insights-israel-hamas-war.

European Union, World Bank, and United Nations. 2024. "Gaza Strip Interim Damage Assessment." Summary note. https://thedocs.worldbank.org/en/doc/14e309cd34e04e40b90eb19afa7b5d15-0280012024/original/Gaza-Interim-Damage-Assessment-032924-Final.pdf?_gl=1*353010*_gcl_au*MTA4MjAxNDM0NS4xNzIwODEzNjE5.

Hermann, Tamar, and Yaron Kaplan. 2024. "Most Israelis: an 'Absolute Victory' to the War is Unlikely." War in Gaza Survey 11. Jerusalem: The Israel Democracy Institute. https://en.idi.org.il/articles/52976.

Huwart, Jean-Yves, and Loïc Verdier. 2013. *Economic Globalisation: Origins and Consequences*. 1. Aufl. OECD Insights. Paris: OECD.

Jamaluddine, Zeina, Hanan Abukmail, Sarah Aly, Oona M R Campbell, and Francesco Checchi. 2025. "Traumatic Injury Mortality in the Gaza Strip from Oct 7, 2023, to June 30, 2024: A Capture–Recapture Analysis." *The Lancet*, January, S0140673624026783. https://doi.org/10.1016/S0140-6736(24)02678-3.

Johnson, Neil F. 2012. Simply Complexity: *A Clear Guide to Complexity Theory*. 2. publ. in trade paperback. A Oneworld Book. Oxford: Oneworld.

Kahane, Adam. 2012. *Transformative Scenario Planning: Working Together to Change the Future*. 1st ed. San Francisco: Berrett-Koehler Publishers.

Keller-Lynn, Carrie. 2022. "Jewish Israeli Voters Have Moved Significantly Rightward in Recent Years, Data Shows," August 29, 2022, Online edition. https://www.timesofisrael.com/israeli-jewish-voters-moved-significantly-rightward-in-recent-years-data-shows/.

Khanna, Parag. 2016. *Connectography: Mapping the Future of Global Civilization*. First edition. New York: Random House.

Khatib, Rasha, Martin McKee, and Salim Yusuf. 2024. "Counting the Dead in Gaza: Difficult but Essential." *The Lancet* 404 (10449): 237–38. https://doi.org/10.1016/S0140-6736(24)01169-3.

Kubovich, Yaniv, and Michael Hauser Tov. 2024. "Haaretz Investigation: Israeli Army Uses Palestinian Civilians to Inspect Potentially Booby-Trapped

Tunnels in Gaza." *Haaretz*, August 13, 2024, sec. Israel News. https://www.haaretz.com/israel-news/2024-08-13/ty-article-magazine/.premium/idf-uses-gazan-civilians-as-human-shields-to-inspect-potentially-booby-trapped-tunnels/00000191-4c84-d7fd-a7f5-7db6b99e0000.

Leroux, Pieter, and Vincent Maphai. 1992. "The Mont Fleur Scenarios." Volume 7 Number 1. Deeper News. Emeryville: Global Business Network.

Magid, Jacob. 2024. "Knesset Votes Overwhelmingly against Palestinian Statehood, Days before PM's US Trip." *Times of Israel*, July 18, 2024, Online edition. https://www.timesofisrael.com/knesset-votes-overwhelmingly-against-palestinian-statehood-days-before-pms-us-trip/.

Masters, Jonathan, and Will Merrow. 2024. "U.S. Aid to Israel in Four Charts." *Council on Foreign Relations* (blog). May 31, 2024. https://www.cfr.org/article/us-aid-israel-four-charts.

Mishra, Pankaj. 2024. "The Shoah after Gaza." *London Review of Books*, March 1, 2024. https://www.lrb.co.uk/the-paper/v46/n06/pankaj-mishra/the-shoah-after-gaza.

Morris, Benny. 1999. *Righteous Victims: A History of the Zionist-Arab Conflict, 1881-1999*. 1st ed. New York: Knopf.

Nusseibeh, Sari. 2009. *Once Upon a Country: A Palestinian Life*. London: Halban Publishers Ltd.

Pappé, Ilan. 2024. *Lobbying for Zionism on Both Sides of the Atlantic*. London: Oneworld Publications.

Pedahzur, Ami. 2012. *The Triumph of Israel's Radical Right*. New York: Oxford University Press.

Pelham, Nicolas. 2024. "Marwan Barghouti, the World's Most Important Prisoner." *1843 Magazine The Economist*, July 27, 2024. https://www.economist.com/1843/2024/07/22/marwan-barghouti-the-worlds-most-important-prisoner.

Said Aly, Abdel Monem, Shai Feldman, and Khalīl Shiqāqī. 2013. *Arabs and Israelis: Conflict and Peacemaking in the Middle East*. Houndsmills, Basingstoke, Hampshire ; New York, NY: Palgrave Macmillan.

Said, Edward W. 2001. *The End of the Peace Process: Oslo and After*. 1. Vintage Books ed. Current Affairs Middle Eastern Studies. New York, NY: Vintage Books.

Salam, Nawaf, and Philippe Gautier. 2024. Legal consequences arising from the policies and practices of Israel in the Occupied Palestinian Territory, including East Jerusalem. International Court of Justice.

Schwartz, Peter. 1996. *The Art of the Long View: Paths to Strategic Insight for Yourself and Your Company*. First Crown Business Edition. New York: Crown Business.

Shaviṭ, Ari. 2015. *My Promised Land: The Triumph and Tragedy of Israel*. Updated Edition. Brunswick, Victoria: Scribe.

Shell Global. 2024. "Shell Scenarios." August 22, 2024. https://www.shell.com/news-and-insights/scenarios.html.

Shir, Efrat. 2024. "State of the Occupation." Joint situation report Year 57. The Platform - Israeli NGOs for human rights. https://reliefweb.int/report/occupied-palestinian-territory/state-occupation-year-57-joint-situation-report-june-2024-enhe.

Sunter, Clem. 1987. *The World and South Africa in the 1990s*. 1st ed. Cape Town: Human & Rousseau : Tafelberg.

Taleb, Nassim Nicholas. 2010. The Black Swan: *The Impact of the Highly Improbable*. 2nd ed., Random trade pbk. ed. New York: Random House Trade Paperbacks.

Thrall, Nathan. 2017. *The Only Language They Understand: Forcing Compromise in Israel and Palestine*. First edition. New York: Metropolitan Books, Henry Holt and Company.

Tetlock, Philip E., and Dan Gardner. 2016. *Superforecasting: The Art and Science of Prediction*. London: Random House Books.

Van der Heijden, Kees. 2005. *Scenarios: The Art of Strategic Conversation*. 2nd ed. Chichester, West Sussex ; Hoboken, N.J: John Wiley & Sons.

Van Veen, Erwin. 2024. "Israel's Strategic Peril." *Clingendael* (blog). May 28, 2024. https://www.clingendael.org/publication/israels-strategic-peril.

Van Veen, Erwin, and Azizi Hamidreza. 2024. "Playing with Fire: Patterns of Iranian-Israeli Military Confrontation." *War on the Rocks*, June 25, 2024. https://warontherocks.com/2024/06/playing-with-fire-patterns-of-iranian-israeli-military-confrontation/.

Visualizing Palestine. 2024. "How Israel Is Arming Israeli Settlers." *Visualizing Palestine* (blog). August 2024. https://visualizingpalestine.org/visual/how-israel-is-arming-israeli-settlers/.

Wagemakers, Joas. 2024. *Hamas: Palestijns Nationalisme en Militant Pragmatisme*. Amsterdam: Amsterdam University Press.

Weizman, Eyal. 2012. *Hollow Land: Israel's Architecture of Occupation*. London; New York: Verso.

Wilkinson, Angela, and Roland Kupers. 2013. "Living in the Futures." *Harvard Business Review*, May 1, 2013. https://hbr.org/2013/05/living-in-the-futures.

Yizhar, S. 2011. *Khirbet Khizeh*. 1. publ. in Great Britain. London: Granta.

Young, Michael. 2024. "Israel's Exceptionalism Is Untenable." *Carnegie Diwan* (blog). August 14, 2024. https://carnegieendowment.org/middle-east/diwan/2024/08/israels-exceptionalism-is-untenable?lang=en.

Open Access This chapter is licensed under the terms of the Creative Commons Attribution 4.0 International License (http://creativecommons.org/licenses/by/4.0/), which permits use, sharing, adaptation, distribution and reproduction in any medium or format, as long as you give appropriate credit to the original author(s) and the source, provide a link to the Creative Commons license and indicate if changes were made.

The images or other third party material in this chapter are included in the chapter's Creative Commons license, unless indicated otherwise in a credit line to the material. If material is not included in the chapter's Creative Commons license and your intended use is not permitted by statutory regulation or exceeds the permitted use, you will need to obtain permission directly from the copyright holder.

PART I

Direct Conflict Stakeholders

CHAPTER 3

Hamas Walking the Path of Thorns

Abdalhadi Alijla

Abstract The deep interwovenness of Hamas with Palestinian society makes it difficult to eradicate the movement in its capacity as a militant and Islamist expression of resistance against Israel's unlawful occupation. The Israeli military effort in Gaza to eradicate all institutions of social life and its mass killing of civilians aims at undercutting the popular and social bases of Hamas without, however, any accompanying political effort to change the fundamentals of occupation. The carnage Israel has caused makes it more likely than not that Hamas, or a look-alike, will emerge from the rubble unless Israel takes its mass assassinations and forced displacements to their ultimate conclusion. This also means that Hamas will play a role in the future governance of Gaza, and indeed of the state of Palestine as a whole if the objective is durable peace. The dysfunction of the Palestinian Authority and the destruction of Gaza will only make militant resistance a more attractive option for many Palestinians and Hamas is well placed to take advantage of such a development. Israel will probably welcome it since Palestinian militancy enables iron-fisted repression with the excuse of fighting terrorism.

A. Alijla (✉)
Arab Reform Initiative (ARI), Paris, France
e-mail: abid.ijla@gmail.com

© The Author(s) 2025
E. van Veen (ed.), *The Future of the Occupation of the Palestinian Territories after Gaza*,
https://doi.org/10.1007/978-3-031-93798-9_3

Keywords Al-Aqsa flood · Yahya Sinwar · Axis of resistance · Second intifada · Al-Qassam brigades · Fatah · Palestinian Liberation Organization (PLO)

INTRODUCTION

In January 2024, the International Court of Justice (ICJ) assessed that there was a real and imminent risk of the onset of genocide in Gaza. A year later, the official death toll among Palestinians has surpassed 46,000, the majority of whom are women and children. Scientific estimations put the total number of victims at over 189,000 and counting (Khatib et al. 2024). In addition to known victims, there are over 8,000 missing persons. Israel also destroyed all academic institutions in Gaza, as well as all major hospitals. Hence, the Israeli military campaign constitutes a war not only on Hamas but also mortgages Gaza's future by making it unlivable. Within weeks after 7 October 2023, it became evident that Israel was waging a comprehensive war on Gaza, targeting its infrastructure, its people and its prospects. Despite the many attempts by the Qatari and Egyptian governments to stop the slaughter and negotiate a ceasefire—efforts that the American administration pretended to join while condoning Israeli atrocities—Israel persists in its stated desire to eliminate Hamas and maintains that the movement cannot be part of any future governance mechanism in Gaza. But if Hamas cannot be eradicated, it is not clear how the future governance of Gaza can be organized. This essay seeks to answers both issues. First, I examine whether Hamas can be eradicated. Second, I discuss governance options for Gaza once the slaughter stops, if it does.

CAN HAMAS BE ERADICATED?

The short answer to the question whether Hamas can be eradicated in Gaza is no. This is the case because such an objective lacks an understanding of Hamas's nature, its role, and its interwovenness with Palestinian society—both in Gaza and beyond. Neither methods used previously by the Palestinian Authority (PA) nor Israel's coercive power are likely to dismantle Hamas completely. The Palestinian Authority has come down hard on Hamas before, especially between 1994 and 2002. It disrupted the group's finances, restricted the movements of its members, and barred them from public employment, including in the educational and health sectors (Robinson 2004; Hroub 2009). Despite these measures, Hamas managed to survive. It established parallel and clandestine institutions that ensured continuation of its activities at various levels and in different ways within Gaza. Years-long efforts, undertaken by several Palestinian security agencies in collaboration with Israel, failed to dismantle the movement. Hamas taking control over Gaza in 2007 marked the anti-climax of this effort.

In similar vein, Israel's current military campaign in Gaza will certainly weaken Hamas's military capacity for some time, including its ability to launch rockets. But it will not end its support among Palestinians, especially outside of Gaza. Recent polls in the West Bank and Gaza indicate a relatively steady level of support for Hamas. In December 2023, support for Hamas in Gaza stood at 42% (up from 38% in September 2023). Support for Fatah stood at 18% (down from 25% in September 2023). In September 2024, support for Hamas in Gaza stood at 35% and Fatah at 26% (PCPSR 2024a). However, based on my own experience and research, such figures should be approached with skepticism since they are not just the result of Hamas's leading role in the current conflict with Israel, but also reflect other factors like mounting grievances amid destruction and slaughter.

In 2022, I visited Gaza after sixteen years living abroad. It was evident that the local population was dissatisfied with Hamas governance. According to the 2022 Arab Barometer, approximately 23% of respondents expressed significant trust in Hamas whereas 52% reported having no trust in the movement at all. It is crucial to note that this lack of trust extends to other Palestinian political parties, including Fatah. In March 2023, 71% of Gaza's population perceived Hamas's institutions as corrupt, while 81% believed the PA was corrupt (Arab Barometer 2022). Over the last decade, Palestinians in Gaza have protested against Hamas's governance performance, particularly criticizing imposed taxation, lack of opportunities, and poor services. This sentiment, however, does not equate to an outright rejection of Hamas as a resistance movement. Despite resentment toward Hamas for 15 years of alleged authoritarian control and corruption, not all Gazans want to see it gone. Gazans desire change, but not necessarily a return to the PA and Fatah, which have far lower levels of trust. What they seek is a partnership between Hamas and Fatah that embraces democratic governance and the rule of law. Yet, this requires an end of the Israeli occupation. For instance, President Abbas canceled the presidential and parliamentarian elections in 2021 due to Israel refusing to enable the inclusion of East Jerusalem, which was similar to what has happened during previous elections (Al-Mughrabi 2021).

Many of the Palestinians in Gaza who are critical of Hamas distinguish between its military resistance, represented by the movement's Al-Qassam military wing, and its governance of Gaza. Essentially, they support Hamas' resistance against occupation, but do not necessarily agree with the way Hamas administers civil affairs. This distinction is reflected in a PCPSR opinion poll of December 2023: while 37% of Gaza residents disagreed with the actions taken on 7 October, a majority— 56%—believe that armed struggle is the only path to an independent Palestinian state and the end of Israel's occupation—a rise from 50% in September 2023 (PCPSR 2024a). Support for Hamas therefore arises directly from Palestinian grievances and the absence of any meaningful political settlement with Israel. In the West Bank, with a population approaching 3 million, Hamas enjoys significantly greater popularity than in Gaza. This can be attributed to the inaction of the PA, the aggressive behavior of Israeli settlers, and the daily confrontations Palestinians experience with the Israeli army.

The failure of the Oslo Accords, coupled with corruption within the PA, has led the majority of Palestinians to agree that Hamas' agenda of military struggle is the only remaining viable option to resist occupation. Such sentiments sustain support for Hamas operations despite significant challenges. In 2017, Hamas decoupled itself from the Muslim Brotherhood, which further enhanced its nationalist credentials (Al-Mughrabi and Finn 2017). As the war on Gaza continues, over 79% of the population has at least one family member who is killed or injured by June 2024. Belief in the legitimacy of armed resistance will probably increase as a result (PCPSR 2024b). Unless an alternative to Hamas emerges, the majority of Palestinians are likely to maintain their support for armed struggle. This does not necessarily imply active membership or even sympathy with Hamas, but rather a belief in armed resistance as last resort. But there is potential for sympathizers to become more active if no alternatives present themselves. Fatah, Islamic Jihad, the Palestinian Front for Liberation of Palestine (PFLP), and others do already provide alternatives of course, but these groups lack the necessary resources, experiences, and mobilization capacity.

Another important factor that makes eliminating Hamas impossible is its characteristics. Hamas is akin to a chimera from Greek mythology, embodying traits of various entities: it operates as a social movement, military organization, rebel group, governing body, political party, and has been labeled both a terrorist group and as freedom fighters. These multifaceted characteristics have enabled it to ingrain itself deeply in Palestinian society and to adapt its form and function to meet different challenges and opportunities. In her study of Hamas institutions and their development, Sara Roy found that their embeddedness in civil society is more developed than previously thought (Roy 2002). In his analyses of Hamas's security forces after 2007, Yezid Sayegh examined how they professionalized while acting as state-run police and security apparatus (Sayigh 2011). Hence, Hamas is a visible yet also an elusive target. While it can be attacked, pinpointing it with sufficient precision for a coup de grace is difficult. In addition, Hamas has long employed political "clannism", leveraging the loyalty of strong clan members. This approach facilitates mobilization through family networks, mosques, and community engagement at neighborhood and street levels. Such social structures cannot be dismantled without extreme measures. The complete elimination of this network would require action against every single Palestinian in the West Bank and Gaza.

Yet another factor is regional dynamics. Hamas is a member of a regional alliance that includes Iran, Hezbollah, Iraqi Islamist militias, and the Houthis in Yemen. This "axis of resistance" acts as a protective network that helps Hamas survive by providing it with tactics, resources, weapons, and mobility. As long as this network endures, eliminating Hamas is not feasible. It effectively ensures Hamas can maintain a minimum level of functionality and operational activity, even when it is weakened. As we have seen over the past months, Hezbollah, the Houthi, and the Iraqi Islamic resistance engaged out of solidarity with Hamas as well as on the basis of their own interests, signaling that Hamas's war is their war, at least in part.

Taking all of this into consideration suggests it is possible to weaken Hamas, but very difficult to eliminate. Historical experience also suggests that force and violence can yield counterproductive outcomes, as evidenced by previous crackdowns and Israel's 16-year siege of Gaza actually having bolstered Hamas prior to 7 October 2023. Hamas is an integral part of the fabric of Palestinian society. This interwovenness explains, incidentally, why Israel's current military operation in Gaza targets its civilian populations and institutions and not just Hamas. It is a wholesale effort to render the Gaza Strip uninhabitable and eradicate the social support basis of the movement with forced displacement and mass slaughter as additional gains.

The Myth of "The Day After" and Future Governance in Gaza

Now that I have argued that Hamas will remain present in Gaza one way or another in all likelihood, several further factors must be considered before discussing what is called the "day after" or "the future governance of Gaza". First, the future of the Palestinian Authority in relation to prospects for reconciliation between Hamas and Fatah. Second, the role and acceptance of Hamas as de facto governing authority in Gaza. Third, prospects for the reconstruction of Gaza as part of negotiations about a broader political solution that paves the way for a Palestinian state.

Prior to the current mass slaughter and forced displacement in Gaza, Hamas and Fatah faced several barriers that hindered their administrative and bureaucratic reconciliation. The most significant obstacle was their parallel political agendas (Alijla and Al-Masri 2019). Hamas foregrounds militant resistance against occupation whereas Fatah has worked faithfully with Israeli forces as part of the PA's security collaboration. This matter remains unresolved although the polling figures cited above indicate a shift among Palestinians toward the position of Hamas. However, other differences that have made reconciliation difficult include Hamas its desire for control over the security apparatus in Gaza and for greater influence in the PLO—e.g., 50% of PLO posts. The Israeli invasion of Gaza is likely to have softened Hamas's position on its objective of maintaining security control over Gaza, however, and has made it more amenable to integrate into the PA's security structures and institutions. This is also the case because the Hamas activists that were involved in the 2007 killings of Fatah members, security officers, and repression of Gazan clans,[1] and who subsequently moved into leadership positions in the movement, are no more and hence cannot veto Hamas reconciliation with, or participation in, the PA security apparatus as part of a future government of national

---

[1] After 2012, reconciliation efforts between Mohamed Dahlan and Hamas included paying "Fidya," a form of compensation, to families of those killed, to mend relations between Hamas and key clans in Gaza.

unity government. Finally, Hamas has lost thousands of its militants in the recent fighting and lacks the resources to fast-track recruitment and rebuild its military capabilities, which may serve as an additional motivator for considering security integration with Fatah into PA structures (Mehvar and Khdour 2024). Nevertheless, Hamas is likely to stand firm on the issue of PLO representation. The movement continues to believe that it deserves greater representation within PLO bodies, especially compared to other political parties that are almost inactive or non-existent on the ground.

The "day after" question is about who will govern Gaza during and after the Israeli military campaign. Answering these questions requires examination of earlier governance structures and governance alternatives in Gaza. Even before the Israeli military campaign of mass slaughter and forced displacement, no one was interested in controlling and governing Gaza except Hamas. The Palestinian Authority (PA) showed little interest in governing Gaza or coexisting with Hamas. President Abbas and his security apparatus would likely face significant challenges in governing Gaza if they regained control, as new rivalries would rapidly emerge within Fatah. In the past two decades, Fatah has fragmented in both Gaza and the West Bank with new local "lords" emerging. Regional powers such as Egypt and Jordan have similarly shown limited interest in governing Gaza, focusing mainly on coordinating ceasefires, humanitarian aid, and reconstruction efforts—but without engaging in security or service provision. Finally, Israel maintained a siege and control modus operandi over the territory after withdrawing from Gaza in 2005, but has shown no interest in governing either. Its primary focus has been on maintaining security control over specific areas and creating buffer zones. This leaves Hamas as the only party willing and prepared to govern.

The structure of governance in Gaza that must be managed has two layers. The first level consists of the Palestinian Authority (PA) and the de facto Hamas authorities who oversee the police and manage education and health services. After Hamas took control of Gaza in 2007, the PA continued to pay the salaries of civil employees, including teachers and health workers, even though many were instructed to stay home. The PA maintained these payments to retain some influence, leverage international aid directed at Gaza, and because it collects taxes on goods imported via Israel into Gaza. Therefore, Gaza was also a financial resource for the PA. While Hamas took over responsibilities such as the appointments of public employees, some aspects of social protection services, and some administrative functions, it was primarily a security provider. Hamas's revenue mainly came from direct taxation. However, in recent years, Hamas struggled to pay its employees regularly. Despite these challenges, Hamas and the PA have shared governance over certain services such as hospitals and schools as well as the issuance of birth certificates and passports.

The second level of governance in Gaza involves its municipalities, which are responsible for essential services like water, electricity, sanitation, and cultural programs. There are about ten municipalities in Gaza, some democratically elected and others appointed by Hamas. These municipalities have continued to receive international funding until 7 October 2023 and have coordinated directly with both the PA and Hamas. During the war, these municipalities have sought to keep providing services despite the targeting of their employees, the destruction of their buildings, and the loss of vehicles. They are the only formal institutions working to deliver services under extreme circumstances. This means that Hamas can leverage their existence to rebuild, to an extent, its bureaucratic apparatus and reconfigure its administrative structure to fit new realities while maintaining itself as the only realistic security institution at the local level. The failure of Israeli attempts to recruit local leaders or tribes illustrates Hamas' influence and capabilities.

Well over a year into the Israeli war on Gaza, Hamas is still able to fight and launch rockets into Israel, even though far more sporadically and in a more guerilla-style fashion. To some extent, Hamas has also attempted to rebuild administrative mechanisms in Gaza. However, Israel's military strategy of targeting civilians seeks to undermine efforts by Hamas to reestablish civilian administration. Even with the possibility of a ceasefire and the return of over a million people to the northern part of Gaza, what seems likely is continuous low- to mid-intensity combat without structured governance and continuous Israeli killing of civilians. Amid such chaos and violence, regional actors like the UAE, Egypt, Jordan, Qatar, and Turkey may seek to strengthen their regional and international positions by getting involved in Gaza after all. Yet, this could lead to further insecurity, a complete breakdown of the rule of law as well as competition between regional actors to deliver aid through their agents to build clientelist networks, increasing the chaos. The outcome will depend on how the situation in Gaza develops and what roles these actors choose to play. It is unlikely that regional Arab states will provide forces on the ground to maintain order, which is what Israel seems to prefer, without a political horizon for a two-state formula. Israeli politicians, including Prime Minister Netanyahu, have suggested that some Arab states might be willing to send troops to Gaza, but this was already refused by both Egypt and Jordan (Jeffery and Magdy 2023). The UAE is the only country that has indicated it might consider sending troops, but Hamas and other Palestinian factions have made it clear that they would treat such troops as "Israeli troops," signaling that international forces are not welcome in Gaza (Middle East Eye n.d.).

A War on the Future

The Israeli strategy regarding Gaza appears to lack a long-term plan for its civil governance. But this might in fact be the plan. Plainly put, Israel first seeks to cause as much destruction as it can and make Gaza as unlivable as possible. Next, Israel will use these conditions to ethnically cleanse northern Gaza and enable the establishment of indirect rule over the rest of Gaza via groups of criminals it supports and protects. In this manner, the purposeful absence of civil administration will create a permanent situation of insecurity that invites migration. Israel can further aggravate such a bleak state of play by complicating any reconstruction process, which will be slow in any case. For example, the UN has estimated it may take at least fifteen years to remove just the rubble. If Israel continues its blockade and adopts similar approaches to reconstruction as it used after the 2014 war, fifteen years is an optimistic estimate. Back then, Israel controlled every aspect of rubble removal and the rebuilding of private and public structures. Its current strategy might well be more restrictive, which would make the reconstruction of Gaza exceedingly difficult (Barakat and Masri 2017).

Another critical implication of the ongoing conflict for the future is the Israeli policy of targeted assassinations of Hamas leadership ranks. The focus has been on the second, third, and fourth levels of cadres and particularly the generation that emerged after 2003. It was formed during the second Intifada and the collapse of the peace process. This generation—well-educated and deeply involved in civil society organizations and educational institutions—was instrumental to Hamas's revival and growth. According to a lawyer and activist in Gaza, "It would be naive to believe that Hamas's leadership alone was responsible for all its achievements; rather, it was this generation of young and well-educated activists." This group played a crucial role in building Hamas's strength in Gaza up until 2023, significantly contributing to the organization's rise as a formidable force. Israel has sought to kill and displace this younger and well-educated generation of Hamas members, many of whom are civilians with no ties to the military wing of Hamas. After this conflict, Hamas will be without this generation of leaders and educated members. As a result, the organization may well become dominated by less experienced and more extreme individuals, which could have severe effect on society in terms of its Islamization and securitization, inclining it toward more extremist violence.

A final implication of the present conflict for the future is the direct or indirect killing of hundreds of civil society activists, including those involved in human rights and women's organizations, while many others have been forced to flee Gaza. This will create a significant vacuum in civil society organizations (CSOs) that have historically acted as a counterbalance to Hamas' more totalitarian tendencies and resisted the Islamization of Gazan society. The war has also exposed the weaknesses of many Western-funded CSOs, which ceased operations or disappeared entirely once the conflict began. In contrast, locally funded or Arab-funded CSOs have managed to continue their work, often at maximum capacity. As a result, many in Gaza have become distrustful of NGOs that were active before the conflict but disappeared once it started, or whose leaders fled. On the whole, Gaza is likely to experience a permanent decline in the presence of Western-funded NGOs as locally led NGOs take over.

Is There Political Will for a Peaceful Solution?

Before 7 October 2023, Hamas governed Gaza with an iron fist, effectively establishing a police state within a de-facto semi-state. This structure was largely modeled on the Palestinian Authority (PA), particularly in terms of its security apparatus. Hamas retained much of the PA's organizational framework after 2007, merely rebranding agencies and appointing new members. Although this governance and security structure has been destroyed, existing hierarchies and connections with the West Bank government could rapidly reconstruct it. Hence, one critical question for the prospects of realizing a political solution is under what conditions Hamas might dissolve its military wing and transform into a political party. Historical precedent suggests this is possible: the Palestinian Authority cracked down on Hamas in 1994 when hopes for peaceful conflict resolution based on the Oslo Accords were high, which led to a significant decline in Hamas's popularity. At that time, some Hamas leaders, including the head of Hamas political bureau, Ismail Haniya, assassinated in Tehran, resigned and formed a new Islamic party called the "Islamic Salvation National Party" with direct support from Yasser Arafat. This indicates that Hamas, along with other political groups, might shift to political participation and abandon armed resistance if there is the prospect of a political solution and a measure of pressure. Conversely, without a political solution, Hamas or other militant groups could grow stronger. Even though Hamas was not the most popular party in Gaza before 7 October 2023, particularly not among youth— in fact, most youth indicated distrust in all parties and answered that "no party" represents them (Arab Barometer 2022)[2]—the deep grievances resulting from the 2023–2024 Gaza conflict could easily incentivize youth to join Hamas after all, perpetuating the cycle of violence and resistance.

In conclusion, the future governance of Gaza is uncertain at the moment as there are too many unsettled variables. However, certain elements are predictable. Politically, Hamas will continue to play a role, whether as part of a governing body or by exerting influence over the decision-making processes of others. Without an end to the Israeli occupation and a clear political horizon, Hamas's military wing and capacities, along with those of other groups, are likely to be rebuilt or even strengthened, especially given the unprecedented levels of grievances and the absence of hope for new generations. Economically, Gaza faces enormous challenges. Capital is fleeing the region with many business owners relocating to Egypt or losing their businesses entirely. Rebuilding Gaza's economy will be extremely difficult without robust international and regional support. Ultimately, the decisive factor is the Israeli occupation and the political will within Israel to end it.

Conflict of Interest The author has no conflict of interests to declare that are relevant to the content of this chapter.

---

[2] According to the author's analysis and unpublished work, there were more than a dozen uprisings against Hamas its rule between 2007 and 2023 (Alijla 2023).

Bibliography

Arab Barometer. 2022. "Arab Barometer Wave V 2021–2022." The Arab Barometer. https://www.arabbarometer.org/surveys/arab-barometer-wave-vii/.
Abdalhadi, Alijla, and Aziz Al-Masri. (2019). New Bottles, Old Wine: The Contemporary Palestinian Political Division 6(1): 2. https://doi.org/10.17077/2168-538X.1116.
Alijla, Abdalhadi. "The (Semi) State's Fragility: Hamas, Clannism, and Legitimacy." Social Sciences 10, no. 11 (2021): 437.
Alijla, Abdalhadi. 2023. "Thorny Identity? Non-State Actors, Service Provision, Identities, and Hamas in Gaza." *Small Wars & Insurgencies* 34 (1): 195–220. https://doi.org/10.1080/09592318.2022.2097399.
Al-Mughrabi, Nidal, and Tom Finn. 2017. "Hamas Softens Stance on Israel, Drops Muslim Brotherhood Link." *Reuters*, May 1, 2017, sec. World. https://www.reuters.com/article/world/hamas-softens-stance-on-isr ael-drops-muslim-brotherhood-link-idUSKBN17X1N9/.
Al-Mughrabi, Nidal. 2021. "Palestinian Leader Delays Parliamentary and Presidential Elections, Blaming Israel." *Reuters*, April 30, 2021, sec. Middle East. https://www.reuters.com/world/middle-east/palestinian-elections-del ayed-says-president-mahmoud-abbas-2021-04-29/.
Barakat, Sultan, and Firas Masri. 2017. "Still in Ruins: Reviving the Stalled Reconstruction of Gaza." Doha: Brookings. https://www.brookings.edu/art icles/reviving-the-stalled-reconstruction-of-gaza/.
Hroub, Khaled. 2009. *Hamas*. The Other Press.
Jeffery, Jack, and Samy Magdy. 2023. "Why Egypt and Other Arab Countries Are Unwilling to Take in Palestinian Refugees from Gaza | AP News." October 19, 2023. https://apnews.com/article/palestinian-jordan-egypt-isr ael-refugee-502c06d004767d4b64848d878b66bd3d.
Khatib, Rasha, Martin McKee, and Salim Yusuf. 2024. "Counting the Dead in Gaza: Difficult but Essential." *The Lancet* 404 (10449): 237–38. https://doi.org/10.1016/S0140-6736(24)01169-3.
Mehvar, Ameneh and Nasser Khdour. 2024. "After a Year of War, Hamas Is Militarily Weakened — but Far from 'Eliminated.'" *ACLED* (blog). October 6, 2024. https://acleddata.com/2024/10/06/after-a-year-of-war-hamas-is-militarily-weakened-but-far-from-eliminated/.
Middle East Eye. n.d. "UAE Signals Willingness to Send Troops to Gaza." Middle East Eye. Accessed October 18, 2024. https://www.middleeasteye. net/live-blog/live-blog-update/uae-signals-willingness-send-troops-gaza.
PCPRS. 2024a. "Public Opinion Poll No (93)." 93. Ramallah. https://pcpsr.org/en/node/991.
PCPSR. 2024b. "Public Opinion Poll No (92) | PCPSR." 2024. https://pcpsr.org/en/node/980.

Robinson, Glenn E. "Hamas as social movement." Islamic activism: a social movement theory approach (2004): 112–139.
Roy, Sara. "Between Hamas and the Palestinian authority: Islamic movements and Palestinian development in the Gaza Strip." In Structural Flaws in the Middle East Peace Process: Historical Contexts, pp. 178–199. London: Palgrave Macmillan UK, 2002.
Sayigh, Yezid. 2011. We Serve the People" - Hamas Policing in Gaza. 1st ed. Waltham: Crown Center for Middle East Studies.

Open Access This chapter is licensed under the terms of the Creative Commons Attribution 4.0 International License (http://creativecommons.org/licenses/by/4.0/), which permits use, sharing, adaptation, distribution and reproduction in any medium or format, as long as you give appropriate credit to the original author(s) and the source, provide a link to the Creative Commons license and indicate if changes were made.

The images or other third party material in this chapter are included in the chapter's Creative Commons license, unless indicated otherwise in a credit line to the material. If material is not included in the chapter's Creative Commons license and your intended use is not permitted by statutory regulation or exceeds the permitted use, you will need to obtain permission directly from the copyright holder.

CHAPTER 4

The Palestinian Authority Watches Gaza Burn

Mouin Rabbani

Abstract Originally conceived of as the administrative arm of the PLO in the occupied territories, the Palestinian Authority became the seat of Fatah's political leadership after the Oslo Accords. This had the effect of marginalizing the Palestinian diaspora and Palestinian citizens of Israel within the Palestinian national movement. Under President Abbas, moreover, a deep rift between Hamas and Fatah developed while he persisted with the strategy of delivering security for Israel in a bid to show the PA as a reliable partner capable of implementing the Oslo Accords. Israel's response was to further accelerate settlement and consolidate its occupation. Together with the increasingly authoritarian leadership style of Abbas, the absence of meaningful resistance gradually put the PA on the path to illegitimacy and irrelevance. After 7 October 2023, it dropped off a cliff as the PA and Fatah's leadership not only became bystanders to the carnage in Gaza and obstructed meaningful national reconciliation, but also mobilized Palestinian security forces against Palestinian militants in the West Bank. As Israeli strategy shifts toward a dissolution of the PA,

M. Rabbani (✉)
Jadaliyya, Fairfax, Virginia, USA

© The Author(s) 2025
E. van Veen (ed.), *The Future of the Occupation of the Palestinian Territories after Gaza*,
https://doi.org/10.1007/978-3-031-93798-9_4

effective Palestinian resistance will require a revitalization of the national movement, incorporating Hamas, to pursue a strategy against occupation that is consistent with international law.

Keywords Oslo Accords · Yaser Arafat · Mahmoud Abbas · Security coordination · Palestinian Liberation Organization (PLO) · Second intifada · Gaza · West Bank · Fatah

Introduction

For the Palestinian Authority (PA), the crisis that erupted on 7 October 2023 could not have come at a worse time or occurred under worse circumstances. The manner in which the situation in Gaza has developed since has further weakened the PA, rendering achievement of its objectives ever more remote and contributing to its likely wholesale collapse in the medium-term. Understanding why this is the case requires a short analysis of the origins, evolution, and role of the Palestinian Authority; the strategic agenda adopted by PA President Mahmoud Abbas; relations between Fatah and Hamas; as well as the role the PA has played since 7 October 2023.

Situating the PA in Its Historical Context

The PA was established in 1994 by the Palestine Liberation Organization (PLO) pursuant to the 13 September 1993 Declaration of Principles on Interim Self-Government Arrangements (the Oslo Accords). Its functions, authorities, and responsibilities were further specified in the Agreement on the Gaza Strip and Jericho Area of 4 May 1994 (the Gaza-Jericho Agreement), its annex on Economic Relations between the Government of the State of Israel and the PLO of 29 April 1994 (the Paris Protocol) and the Israeli-Palestinian Interim Agreement on the West Bank and the Gaza Strip of 28 September 1995 (the Oslo

II Agreement).[1] Officially a subsidiary agency of the PLO with a limited geographical and primarily administrative mandate including local policing, the PA's formal role was to assume and discharge those responsibilities transferred by Israel to the PLO in the West Bank and Gaza Strip on the basis of the agreements cited above. In practice, the locus of Palestinian leadership and decision-making shifted from the PLO to the PA during the mid-1990s, particularly after Palestinian leader Yasir Arafat assumed the leadership of the new institution and relocated from Tunisian exile to Palestinian soil, alternating between Gaza City and Ramallah.

Since the late 1960s, the PLO had served as an umbrella organization for a variety of Palestinian guerilla movements. The Palestinian National Liberation Movement (Fatah), a broad-based nationalist movement, was the largest group at the time and hence, the PLO's most powerful and dominant member. It was followed by the Marxist Popular Front for the Liberation of Palestine (PFLP) and a host of smaller movements, a number of them operating as surrogates for various Arab governments. The Palestine Communist Party (PCP, currently known as the Palestine People's Party, PPP), was admitted only in 1987. In contrast to the others, its center of gravity had always been in the occupied territories and it retained only a limited presence in exile.

The Islamist Islamic Resistance Movement (Hamas) and Palestinian Islamic Jihad (PIJ), which were also primarily based within the occupied territories, were not part of the PLO and have yet to be incorporated. Historically, this was the case because the Muslim Brotherhood, which established Hamas in the late 1980s, adopted a quiescent attitude toward the occupation and prioritized the Islamization of Palestinian society over confrontation with Israel. By the time serious discussions about its incorporation commenced during the late 1980s, Fatah was weary of Hamas's growing size and popularity. Hamas was also viewed as making excessive demands in terms of allocations under the PLO quota system that

---

[1] The indicated agreements can be found at the following links: https://www.usip.org/sites/default/files/file/resources/collections/peace_agreements/oslo_09131993.pdf; https://peacemaker.un.org/sites/default/files/document/files/2024/05/il20ps940504agreement20on20the20gaza20strip20and20the20jericho20area2028cairo20agreement29.pdf; https://unctad.org/system/files/information-document/ParisProtocol_en.pdf (although the Paris Protocol was signed a week before the Gaza-Jericho Agreement, it was nevertheless incorporated into this document as an annex); https://www.usip.org/sites/default/files/file/resources/collections/peace_agreements/interim_agreement_09282005.pdf (all accessed on 5 January 2025).

apportioned seats to constituent organizations within its various organs (Hroub 2014; Baconi 2018). PIJ retained better relations with the PLO, in part because many of its members were previously in one or another PLO faction, and because its program of confronting Israel was more compatible with that of the PLO (Milton-Edwards 1999; Skare 2021).

While the PLO retained its internationally recognized status as the sole legitimate representative of the Palestinian people after Oslo, it was wholly eclipsed by the PA in practice. This had multiple repercussions. First, Palestinians living in exile were severed from the Palestinian proto-state that the PA sought to run as their national movement and its decision-making structures—the PLO—gradually became marginalized. As this group constituted approximately half of the global Palestinian population and had sustained the national liberation movement over previous decades, providing most of its cadres and fighters, its omission negatively influenced the PA's legitimacy. Second, Palestinian citizens of Israel residing within its pre-1967 borders were also left to fend for themselves within the Israeli political arena. Third, the shift from the PLO to the PA—and from operating from exile to operating under conditions of occupation—brought the Palestinian leadership fully in Israel's reach and under its latent control. These factors caused a gradual decrease of PA legitimacy among Palestinians and an increase in its dependence on Israel and Western funders (Tartir 2011). Both processes were accelerated by the PA's gradually growing authoritarianism (Hijazi and Lovatt 2017).

The Fateful Rise of Mahmoud Abbas

By the time Mahmoud Abbas (Abu Mazin) succeeded Yaser Arafat as Palestinian leader in 2004–2005, the PLO had effectively been reduced to an auxiliary of the PA. Although, for example, the PA was barred by the provisions of the Oslo agreement from conducting foreign relations except for purposes of securing development assistance for the territories it administered, Palestinian diplomats were appointed by the PA's Ministry of Foreign Affairs rather than the PLO's marginalized and largely defunct Department of Political Affairs. Given Abbas's fraught relationship with Arafat, as well as the West's open campaign in favor of his succession, Abbas's assumption of power was surprisingly smooth. He claimed the posts of Chairman of the Executive Committee of the PLO, President of the PA, and Chairman of the Fatah Central Committee quickly and virtually without opposition. Rival Fatah power centers that were still consequential at this point—they often controlled a PA security force or a militia—united behind Abbas as consensus candidate. This was in significant part because they perceived him as too weak to challenge their power and interests. Arafat's style of rule had been to promote multiple competing power centers with himself at the apex, allocating resources and acting as ultimate arbiter of their conflicts. Arafat encouraged pluralism as a mechanism of control as it enabled him to act as power broker. His iconic status made this possible, which Abbas lacked. The various Fatah power centers at that time also represented and promoted the interests of various Palestinian ideological platforms, geographical regions, institutions, and even individuals. In contrast to Arafat, Abbas sought to control this diversity by gradually restricting the resources of these rival power centers, marginalizing their institutions, and isolating rivals. Abbas' approach to rule turned out to be more centralized and authoritarian than that of Arafat. Nevertheless, a number of key individuals have managed to retain relevance within the PA, at times even from Israeli prison or in exile, such as Marwan Barghouti and Muhammad Dahlan. They are expected to make a return once Abbas departs the scene. A final reason for Abbas's acclamation by consensus was the rise of Hamas during the 2000–2004 Al-Aqsa Uprising (also known as the second Intifada), which made it essential for Fatah to close ranks lest it lose influence to its Islamist rival. In this context, the sudden demise of Arafat in 2004 put a further premium on a smooth leadership transition (Sayigh 1999; Elgindy 2024).

Hamas, Hamas, and Less Hamas

Abbas recognized that he could become a credible and effective leader only if he subordinated both an increasingly unruly Fatah and an ascendant Hamas to his control. The method he chose to accomplish this was the ballot box: PA presidential elections were conducted in 2005 to confirm his political primacy within the Palestinian political arena. Elections to the Palestinian Legislative Council (PLC, the legislature of the PA) were held in 2006 to weaken Fatah power centers by incorporating Hamas while simultaneously committing Hamas to the decisions of PA institutions. The notion that Hamas could be subordinated in this manner backfired spectacularly when it won a veto-proof majority of the PA parliament. With Fatah refusing to relinquish its hegemony over the PA and Hamas feeling entitled to replace it, relations soured. The growing discord between Fatah and Hamas ultimately caused efforts at accommodation and power-sharing, such as the February 2007 Mecca agreement, to fail (International Crisis Group 2007a).

Compounding tense relations between these rival Palestinian movements was the stance of the international community against Hamas in response to its electoral victory. The Quartet conditions, formulated as ideological positions designed to be refused by Hamas, played a particularly noteworthy role in amplifying intra-Palestinian distrust because they gave Abbas a pretext to reject accommodation by arguing that Hamas non-acceptance of these conditions would lead to Western sanctions that would paralyze the PA. Amidst mounting confrontation, Hamas got wind of a US- and Israeli-sponsored effort, to be led by Dahlan, to mobilize PA security forces and militias to unseat it (Rose 2008). The first democratically elected Islamist movement in the Arab world to assume office was to be deposed by a coalition consisting of the self-proclaimed leader of the free world (the United States), the self-proclaimed only democracy in the Middle East (Israel), and the Palestinian partner for peace both had been nurturing (the PA). The pre-emptive seizure of power by Hamas in the Gaza Strip in June 2007 marked the formal start of the Hamas-Fatah schism (International Crisis Group 2007b).

Abbas's antipathy to Hamas notwithstanding, his interest in reclaiming the Gaza Strip has been minimal since 2007. While he wants to see Hamas removed from power, he considers taking responsibility over the Gaza Strip as all burden and no benefit. From Abbas's perspective, a resumption of PA administration over the territory and its residents represents an impossible challenge. Appointed with the task of rooting out Hamas from the West Bank, Prime Minister Salam Fayyad (2007–2013) found himself resisting proposals from Abbas on several occasions that would simply have cut Gaza off, for example by ending salary payments to PA loyalists in the area that had gone on strike at Ramallah's behest and who had been replaced by Hamas. Abbas never formally renounced PA claims to be the legitimate authority of Gaza, but made no effort to promote this claim in practice either. In fact, Abbas has not visited Gaza once since 2007, being entirely comfortable with the idea that Gaza was and will remain Hamas's problem. Numerous interviews conducted by the author of this essay suggest that this also meant he was not interested in national reconciliation or power-sharing with Hamas, which in turn ensured that the various agreements negotiated between Hamas and Fatah to this effect, came to nought.

Putting All the PA's Eggs in an Israeli Basket

Analysis of the 2006 election result has often focused on PA corruption and mismanagement as the leading causes of Fatah's defeat at the ballot box. While certainly relevant, the more important and decisive factor was the PA's failure to achieve its strategic objectives: establishing a sovereign and independent Palestinian state in the occupied territories via bilateral negotiations with Israel under US auspices. While primarily the result of Israeli-US policy, this failure has in no small part been the result of the personal and political convictions of Abbas. Upon assuming leadership, according to author interviews, he believed the key task was to demonstrate that the PA could be a reliable partner. Proving this, he was convinced, would either persuade the Israelis to accept a two-state settlement, or sufficiently impress the United States to pressure Israel to end occupation. This political outlook helps explain Abbas' consistent refusal to implement any of the reconciliation agreements reached with Hamas since 2007 and also the persistence of the PA's ongoing security coordination with Israel. It has been described by Abbas as "sacred," even in the face of systematic Israeli provocations. In fact, interviews and analysis conducted by the author suggest that Abbas still considers the suppression of Hamas in the West Bank and the disarming of Fatah's Al-Aqsa Martyrs' Brigades after 2007 as his crowning achievements on the road toward Palestinian sovereignty. Both moves were executed in close coordination with Israel. By the same logic, Abbas' repeated endorsement of "popular resistance" was never intended to promote confrontation with Israel. The term, which refers to organized civil resistance campaigns such as that in the West Bank village of Bil'in against the Israel's West Bank Wall, was constantly highlighted by Abbas without providing any support to such initiatives. Abbas used it instead as a rhetorical device to delegitimize *armed* resistance. Despite Israeli unwillingness to seriously engage with the Palestinians on the permanent status agreement foreseen by Oslo and by Washington's and Brussels' refusal to turn the screws on Israel to cease settlement expansion or champion Palestinian statehood beyond occasional statements, Abbas simply stayed the course. There are, however, two mitigating circumstances that need to be considered.

To begin with, Abbas had the misfortune to assume leadership of the Palestinian national movement after Israel had already started a concerted campaign to convince the world and itself that "there is no Palestinian partner for peace." The Israeli political class committed itself to an intensified program of annexation after the second intifada and, with rare exceptions, was no longer interested in a bilateral resolution. It responded to each of Abbas' efforts to demonstrate the possibilities of reliable partnership with new and increasingly extravagant demands. For example, it began to insist that the Palestinians not only recognize Israel and its "right to exist," but also that they recognize Israel as a Jewish state. In effect, the Palestinian leadership was required to issue a halal certificate for the Nakba, and formally endorse permanent second-class status for Israel's Palestinian citizens. More importantly, Israel raised this demand in the full knowledge it was a non-starter, which would nevertheless receive sufficient Western support to help portray the Palestinians as rejecting peace. A second mitigating circumstance was that Abbas saw his "resistance toolkit" in the post-Oslo political arena as limited to negotiations. One Egyptian analyst on BBC Arabic radio acerbically described this a decade ago as: "negotiations or death, negotiations until death." This approach proved to be a complete mismatch with Israel's unilateral post-intifada strategy that had no need for a Palestinian partner. In fact, it required the absence of one. By spurning Abbas's efforts, Israel's position became a self-fulfilling prophecy with the side-effect of gradually increasing the level of disillusionment among Palestinians with Abbas. Those unilateral initiatives that Abbas undertook other than negotiations, such as the statehood initiative or international legal efforts, were often advanced reluctantly and under pressure. They were also designed to minimize friction with Israel and the United States.

By 2023, Abbas and his PA had little to show for their efforts. Despite the 2004 Advisory Opinion of the International Court of Justice on the West Bank Wall confirming the illegality of many Israeli practices including settlement, the enhanced status of Palestine at the United Nations and developments at the International Criminal Court, Abbas remained powerless to resist accelerating Israeli expansion within the occupied territories. Primarily because he chose not to, just as Abbas chose to ignore mounting evidence that his strategy was failing. He proved incapable of adjusting it to a changing context, preferring to persist in the belief that delivering more of the same would produce a better outcome. At one level, Abbas appeared convinced that if he kept trying, his approach would bear fruit. At another level, he proved to be incapable of formulating an alternative that would entail confrontation with Israel or his Western sponsors, or the mobilization of his people. As the Palestinian sociologist Jamil Hilal noted during a conference in the context of the Fatah-Hamas schism: "both are suspicious of any popular mobilization, including against Israel, for fear it could challenge their own rule." However, Abbas's awareness of the PA's vulnerabilities doubtlessly also played a role. After all, Israel and the West could immobilize it in an instant by starving it of the funds required to pay the civil service and security forces, or by bringing economic life to a halt.

ISRAEL WATCHES PA FAILURE WITH SATISFACTION

Prioritizing Palestinian fragmentation over partnership with the PA, Israel was content to see Hamas maintain its hegemony over the Gaza Strip. Settlement construction kept accelerating. President Obama had checked out of Arab–Israeli diplomacy during his second term and Trump simply ignored the Palestinians by formally recognizing the fruits of Israeli unilateralism, relocating the US embassy from Tel Aviv to Jerusalem; ordering the closure of the PLO mission in Washington and expelling its diplomats; recognizing Israel's claim of sovereignty over all of Jerusalem as well as the Syrian Golan Heights; intensifying the campaign against UNRWA; and launching his "Peace to Prosperity" initiative in 2020, which promoted formal Israeli annexation of at least a third of the West Bank. No less alarming to the Palestinians, Washington also brokered a number of Arab–Israeli normalization agreements designed to marginalize them.

As the PA increasingly served as Abbas' personal power bastion, it came to be viewed by ordinary Palestinians as autocratic, sclerotic, venal, and wholly out of touch. Abbas's popularity plumbed new depths with every successive public opinion poll and he dragged the PA down with him.[2] By 7 October 2023, there was very little left of the PA as a recognizably national Palestinian institution. To make matters worse, it continued with business as usual despite being confronted with an openly annexationist Israeli government in 2022. Its security forces habitually deferred to the Israeli military and even turned their guns on their own people rather than protect them from Israel's violent settlers.

---

[2] See for example the successive polls conducted by the Palestinian Center for Policy and Survey Research (PCPSR). Most of these can be accessed here: https://pcpsr.org/en/node/154.

The Main Effects of 7 October 2023 on the Palestinian Authority

The attack of 7 October 2023 and Israel's subsequent genocidal onslaught in Gaza cast the contrast between Hamas and the PA into starker relief. Hamas was seen as actively resisting Israeli occupation while the PA was busy accommodating it. Today, PA survival depends on maintaining the symbiotic relation it has developed with occupation. As the carnage in Gaza unfolded while Israeli raids in the West Bank intensified, the PA and its leaders assumed the role of spectators. Cooperation with Israel against Palestinian militancy continued as if nothing had changed. In response to growing demands for a national unity government, Abbas replaced his prime minister, the prominent Fatah leader Muhammad Shtayyeh, with Muhammad Mustafa, his money man. Mustafa promptly issued a plan for Gaza that pretended Hamas simply did not exist, once again giving reconciliation and cooperation initiatives short shrift. A few meetings in Moscow and Beijing to unify Palestinian political ranks produced anodyne communiques without tangible action. Next to Abbas' usual recalcitrance, Egypt's absence in spite of its habitual role as custodian of Palestinian reconciliation also played a major role. This state of play notwithstanding, November–December 2024 brought the potential of a shift. Meeting in Cairo under Egyptian auspices, Hamas and Fatah reached a fairly detailed agreement about post-war Gaza governance and administration.[3] Pursuant to this accord, Gaza would be ruled by a committee consisting of politically unaffiliated individuals who would each be endorsed by the leadership of both movements. Although nonpartisan, the committee would be formally appointed by the PA and operate under its auspices. The agreement represented a recognition on the part of Hamas that it is incapable of addressing the monumental task of reconstruction without the PA, as well as a recognition on the part of the PA that it cannot play a significant role in the Gaza Strip without the consent of Hamas. The missing element is, yet again, Abbas' willingness to endorse the text produced by his negotiators.

---

[3] Aljazeera, "Hamas and Fatah Sign Unity Deal in Beijing Aimed at Gaza Governance", 23 July 2024. https://www.aljazeera.com/news/2024/7/23/palestinian-rivals-hamas-and-fatah-sign-unity-deal-brokered-by-china; Beth McKernan, "Hamas and Fatah Agree to Create Committee to Run Postwar Gaza Strip", *The Guardian*. 3 December 2024. https://www.theguardian.com/world/2024/dec/03/hamas-and-fatah-agree-to-create-committee-to-run-postwar-gaza-strip.

Naturally, this Fatah-Hamas agreement depends on the successful conclusion of Hamas-Israeli negotiations. Moreover, Abbas ordered PA security forces to launch an unprecedented campaign in the wake of the Cairo agreement to secure control of the northern West Bank and the Jenin refugee camp where Hamas and PIJ maintain a significant presence. His motivations were not difficult to discern. Abbas does not want to be tainted by any association with the Islamist movement, particularly with Donald Trump back in the White House, and he intends to demonstrate that he can confront and disarm Hamas. However, the images of Palestinian security forces killing Palestinians in the West Bank, while Israel cleanses Gaza and reduces it to rubble, destroyed any legitimacy Abbas may still have had. Indeed, it is difficult to see how the PA can survive in the longer term. Israel's annexationist agenda requires its dissolution after which it is likely to try to prevent the emergence of a new national leader to facilitate occupation of a fragmented West Bank. Israel might seek to put local strongmen in place that can act as glorified municipal governments with local authority, but who ultimately operate under Israeli control. Anticipating criticism, Israel may allow the PA to persist in name, but empty it of substance. Israel's finance minister, the settler Bezalel Smotrich, is using various mechanisms to bankrupt the PA on the premise that starving it of funds will cause its implosion more effectively than formal disbandment. Israel will only back off if confronted with US opposition, or an organized campaign to maintain the PA by the leadership of its own security forces.

Looking Ahead

The Gaza genocide has demonstrated the urgent need to reconstruct the Palestinian national movement and its institutions. It has become clear that neither Hamas nor Fatah, nor the PA, can successfully exercise hegemony over the Palestinian national movement or the Palestinian people. Rather, they will need to come to a power-sharing arrangement if these movements want to achieve Palestinian national objectives. The prospects of achieving this outcome within the framework of the PA are limited at best. It functions under direct Israeli control, has become hostage to vested interests, and is too dependent on US and European support. Even if Hamas and Fatah were to reach an agreement and proceed to implement it, Israel can easily prevent its realization in both the West Bank and Gaza. Israel probably envisages separate arrangements, which has the advantage of undermining the territorial integrity of the occupied territories and facilitates its agenda of fragmentation.

A more constructive approach would therefore be to focus on the revival of national institutions, especially the PLO. This would shift the focus from the allocation of personnel, positions, and resources within the PA—vested interests—to broader strategic questions of leadership and strategy. In other words, Hamas and PIJ need to be incorporated into the PLO on the basis of a consensual political program and strategy. A program, in other words, that reflects the priorities of Palestinians everywhere. In such an approach, the PA would once again be subordinated to the PLO and shorn of its political aspects, such as the office of president, and focus instead on its original core function: the administration and provision of services to its people. The key question is whether Hamas could commit to such a formula rather than establishing new institutions of its own. The aforementioned negotiations in Cairo suggest it may be cooperative.

Parts of the West—such as the United States, UK, Germany, and the Netherlands—are certain to respond with hostility. Yet, if the Palestinians stay united, adopt a political program consistent with international law and the international consensus on the desired resolution of the Palestine question—such as expressed in the July 2024 ICJ Advisory Opinion confirming the unlawfulness of the occupation—even these countries may find it necessary to engage in order to ensure security and stability in the Middle East.

Conflict of Interest The author has no conflict of interests to declare that are relevant to the content of this chapter.

References

Alaa Tartir, *The Role of International Aid in Development: The Case of Palestine 1994–2008* (Lambert, 2011).
Beverly Milton-Edwards, *Islamic Politics in Palestine* (I.B. Tauris, 1999).
David Rose, "The Gaza Bombshell", *Vanity Fair*, 3 March 2008 https://www.vanityfair.com/news/2008/04/gaza200804?srsltid=AfmBOopQxa1x_hmJ jHjIKTRSiOKSy1DuTjcTx_4t6eh7BT9h89F-FmNw.
Erik Skare, *A History of Palestinian Islamic Jihad: Faith, Awareness, and Revolution in the Middle East* (Cambridge University Press, 2021).

International Crisis Group, *After Mecca: Engaging Hamas*, 28 February 2007a https://www.crisisgroup.org/sites/default/files/62-after-mecca-engaging-hamas.pdf.
International Crisis Group, *After Gaza*, 2 August 2007b https://www.crisisgroup.org/sites/default/files/68-after-gaza.pdf.
Khaled Elgindy, "The Fall and Fall of Mahmoud Abbas", *Foreign Affairs* (30 August, 2024) https://www.foreignaffairs.com/palestinian-territories/fall-and-fall-mahmoud-abbas.
Khaled Hroub, *Hamas: Political Thought and Practice* (Institute for Palestine Studies, 2014).
Saleh Hijazi and Hugh Lovatt, "Europe and the Palestinian Authority's Authoritarian Drift", European Council on Foreign Relations (20 April 2017) https://ecfr.eu/article/commentary_europe_and_the_palestinian_authoritys_authoritarian_drift_7274/.
Tareq Baconi, *Hamas Contained: A History of Palestinian Resistance* (Stanford University Press, 2018).
Yezid Sayigh, *Armed Struggle and the Search for State* (Oxford University Press, 1999).

Open Access This chapter is licensed under the terms of the Creative Commons Attribution 4.0 International License (http://creativecommons.org/licenses/by/4.0/), which permits use, sharing, adaptation, distribution and reproduction in any medium or format, as long as you give appropriate credit to the original author(s) and the source, provide a link to the Creative Commons license and indicate if changes were made.

The images or other third party material in this chapter are included in the chapter's Creative Commons license, unless indicated otherwise in a credit line to the material. If material is not included in the chapter's Creative Commons license and your intended use is not permitted by statutory regulation or exceeds the permitted use, you will need to obtain permission directly from the copyright holder.

CHAPTER 5

Israel: From Creeping to Decisive Annexation

Gil Murciano

Abstract Israel's 37th government has adopted an explicit policy of full annexation of the West Bank, making it a central national project. Even before the attack on 7 October 2023, key figures in the government were laying the legal, operational, and financial groundwork to advance this agenda, in particular Minister of Finance Bezalel Smotrich. The 7 October 2023 massacre further emboldened the government to intensify these efforts, leveraging public hostility toward Palestinians and diverting public attention from the West Bank to Gaza. This strategy seeks to dismantle the last remnants of the two-state solution framework, which includes the bankrupting of the Palestinian Authority. The far-reaching consequences of such a policy—i.e., rendering the two-state solution unviable as a framework for conflict resolution—are a rallying call for the international community to form a unified coalition against annexation. Such a coalition could in turn serve as a foundation for renewed efforts to promote an Israeli-Palestinian political process at a later stage.

G. Murciano (✉)
Mitvim Institute, Petah Tikva, Israel

© The Author(s) 2025
E. van Veen (ed.), *The Future of the Occupation of the Palestinian Territories after Gaza*,
https://doi.org/10.1007/978-3-031-93798-9_5

Keywords Oslo Accords · Decisive plan · Bezalel Smotrich · Settler violence · Benjamin Netanyahu · Religious Zionism · Palestinian Authority · Settlements · Coalition against annexation

Introduction

Under its 37th government, Israel's policy in the West Bank has shifted from "creeping annexation"—a discreet, gradual approach to settlement expansion meant to avoid domestic or international backlash—to a much more explicit and assertive strategy of annexation. The inclusion of far-right politicians in key executive positions, particularly Minister of Finance Bezalel Smotrich, has transformed Israel's occupation agenda. Smotrich's "decisive plan" aims to annex the West Bank outright and in an overt fashion, dismantle any remaining vestiges of the Oslo Accords and render the prospect of a two-state solution impossible. This represents a fundamental change as it turns settlement and annexation efforts from a covert operation into a national priority.

Annexation: Public Sentiment Meets Government Intent

While the far-right's direct executive influence began with the government's inauguration in late 2022, the events of 7 October 2023 and thereafter marked a significant tipping point in the speed and scope with which its annexation agenda has been implemented. Ironically, the Hamas attack facilitated a convergence of public sentiment and government intent that allowed acceleration of annexation in a more open and aggressive manner. To begin with, the atrocities committed by Hamas, coupled with the Palestinian public support for these actions in the West Bank (Reuters 2023), have stoked public animosity toward Palestinians. This has allowed Israeli far-right elements to gain broader public support for their policies. The Hamas attack on 7 October 2023 is not just a day that will forever live in infamy in the history of the Israeli-Palestinian conflict, it is also the starting point of a destructive war that turned the conflict from a political conflict into an inter-communal one. An immediate effect of 7 October 2023 on Israeli public discourse has been the conflation of Hamas as an organization and the Palestinians as a people. The celebrations in the West Bank after the massacre, the Palestinian Authority's denial of the murder of Israeli citizens weeks after the attack and the visible participation of ordinary Gazans in the atrocities have fostered a zero-sum perception among Israelis of the entire Palestinian population (Nitzan (@IsraelNitzan) 2023). This perception has sidelined discussions of a two-state solution. Surveys that showed widespread Palestinian support for Hamas' actions in the following months further deepened these sentiments (Yaari 2023). This public atmosphere in Israel has created an optimal context for the far right-wing part of the Netanyahu government to step up its efforts to annex the West Bank and remove all existing traces of "Oslo" on the ground.

Moreover, domestic and international attention shifted away from the far-right for half a year or so after 7 October 2023. Before this date, the far-right faced close domestic and international scrutiny for its role in seeking to bring judicial reforms about, but the war refocused Israeli public priorities on Gaza and Lebanon. Internationally, the first months of the conflict centered on the humanitarian crisis in Gaza and the potential of Israeli-Hezbollah escalation. It was only after mid-2024 or thereabouts that global attention started to shift back to the situation on the West Bank, particularly settler violence and the fiscal crisis of the Palestinian Authority. Meanwhile, the current Israeli government, widely regarded as the most hawkish in the country's history, has turned settlement expansion and annexation into a top priority. Dubbed the "full-fledged right-wing government" by its members, it has channeled both political energy and significant resources into this agenda. In contrast to the absence of clear long-term strategies in Gaza or Lebanon, the government's approach to settlements stands out as coherent, clear, and decisive. Israel may not have a political strategy for two ongoing wars, but it does have a settlement strategy. Despite severe financial constraints and cuts to other parts of the budget due to wartime conditions, the government has continued to allocate vast resources to settlements. It is worth noting that aggressive settlement proceeds even as Israel's dependence on U.S. and Western support increases, highlighting a growing risk of a clash between Israel's West Bank policies and international policy preferences.

Israel's 37th Government: The Perfect Place for Smotrich's "Decisive Plan"

"These are miraculous times…we want to get as much as possible done in Eretz Israel in general and specifically on Hebron Mountain. For me it is a holy mission." Orit Strook, July 2024 (יאלוזא 2024). The Minister of Settlements and National Missions.

As overarching national policy, settlement and annexation are promoted by a wide range of ministries and government bodies. However, the driving factor is Bezalel Smotrich—the leader of National Religious Party—Religious Zionism. In 2017, Smotrich was the "architect" of the "Decisive Plan" (Smotrich 2024). The core of the plan is to exercise full and long-term Israeli sovereignty over the West Bank by "flooding" the areas of Judea and Samaria with Jewish settlers. The composition of Israel's 37th government provided an ideal political environment for Smotrich to advance his views. The coalition's survival largely hinges on the support of Smotrich's party and Ben Gvir's far-right "Otzma Yehudit," which gives Smotrich the ability to exert influence beyond his electoral base and to shape national strategies. Since taking office, Smotrich has utilized his two ministerial roles to further his objectives. As Minister of Finance, he oversees budgetary planning and allocation. Meanwhile, as an "additional Minister" in the Ministry of Defense with responsibility for civilian oversight of the West Bank (including the planning and approval of settlement activity), he wields considerable authority over Israel's policies in this area (קיבוביץ 2023).

Smotrich's key role in maintaining coalition stability restricts the more moderate factions of the government in countering his initiatives. For example, when Defense Minister Yoav Gallant attempted to curtail Smotrich's executive authority within the ministry, the issue was resolved through compromises aimed at preserving the coalition rather than by limiting Smotrich's policy impact (ולש 2023). This has become the government's typical modus operandi. Smotrich's "Decisive Plan" operates in the West Bank across three main dimensions: political, economic, and on the ground. Each dimension complements the others and all leverage the full powers of the government to create irreversible transformation.[1] I will briefly examine each dimension in turn below. They include:

- laying the groundwork for large-scale expansion of the settlement enterprise;
- legislation aimed at dismantling the remaining vestiges of the Oslo Accords;
- tacit approval of settler violence as unofficial policy to constrict Palestinian living space;
- a direct effort to push the Palestinian Authority toward financial collapse.

Building the Infrastructure for Annexation

Preparing for the expansion of settlement activity has become a primary focus across various ministries since 7 October 2023. Data collected on the settlement enterprise over 2024 indicates key parameters that will enable dramatic growth are being set. One notable example is the sharp increase in the appropriation of "state land" by Israeli authorities (Mauricio 2024). The 24,193 dunams claimed over the last year amounts to nearly half of all land appropriated as state land between the Oslo Accords (1993) and today. This appropriation clearly reflects the government's intention to expand settlements at scale in the near future. In parallel, the government has doubled the budget of the Ministry of Settlement and increased funding for its Settlement Division by 302 million shekels, with an additional 409 million shekels allocated for special settlement projects. Beyond land and funds for settlements, a significant effort has been made to erase legal and practical distinctions between "legal" settlements and "illegal" outposts. Over the past year, an unprecedented 43 new outposts have been established in comparison with the previous decade's yearly average of fewer than 10 new outposts per year (Mauricio 2024). In several instances, this has led to the expulsion of Palestinians from the relevant areas. Additionally, the government has

---

[1] While advancing these four goals, Smotrich and other government members have also been pushing a fourth dimension in recent months, namely the re-occupation and re-settlement of Gaza, which is otherwise left out of account of this analysis.

formally legitimized many existing outposts and integrated them into Israel's administration of the West Bank by providing basic services such as water, electricity, and other utilities. Over 70 illegal outposts have now been recognized as eligible for funding and infrastructure support. National transportation infrastructure between settlements in the West Bank has also been expanded, which has facilitated seizure of more Palestinian land as well as enhanced connectivity between illegal outposts (Mauricio 2023). Last June, Smotrich announced a major agreement with the Ministry of Transportation to invest 7 billion shekels over the next five years in intercity road development between settlements.

Removing the Vestiges of Oslo

Since the current government took office, key political actors from Israel's right-wing parties have worked to enable annexation through legislation, aiming in particular to erase the concept of the two-state solution. Smotrich himself has openly expressed his intention to promote laws that extend Israeli sovereignty over the entire West Bank (Diaz 2024). As he stated, *"We need to eliminate the existential threat of a Palestinian state... Before joining the government, I could only shout and warn. Today, I am in a position to fully exercise my executive power."* However, Smotrich is not acting alone in this endeavor. Over the past year, efforts to suppress the very idea of a two-state solution have gained support from members of both the Israeli right and center-right, including even figures from the center and center-left opposition. Efforts by the Israeli right to eliminate the possibility of a two-state framework began well before the current conflict in Gaza, however. In March 2023, the Knesset voted to repeal parts of Ariel Sharon's 2005 Disengagement Law, specifically concerning Northern Samaria, which had prohibited Israeli entry and settlement in that area (Sharon 2023). This move, aimed at legalizing the settlement in Homesh, signaled a significant departure from the disengagement policy. An even blunter step toward comprehensive rejection of the two-state framework was taken on July 2024 when the Knesset voted overwhelmingly for a motion rejecting the establishment of a Palestinian state (Magid 2024a, b). Receiving the support of Benny Gantz's centrist National Unity party, the motion echoed a new broad front within the Israeli right and center-right against Palestinian statehood. It marked a major success for the government in setting the tone in the Knesset regarding Palestinian rights. Beyond the declarative level, efforts to expand settlement activity have also shaped general legislation with an emphasis on efforts to blur the distinction between Israeli settlements and the state of Israel within its 1967 internationally recognized boundaries. A recent reform involved the redistribution of property tax among municipalities by including settlements in this framework (Spiegel 2024). This change not only sets a significant legal precedent, but also enables settlements to draw from the national property tax fund for their development projects. Such measures effectively integrate settlements into the core Israeli economic system, further solidifying their status.

SETTLER VIOLENCE TO SHRINK PALESTINIAN SPACE THROUGH INTIMIDATION AND SEIZURE

Settler violence, from verbal threats and property destruction to deadly assaults on Palestinians, has increased alongside settlement expansion in the West Bank. It occurs both randomly and as retaliation for Palestinian attacks. Previously, Israeli right-wing governments publicly condemned such violence, citing damage to the rule of law and the settler movement's image. However, the current government often turns a blind eye while some far-right leaders even endorse violence.[2] This tacit support encourages settler violence that aims to further shrink Palestinian living spaces.[3] The aftermath of 7 October 2023 saw a spike in settler violence amounting to over 1,000 incidents in a year, in which over 1,300 Palestinians were driven from their homes (Crisis Group 2024). Reports indicate that incidents of settler violence more than doubled in the months following the 7 October 2023 attack, increasing from an average of three incidents per day to seven (United Nations Office for the Coordination of Humanitarian Affairs 2023). Some reports have linked the surge in violence to the IDF's decision to expand territorial defense units

---

[2] Several politicians from the far-right Otzma Yehudit party endorsed the settler riot in Huwara In February 2023. For example, MK Zvika Fogel referred to the riot as an effective "deterrence" method.

[3] UN OCHA official, 20 June 2024. UN OCHA reported at the end of October 2023 that at least 98 households in fifteen herding communities in the West Bank had been forced from their homes since 7 October. "The Other Mass Displacement".

fivefold across the West Bank after 7 October 2023.[4] This has included distributing over 7,000 military-grade weapons to settlers, some of whom were involved in prior violence.

The government's support for settler violence has deepened the rift between Israel's political leadership and its security agencies, particularly the IDF and Shin Bet (Crisis Group 2024). Shin Bet has long warned that "nationalist terrorism," i.e., settler violence, could trigger escalation in the West Bank and harm Israel's global image. Its Director Ronen Bar publicly criticized the government, accusing some officials of legitimizing "Jewish terror." Settler violence has already triggered unprecedented international actions, including direct sanctions. One of the U.S. justifications for sanctions under President Biden was the harm settler violence does to the "viability of a two-state solution" (United States Department of State 2024). Initially, travel bans targeted individuals involved in the violence. But President Biden escalated with an executive order in February 2024 that imposed financial sanctions on entities involved in West Bank violence. This policy was soon adopted by the UK, France, Canada, and the EU, sanctioning organizations and outposts linked to the violence (וביה and חייף 2024). Despite giving a clear international signal of disagreement, sanctions have so far had little impact on Israeli government actions. Instead, far-right members have launched campaigns to financially compensate those affected by the sanctions (יאלוזא .מ .ל .ג 2024).

A Concerted Push to Trigger the PA's Financial Collapse

The far-right elements of the Israeli Government, led by Smotrich, are also actively working to undermine the financial resilience of the Palestinian Authority (PA), exploiting public outrage over its response to the 7 October 2023 massacre. While the right-wing elements of Netanyahu's government view the PA as a "necessary evil" to prevent West Bank instability, the far-right aims to dismantle it as part of erasing the legacy of the Oslo Accords. Considering the PA's fragile state before the October attack—marked by an unprecedented fiscal crisis and a deep

---

[4] Stemming Israeli Settler Violence at Its Root | Crisis Group. Territorial Defense Units are composed of citizen volunteers and designed to serve as a rapid-response force to protect local communities until the IDF intervenes.

crisis of legitimacy—these efforts pose a serious threat to its ability to govern, let alone to international attempts to "revitalize" it. The far-right campaign to undermine the PA's financial stability has primarily been driven by Smotrich in his role as Minister of Finance. His efforts have concentrated on two key aspects of the PA's reliance on Israel for financial cooperation under the Oslo Accords and the Paris Protocol (1994).

- *Halting transfers of tax revenue:* Tax transfers by Israel account for 60–70% of the PA's revenue (Israel withholds customs duties on behalf of the PA, which it is subsequently obliged to transfer) (Shrock et al. 2022). After the PA refused to condemn the 7 October attacks, Smotrich suspended these transfers, later allowing partial payments but withholding funds related to Gaza and stipends for families of individuals having committed terrorist acts (Ravid 2023).[5] In August 2024, he also withheld NIS 100 million from the tax transfers, citing continued PA payments to families of such individuals.
- *Refusing to renew banking protections:* In response to U.S. sanctions on violent settlers, Smotrich refused to renew protections for Israeli banks handling transactions with the PA, threatening to sever the financial link between the two economies (Kahana 2024). In June 2024, he granted a four-month extension instead of the usual year (Magid 2024a, b). Only after significant international pressure in November 2024 did Smotrich agree to extend the protection for another year (חדש, 2024).

A Defining Moment for Israeli Pragmatists and Their Global Allies

If there is any positive aspect to the government's policy shift toward overt annexation, it is that it compels Israeli moderates and the international community to take action in order to preserve the viability of a two-state solution before it is irreparably damaged. Over the past decade, it was not Smotrich's "decisive plan that silenced talks of Palestinian

---

[5] "Terrorist acts" refer to the cold-blooded murder of civilians not participating in violence at the time of such incidents, i.e., "non-combatants" in the language of the laws of war.

statehood but the so-called conflict management approach. Proposals like Micah Goodman's "initiative for shrinking the conflict" gave Israelis the false comfort that the conflict could be subdued by reducing daily tensions (Tzimzum, n.d.). This allowed many to sidestep the hard political debate about a long-term solution. Meanwhile, "creeping annexation" of the West Bank continued, gradually altering facts on the ground but without much public scrutiny. Smotrich's overt push for annexation now forces key stakeholders—both in Israel and internationally—to face reality and take more decisive action. A clear choice must now be made between annexation or committing to a two-state framework.

The "conflict management" approach to the Israeli-Palestinian conflict was one of the first conceptual victims of the 7 October 2023 attack. Following a decade of marginalization in public and political discourse, the absence of an Israeli-Palestinian settlement returned center-stage as a core factor affecting not only regional but also global security. The war created a clear public desire for decisive solutions to Israel's conflict with the Palestinians. A recent survey of the Mitvim Institute found that only 12% of Israelis still wish to cling to a conflict management approach that avoids strategic decision-making (Mitvim 2024). However, it is the recognition that strategic decisions can no longer be avoided that leads to two radically different perceptions of what decisions are desirable. On one side of the aisle are the fundamentalists, constituting an unprecedentedly large minority (about 30%), that adopt positions considered far-right prior to the war—including annexation of the West Bank and resettlement of Gaza. This growing camp illustrates how the concept of annexation moved from the margins of political debate to the center. It allows Smotrich and his far-right colleagues to argue that their plans enjoy public support. However, on the other side of the aisle there is a large pragmatist camp, which consists of a small plurality of about 40–50% of the Israeli public. It supports agreeing to a political horizon with the Palestinians as part of a broader regional framework. 44% of the Israeli public supports a package deal that includes normalization with KSA, a U.S. security umbrella, and the establishment of a demilitarized Palestinian state. An even larger majority—61% of Israelis—support international sanctions against violent settlers. Hence, when examined in a broader perspective, Smotrich's ambitious vision of "decisive plan" is opposed by most Israelis, including an overwhelming majority of center and center-right voters.

However, turning this finding into an alternative policy proposition requires new political leaders that can develop and present an alternative to annexation. The last two years have provided the Israeli public with an undiluted experience of what it is like to live under a "full-fledged right-wing government." Mistrust and discontent about government performance runs deep and wide among the Israeli public but it is mostly focused on the judicial reform project, the (im)balance between religion and state, and the management of the war in Gaza. Most Israelis recognize the close connection between the Government's judicial reform and the promotion of annexation in the West Bank (Foreign Policy Index 2024), but the topic of settlement expansion nevertheless remains mostly absent from public discourse. Much of this can be attributed to the reluctance of the Israeli opposition to address the topic, which in turn is largely the result of its fragmented nature. Since 7 October 2023, political support among the opposition for the two-state framework has ranged from open rejection to lukewarm endorsement. Even left-wing leaders now present their support in apologetic terms (יקסמוש 2024). A clear example is the Knesset vote of July 2024 that rejected the establishment of a Palestinian state. Most of the National Unity party, the largest opposition faction, supported the motion. Meanwhile, left-wing parties opted not to attend, claiming they did not want to "fall into a right-wing trap." This has left little political resistance to Smotrich's approach and limits debate about the consequences of implementing his "Decisive Plan" for Israel's future.

The shift toward overt annexation and the lack of meaningful debate in Israel about such a course of action highlight the urgent need for increased international involvement. It should focus on two complementary approaches. First, setting clear red lines and "price-tags" for continued settlement expansion could pressure the Israel government to reconsider its policies and spark domestic debate. International actions should delegitimize the far-right agenda and align with growing popular discontent within Israel. Akin to sanctions against violent settlers, this would signal the costs Israel will face if it pursues annexation. Second, the international community must outline and commit to a viable, long-term strategy for gradually promoting the two-state framework, offering a credible alternative to Smotrich's "decisive plan" while safeguarding Israel's security (יקחצ 2024).

For the international community to effectively advance a clear vision and firm red lines on the two-state framework, it must first form a unified front. In other words, a joint international coalition against annexation. This coalition, made up of the U.S., Western, and regional actors, should coordinate their efforts to prevent annexation. A similar joint effort, primarily led by European countries, was partly successful in blocking the far-right's push for annexation during Netanyahu's 2020–2021 government. However, today such a coalition of the willing must do more than just prevent annexation. It has to revitalize efforts to work toward a credible two-state framework instead. Despite differences in methods, opposition to annexation offers a shared platform for international and regional actors, as well as civil society groups, to collaborate on renewing this vision.

Conflict of Interest The author has no conflict of interests to declare that are relevant to the content of this chapter.

Bibliography

Diaz. 2024. ‏זאיד, שלומי. 2024. ‏'מוטרי': נקדם הקיקה תלחהל תונוביר לע יחטש יוש. Hidabroot, 24 ינויל. https://www.hidabroot.org/article/1197595

"Foreign Policy Index 2024: The Israeli Foreign Policy Index for 2024." 2024. *Findings of the Mitvim Institute Survey*. https://mitvim.org.il/wp-content/uploads/2024/09/Mitvim_Israeli-Foreign-Policy-Index-2024.pdf.

"Further Measures to Promote Peace, Security, and Stability in the West Bank— United States Department of State." 2024. United States Department of State, March 12. https://www.state.gov/further-measures-to-promote-peace-security-and-stability-in-the-west-bank/.

Kahana. 2024. ‏אנהכ, אהבנ. 2024. ‏בעקבות הסנקנות לש ביידוג מתמשיותיהם: סמוטריץ' הזוי‏ העיגפ הלכלכב הפלשתינית. IsraelHayom, 14 במרץ. https://www.israelhayom.co.il/news/geopolitics/article/15425756

Magid, Jacob. 2024a. "Knesset Votes Overwhelmingly Against Palestinian Statehood, Days Before PM's US Trip." *Times of Israel*, July 18. https://www.timesofisrael.com/knesset-votes-overwhelmingly-against-palestinian-statehood-days-before-pms-us-trip/.

Magid, Jacob. 2024b. "US Nods at Smotrich's Steps to Ease PA Financial Crisis, But Calls Them Insufficient." *Times of Israel*. 2 July. https://www.timesofisrael.com/us-nods-at-smotrichs-steps-to-ease-pa-financial-crisis-but-calls-them-insufficient/.

Mauricio. 2024. "War and Annexation: How the Israeli Government Changed the West Bank During the First Year of War—Peace Now." Peace

Now, October 14. https://peacenow.org.il/en/war-and-annexation-how-the-israeli-government-changed-the-west-bank-during-the-first-year-of-war.
Mauricio. 2023. "New Roads and Outposts Flourish in the West Bank amid Gaza War—Peace Now." Peace Now, November 22. https://peacenow.org.il/en/new-roads-and-outposts-flourish-in-the-west-bank-amid-gaza-war.
"N12 Report: 6,000 Gazans Crossed into Israel on October 7." Jerusalem Post. 2024. *The Jerusalem Post*, August 31. https://www.jpost.com/israel-hamas-war/article-817176.
Nitzan, Israel (@IsraelNitzan). 2023. X, November 19, 2023, 6:26 p.m. https://x.com/IsraelNitzan/status/1726275835114790942?ref_src=twsrc%5Etfw%7Ctwcamp%5Etweetembed%7Ctwterm%5E1726275835114790942%7Ctwgr%5E4ce23cac2b584e1ea8a6557a227958a452063dc0%7Ctwcon%5Es1_&ref_url=https%3A%2F%2Fwww.i24news.tv%2Fen%2Fnews%2Fisrael-at-war%2F1700470299-palestinian-authority-retracts-statement-denying-hamas-responsibility-for-massacre.
"Poll shows Palestinians back Oct. 7 Attack on Israel, Support for Hamas Rises." 2023. *Reuters*, December 14. https://www.reuters.com/world/middle-east/poll-shows-palestinians-back-oct-7-attack-israel-support-hamas-rises-2023-12-14/.
Ravid, Barak. 2023. "U.S. Asked Israel to Release Withheld Palestinian Tax Revenues." *Axios*, October 31. https://www.axios.com/2023/10/31/israel-hamas-war-tax-palestinian-authority.
Sharon, Jeremy. 2023. Disengagement Repeal Law for Northern West Bank Approved in First Reading. *Times of Israel*, March 14. https://www.timesofisrael.com/disengagement-repeal-law-for-northern-west-bank-approved-in-first-reading/.
"Shrinking the Conflict." n.d. *Tzimzum*. https://www.tzimzum.org.il/wp-content/uploads/2021/03/Shrinking-the-Conflict-About-Us.pdf.
Shrock, Jonah, Epstein, Gabriel, and David Makovsky. 2022. "Responding to the PA's Mounting Fiscal Crisis." The Washington Institute. https://www.washingtoninstitute.org/policy-analysis/responding-pas-mounting-fiscal-crisis.
Smotrich, Bezalel. 2024. "Israel's Decisive Plan." חולישה, January 18. https://hashiloach.org.il/israels-decisive-plan/.
"Stemming Israeli Settler Violence at Its Root." 2024. *Crisis Group*, September 6. https://www.crisisgroup.org/middle-east-north-africa/east-mediterranean-mena-israelpalestine/246-stemming-israeli-settler-violence.
"The other Mass Displacement: Settlers Advance on West Bank Herders." 2023. United Nations Office for the Coordination of Humanitarian Affairs—Occupied Palestinian Territory, November 1. https://www.ochaopt.org/content/other-mass-displacement-while-eyes-are-gaza-settlers-advance-west-bank-herders.

"The Israeli Foreign Policy Index of 2024—Mitvim." 2024. *Mitvim*, September 26. https://mitvim.org.il/en/report/the-israeli-foreign-policy-index-of-2024/.

ביני, ציבובוק. 2023. "סמוטריץ' ממדר את הפרקליטות מבצעית מדיניים גריישי דכ סדקל ביינה הדגב." *Haaretz* ראה, October 4, 2023. https://www.haaretz.co.il/news/politics/2023-10-04/ty-article/.premium/0000018a-f6fa-d12f-afbf-f7ffd5 3b0000.

בלבליסט, Calcalist "קורץ, עמיר. 2023 "פרויקט שובר שיאים: כך הצליחו להקים את המיזם March, 14, 2023. https://www.calcalist.co.il/local_news/article/hkfvua6k2

הלאור", February לט, ולש. 2023. "ונלג באוי'.וחטיבה מסמוכית לע ומכיס ציירטומס לאלצבו טנלג באוי'". 23, 2023. https://news.walla.co.il/item/3560901.

'סנ לש הפוקת ומכ וז': תויולחנתהב הייבנה תרבגה לע קורטס תירוא הרשה". 2024. ורמן, יאלוזא ופצ. | *Ynet*, July 7, 2024. https://www.ynet.co.il/news/article/hyqqkiwdr.

ירטימיד, יקסמוש. 2024. "רתוי תופוחד תויגוס ידמהו יתש ורתפ, תוכחל שי ממישומ, *Haaretz* ראה, July 15, 2024. https://www.haaretz.co.il/opinions/2024-07-15/ty-article-opinion/.premium/00000190-b60c-d7ee-af9c-ff0c79c10000.

יקחצי, ריפ. 2024. "The Israeli Initiative—Mitvim." Mitvim. July 31, 2024. https://mitvim.org.il/en/the-israeli-initiative/.

רימא, ובית, and רגה וזיפ. 2024. "הינטירב הליטה סקנעות לע תעונת 'אמנה' ועל שולשה הדגב." *Haaretz* ראה, October 15, 2024. https://www.haaretz.co.il/news/politics/2024-10-15/ty-article/.premium/00000192-9065-d8fa-a9df-f96d90360000.

חישב: 'ידייב לש תויצקנסה תא ףוקעל לעופ אוהש הדומ 'ץירטומס". 2024. ורמן, רואיל דג, יאלוזא עמ הקפמה לע הניבקמ." *Ynet*, February 5, 2024. https://www.ynet.co.il/economy/article/bjzoyp05a.

Spiegel. 2024. לגיפש, העוג. 2024. ודעת הפינמ אישרה העצה תשפאתר לישוראל בתשחימ ורמב 26. Haaretz. https://www.haaretz.co.il/news/politi/2024-03-26/ty-article/0000018e-7b62-d9f5-a7ae-7f6f4a 530000

שדה, יובל. 2024. הלחץ הבינלאומי הבריע: סמוטריץ' מנע את שיתוק הבנקים הפלסטיניים." בלבליסט, 19 בינואר 2024. https://www.calcalist.co.il/local_news/article/bjsobmuxke.

Yaari. 2023. ירעי, דוהא. 2023. רקס שויב וצרבועט הזע: רוב הפלסטיניים םיכמות בטבח 7 רבוטקואב. Mako, 13 רבמצדב 2023. https://www.mako.co.il/news-military/636 1323ddea5a810/Article-b6535b17af36c81026.htm

Open Access This chapter is licensed under the terms of the Creative Commons Attribution 4.0 International License (http://creativecommons.org/licenses/by/4.0/), which permits use, sharing, adaptation, distribution and reproduction in any medium or format, as long as you give appropriate credit to the original author(s) and the source, provide a link to the Creative Commons license and indicate if changes were made.

The images or other third party material in this chapter are included in the chapter's Creative Commons license, unless indicated otherwise in a credit line to the material. If material is not included in the chapter's Creative Commons license and your intended use is not permitted by statutory regulation or exceeds the permitted use, you will need to obtain permission directly from the copyright holder.

CHAPTER 6

America's Enabling of Occupation

Brian Katulis

Abstract For decades, the United States has been Israel's strongest international supporter. Its assistance has been based on three pillars: a deep strategic security partnership between both countries; strong religious ties and shared values at all social levels; and a favorable public opinion maintained by strong lobby organizations. The result has been a level of great power support for an emergent and small nation that has few parallels elsewhere. As the Hamas attack on Israel of 7 October 2023 coincided with the tenure of a self-declared Zionist U.S. President, these ties have only deepened over the past year—despite the shift to the extreme right in Israeli politics and the carnage in Gaza. As a result, the prospects for change in America's long-standing support for Israel remain limited. Yet, in a bid to extract the United States from the Middle East's "forever wars," a Trump Presidency may push for resolution of the Palestinian issue as part of a broader regional stabilization initiative that builds on the Abraham Accords, which would be hard to resist for Israel's political elites. Meanwhile, greater student protests for Palestinian rights and

B. Katulis (✉)
Middle East Institute, Washington, DC, USA
e-mail: bkatulis@mei.edu

© The Author(s) 2025
E. van Veen (ed.), *The Future of the Occupation of the Palestinian Territories after Gaza*,
https://doi.org/10.1007/978-3-031-93798-9_6

more political criticism of Israel are unlikely to produce policy changes that bring U.S.-Palestinian relations on par with U.S.-Israeli relations.

Keywords Strategic security alliance · Evangelical Christians · Biden administration · Qualitative Military Edge · Zionism · Abraham Accords · Iran

INTRODUCTION

The United States has played a central role in enabling Israel's occupation and control of Palestinian territories in the West Bank, Gaza, and East Jerusalem for decades. The historic events of 2023–2024 have done little to alter the role that the United States plays in supporting Israel's policies. However, uncertainties in the region and within U.S. foreign policy as a result of Donald Trump's re-election could impact the future dynamics of the U.S.-Israel relationship. This essay analyzes the views, interests, role, and levers of influence the United States has on Israel. The objective is to explicate the factors that helped produce the situation that has come to characterize the occupied Palestinian territories and Israel after 7 October 2023. The essay also briefly examines the new strategic landscape in the Middle East that has emerged in this period. Examining the factors that shape America's unique role and relationship with Israel and the Palestinian territories serves as a basis for examining what might happen when current conflicts end and future U.S. administrations adapt their approach to new realities on the ground. On balance, the prospects for change in America's long-standing approach to Israel remain quite limited despite recent upheaval in the domestic political environments of both the United States and Israel, major transformations underway in the Middle East, as well as broader shifts in global geopolitics. This is the case even as the likelihood of a two-state solution fades and the risks to the (regional) state system that are associated with the lack of a resolution remain high.

Drivers of U.S. Support for Israel

The United States has viewed Israel as its most important bilateral relationship in the Middle East for several decades now. This relationship has gone through different phases that were impacted by major changes in the regional and geopolitical landscape as well as by domestic politics in both countries. It is in this vein that the Israel-Hamas war and the broader regional conflict between the United States/Israel and Iran/the axis of resistance, which intensified on the back of the Hamas attack on Israel of 7 October 2023, has produced new challenges to bilateral ties. Nevertheless, the foundation of the U.S.-Israel relationship remains fundamentally unaltered due to the depth and breadth of ties between the governments and people of both countries. Three core factors shape this relationship[1]:

Factor 1: Common Security and Strategic Interests

The United States continues to see Israel as its most important security partner in the Middle East. The roots for this strategic relationship have endured the entire period from the founding of the modern state of Israel in 1948 until the present, including the Cold War as well as the post-Cold War periods (Schoenbaum 1993; Oren 2007). In total, the United States has provided Israel with over $300 billion of military and economic assistance since its founding (Masters and Merrow 2024) and this flow of funding has remained mostly unrestricted for decades, even as Israel took decisions on the status of the disputed Palestinian territories in the West Bank, Gaza, and East Jerusalem. The war that began in 2023 between Israel and Hamas has led to more debate and scrutiny about the size and nature of this assistance inside of the United States, particularly among some left-wing circles in the Democratic Party but also among a few voices in the libertarian camp of the Republican Party. However, those voices remain mostly on the fringes of the policy and strategic debate and have not produced major policy shifts by the Biden administration (Katulis 2024).

---

[1] More incidental factors also played a role, such as how the anti-immigration fervor inside of the United States in the first half of the twentieth century shaped U.S. President Harry S. Truman's decision to support the founding of Israel. In part, it was a bid to get Jewish refugees to settle in Israel rather than in the United States.

The security imperatives of the U.S.-Israeli relationship remain strong in the current era of acute security threats to Israel (and to a lesser degree the United States) posed by Iran and its network of partners, including Hezbollah in Lebanon, Hamas and Islamic Jihad in the Palestinian territories and the Houthis in Yemen—even after the recent battering of a number of these groups, as well as Iran itself. Security challenges posed by non-state actors operating in the region, including the remnants of the Islamic State in parts of Syria and Iraq, represent another subfactor that incentivizes U.S. support to Israel with little or no restrictions. Along with these groups, there is a number of non-state actors operating in parts of Africa, such as AQIM, MUJAO, and Ansar Dine, that are problematic. On the military and intelligence fronts, the United States and Israel are deeply intertwined, so much so that even when Israel takes unilateral action that is at odds with U.S. interests and preferences, no U.S. administration has found it advisable to question the overall basis of the bilateral security relationship. Furthermore, the United States benefits significantly from its military, intelligence, and technological relationship with Israel, including access to advanced defense systems like the Iron Dome missile defense system and counterterrorism methods. By and large, the strength of the security dimension of the Israeli-U.S. relationship has made it possible to react to geopolitical events in ways that have further deepened the bond. It is in this vein that dynamics from Cold War competition with the USSR, the global war on terrorism, and more recently competition from Russia and China have created new areas for Israeli-U.S. security cooperation—at times enabling joint action—that has helped innovate this aspect of the relationship and keep it up to date. For example, when Islamic State came to power in parts of Syria and Iraq about a decade ago, the United States and Israel worked together to develop targeted intelligence and military operations in support of the international coalition assembled to defeat Islamic State. In addition, both countries have coordinated to counter threats from a range of Iran-backed groups during the 2023–2024 period, including the Houthis in Yemen and a number of shadowy militias operating in Syria and Iraq. Overall, the United States has relied on a strategic and security paradigm in which Israel forms a small but important piece in the broader puzzle of how the United States approaches the Middle East, as well as the wider world.

FACTOR 2: STRONG RELIGIOUS TIES AND SHARED VALUES

Separate but linked to security interests are the strong religious ties and shared values between the two countries that have deepened over decades. In this regard, a belief in the right to self-determination of the Jewish people after the Holocaust and centuries of persecution serves as a critical historical building block for strong socio-religious relations between the United States and Israel, as it does in a number of European countries (Meade 2022). The associated people-to-people aspect of the relation between Israel and the United States extends well beyond the Jewish community in the United States as many American Christians, particularly evangelical Christians, see the modern state of Israel as core to their world views in religious, moral, and eschatological terms (Gitlin and Leibowitz 2010). Recent shifts inside conservative circles in the Republican Party have brought evangelical Christians ever closer to the centers of power. The naming of former politician and evangelical Christian Mike Huckabee as the U.S. ambassador to Israel by Donald Trump in his second term is an indicator of this trend, just as the appointment of Mike Pompeo as Secretary of State during Trump's first term.

Israel is often described in the United States as the only liberal democracy in the Middle East—even though in reality it is an electoral democracy with limits on freedom and shortcomings for some of its citizens,[2] such as discriminatory laws that exist against its Palestinian/Arab community like the 2018 law on the nation state. Notwithstanding such observations, many Americans support Israel because they see it as a democratic nation with a commitment to freedoms of speech, religion, and press, to name a few. A new dynamic that has emerged over the past years is the sense that Israel's religious and political identity is moving so far to the extremist right that it has stunned parts of America's Jewish community. This seemed particularly acute in the months before the Hamas attack on Israel on 7 October when the debate of the day was the proposed changes to Israel's political and judicial systems, some of which touched upon the issue of religious identity. That development created concern that Israel was moving in a regressive direction in which rightwing extremist perspectives aligned with a settler colonialist mindset were

---

[2] V-DEM downgraded Israel in 2023 from a liberal to an electoral democracy due to the judicial reform plans of the Netanyahu government and government attacks on the judiciary, especially the Supreme Court.

becoming increasingly dominant. This trend runs contrary to trends in other parts of the Middle East, particularly in some of the wealthier Arab countries that are gradually moving in a more socially progressive direction with less emphasis on rigid religious identities narrowly defined by conservative clerical authorities. That battle for the Middle East's broader identity is still very much underway and one can argue that the backward-looking agendas of Iran, Hamas, Hezbollah, and the Houthis threaten to undermine opportunities for greater regional integration and connection across countries and cultures. In a curious way, some of the dominant power elite in Israel's current right-wing politics show remarkable similarities with Iran's rulers and other guides of retrograde Islamist political movements with regard to how narrow and extremist religious doctrine influences their worldview.

Factor 3: Public Opinion and the Impact of Lobbying Groups

U.S. public opinion remains strongly favorable toward Israel, driven in part by the first two factors described above. In addition, Israel has many points of connection with the United States that enable regular maintenance of the relationship at the people-to-people level. Such connective social issue is strong at the elite level including public policy making, but also exists at cultural, societal, and religious levels. Although the debate within the Jewish American, as well as within Christian and Muslim American religious communities, about Israel has become more pluralistic and diverse in recent years, that diversity of views has not yet manifested itself in a major shift in political views, let alone policy trends. Moreover, pro-Israel lobby groups play an important role in shaping U.S. social views and political discourse about Israel, especially organizations like the American Israel Public Affairs Committee (AIPAC). These groups advocate at scale for U.S. support for Israel through public advocacy, lobbying on legislation, and donations. Their work has maintained fairly strong bipartisan support for Israel in Congress and resulted in a steady stream of military aid to Israel, in particular over the past year (OpenSecrets, 1996). The work of such advocacy organizations is facilitated by the enduring favorable opinion of most American people toward Israel, even though public opinion polling has seen some shifts against the dominant pro-Israel attitude, particularly among pockets of younger Americans, college-educated elites, and parts of the left wing of the Democratic party

(Dinesh and Silver 2023; Jones 2024). However, these shifts have not yet produced major changes in the positive consensus view of Israel among the Democratic and Republican parties.

In contrast to the effective lobbying and advocacy work of pro-Israeli organizations, the Palestinian and Arab communities in America have not yet successfully built coalitions capable of articulating a proactive agenda in support of a two-state solution. After 7 October 2023, many of the debates on display inside U.S. society, including at elite universities, have had a mixed or negative effect on the prospects for presenting a more positive image about Palestinians and their cause. Instances when demonstrators and protestors appeared to articulate views not dissimilar from those held by terrorist groups and extremist organizations may well have reinforced traditional pro-Israel views and attitudes. Zooming out from an advocacy point of view, U.S. policy on the Middle East under both Republican and Democratic administrations has tended to treat the U.S. relationship with Palestinians as a subsidiary to U.S.-Israel ties due to a mix of effective lobbying for the Israeli cause, ineffective lobbying for the Palestinian cause and the presence of radical fringes at protests that emphasize Palestinians rights (Elgindy 2019).

In sum, Israel is viewed by vast majorities of American voters and leaders in both its dominant political parties as the most reliable, if sometimes troublesome, security partner in the Middle East. U.S. support for Israel, as well as for the ongoing Israeli occupation of Palestinian territories, that results from this view is centered on three main factors: security interests, religious ties and shared values, and organized public support. These foundations have grown slightly weaker of late, but not as much as advocates for other paradigms might wish for. Especially Israel's core role as a security partner that helps America address threats to global security like Iran and Islamic State remains a key imperative that makes it difficult for U.S. policymakers to accept the idea of using U.S. military assistance as leverage to end occupation. The deep religious ties that key sectors of the American population have with the Jewish state further complicate such a course of action, even as Israel has drifted more rightward over the past decade and a half.

Levers of U.S. Influence and Policy Options for the Second Trump Administration

Given these three main factors shaping America's approach, and considering how they have enabled and underwritten Israel's occupation of Palestinian territories for decades, it is clear that there is strong path dependency in America's support for Israel that limits openings for major shifts. But nothing in life, particularly the Middle East and U.S. politics, is immutable and many dynamics are in play today that have uncertain outcomes. One is that the re-election of Donald Trump as U.S. president introduces a new and impulsive variable into the combustible mix of today's Middle East. Trump has prided himself on his unpredictability in how he operates as a leader, seeking to gain leverage and advantage over friend and foe alike in how he has conducted foreign policy. This could generate a range of unexpected policy options that might come to fruition under the second Trump administration, depending on circumstances.

The second Trump administration's approach to Israel and the Palestinian territories will be dependent in large part on the inheritance that the Biden administration leaves behind and on where things stand on the ground. At the moment, the prospects for any major advances in terms of peace and stability look bleak. Palestinians remain fragmented in three different areas: the West Bank, Gaza Strip, and East Jerusalem. Their condition remains dire in Gaza, where the ongoing conflict and massive recovery and reconstruction effort that will be required has yet to get underway. Israel's current government leans heavily toward the right, with some voices calling for outright annexation of the West Bank. Extremist groups of Israeli settlers continue to threaten Palestinians in the West Bank and similar groups do the same in actions against Palestinians in East Jerusalem. Extremist groups among Palestinians have a symbiotic relationship with Israeli extremists as they feed off of each other and foster greater instability. These conditions, along with wider regional conflict, are likely to shape the Trump administration's policy options and initial actions. Hence, its approach to the Israeli Palestinian question is quite likely to be grounded, at least initially, in the policies of his first term in office.

This included, to begin with, a continuation of strong support for Israel. Trump was the first U.S. president to formally and officially recognize Jerusalem as Israel's capital in 2017 by moving the U.S. embassy there. Trump also backed Israel's claims over the Golan Heights, a territory formerly controlled by Syria that, according to international law and previous peace negotiations, is considered disputed and occupied territory. Hence, in the matter of recognizing rights and territories that Israel claims, Trump may be even more pro-Israel than President Joe Biden, who made clear his support for Israel and the Zionist cause. In addition, the first Trump administration facilitated the 2020 Abraham Accords that led to normalization agreements between Israel and several Arab nations, including the UAE, Bahrain, and Morocco, as well as Sudan for a brief period of time (Rosenberg 2021). This deal temporarily blocked a move by Israel to annex the West Bank. The incoming second term of the Trump administration is likely to seek a pathway for normalization between Israel and Saudi Arabia, but it will find a much-changed regional landscape in which such a move has become more difficult for Riyadh given the destruction of Gaza as well as the annexationist mindset and actions of the Israeli government. Finally, the "Peace to Prosperity" plan[3] that the Trump administration's unveiled in January 2020, which aimed to resolve the Israeli Palestinian conflict and create a pathway for addressing broader issues in the Middle East, might be revived. The plan had several key components, including a concept for a semi-autonomous Palestinian entity doubling as the "State of Palestine." However, it featured major modifications to previous Middle East peace proposals, including making Jerusalem Israel's undivided capital. The concept also proposed a partial annexation by Israel of the West Bank in exchange for a land swap with other territories, and it proposed a demilitarized Palestinian state with major limitations on its sovereignty, including Israeli control of airspace. It furthermore proposed a $50 billion investment in Palestinian infrastructure and businesses over a decade. In addition, it outlined a general scenario for compensating Palestinian refugees while providing for their permanent settlement in third countries.

Israeli leaders generally welcomed the plan while Palestinian leaders rejected it, calling it a one-sided proposal. The plan itself did not become the basis for a wider discussion. Its core was to facilitate a resolution that allowed for Israeli territorial expansion in the West Bank combined with economic incentives for Palestinians. It was generally viewed as falling

---

[3] "Peace to Prosperity: A Vision to Improve the Lives of the Palestinian and Israeli People," The White House of the Trump Administration, January 2020, available at: https://trumpwhitehouse.archives.gov/peacetoprosperity/.

short of meeting the expectations of Palestinians and many others in the region. The fact that this plan has not become a vehicle for a way to move forward on the Israeli Palestinian front makes it unlikely that Trump would gain traction if his second administration returned to this proposal without additional elements to expand its appeal. In addition, the increased human and financial costs of the Gaza war, along with Israeli settlers expanding their control in the West Bank, have likely made the 2020 Trump plan even less viable than it was on release. Given these fundamentals, the scenarios for a major shift in U.S. policy on the Israeli Palestinian front in the next few years seem quite limited, but there are some opportunities.

If the war between Israel and Hamas continues and leads to a long-term Israeli occupation of Gaza, along with continued instability in the West Bank and East Jerusalem, then the ongoing costs of the unresolved situation could lead the second Trump administration to seek a new pathway for stability and an agreement. The security and financial costs of the current U.S. approach to the Middle East have accumulated over the last year and a half, and a new Trump administration appears unwilling to bear the costs of current U.S. policy, which has resulted in simmering conflicts on multiple fronts in the Middle East that risk drawing U.S. troops into the fight. In his re-election campaign, Trump sent many different signals about ongoing wars. One of them was an urgent desire to bring them to an end.

If Trump is motivated to achieve a bigger historical gain for his legacy by means of an Israel-Saudi normalization accord, it will require a clearer and stronger pathway to a two-state solution than the 2020 Trump Middle East plan provided, given the position staked out by Saudi Arabia after 7 October 2023 by demanding a two-state solution. An alternative pathway would involve re-imaging America's power and influence in a way that helps build a more unified, regional, and international collective effort to create the State of Palestine—one in which Trump makes a comprehensive deal involving Israel-Saudi normalization.

The key ingredient is to shift the calculus of Israel's people and leaders in helping them see the possibility that Israel's central choices revolve around stark alternatives: endless war and occupation versus regional integration with greater security and prosperity for all. In order to do this, the United States needs to deepen its commitment to the region and do something it has never done before: Make the Palestinian people a priority in its own policy and in its engagement with key regional partners. It's an ambitious agenda, but trying this alternative pathway is better than the current course.

Conflict of Interest The author has no conflict of interests to declare that are relevant to the content of this chapter.

BIBLIOGRAPHY

"America's Strategic Drift in the Middle East: An Assessment of the Biden Administration's Policy One Year Into the Israel-Hamas War," by Brian Katulis, Middle East Institute, published October 2, 2024, found at America's Strategic Drift in the Middle East: An Assessment of the Biden Administration's Policy One Year Into the Israel-Hamas War | Middle East Institute.

Blind Spot: America and the Palestinians, From Balfour to Trump by Khaled Elgindy (Washington DC, The Brookings Institution, 2019).

Dinesh, Shradha and Laura Silver. 2023. How Americans view Israel, Netanyahu and U.S.-Israel relations in 5 charts. Blogpost: Pew Research. 21 August 2023. Online: https://www.pewresearch.org/short-reads/2023/08/21/how-americans-view-israel-netanyahu-and-u-s-israel-relations-in-5-charts/.

Enemies and Allies: An Unforgettable Journey Inside the Fast Moving & Immensely Turbulent Modern Middle East by Joel C. Rosenberg (Carol Stream, Illinois, Tyndale House Publishers, 2021).

Jones, Jeffrey. 2024. *Americans' Views of Both Israel, Palestinian Authority Down.* Blogpost: Gallup. 4 March 2024. Online: https://news.gallup.com/poll/611375/americans-views-israel-palestinian-authority-down.aspx.

OpenSecrets. 1996. *Your home for money in politics.* OpenSecrets. https://www.opensecrets.org/

"Peace to Prosperity: A Vision to Improve the Lives of the Palestinian and Israeli People," The White House of the Trump Administration, January 2020, available at: https://trumpwhitehouse.archives.gov/peacetoprosperity/.

The Arc of a Covenant: The United States, Israel, and the Fate of the Jewish People by Walter Russell Meade (United states, Alfred A. Knopf, 2022).

The Chosen Peoples: America, Israel, and the Ordeals of Divine Election by Todd Gitlin and Liel Leibowitz (New York, Simon & Schuster, 2010).

The Israel Lobby and U.S. Foreign Policy by John J. Mearsheimer and Stephen M. Walt (New York, Farrar, Straus and Girous, 2007).

The United States and the State of Israel by David Schoenbaum (New York, Oxford University, 1993) and Power, Faith and Fantasy: America in the Middle East 1776 to the Present by Michael B. Oren (New York, W.W Norton & Company, 2007).

"U.S. Aid to Israel in Four Charts," Jonathan Masters and Will Merrow, Council on Foreign Relations, updated on November 13, 2024, found at U.S. Aid to Israel in Four Charts | Council on Foreign Relations.

Open Access This chapter is licensed under the terms of the Creative Commons Attribution 4.0 International License (http://creativecommons.org/licenses/by/4.0/), which permits use, sharing, adaptation, distribution and reproduction in any medium or format, as long as you give appropriate credit to the original author(s) and the source, provide a link to the Creative Commons license and indicate if changes were made.

The images or other third party material in this chapter are included in the chapter's Creative Commons license, unless indicated otherwise in a credit line to the material. If material is not included in the chapter's Creative Commons license and your intended use is not permitted by statutory regulation or exceeds the permitted use, you will need to obtain permission directly from the copyright holder.

PART II

Neighbors

CHAPTER 7

Hezbollah: Shaken to the Core

Joseph Daher

Abstract Hezbollah's origins as an armed resistance movement against the Israeli occupation of southern Lebanon have gradually been diluted over the past decades by its efforts to strengthen the party's domestic power base within Lebanon, its foray into the Syrian civil war and its pursuit of regional objectives together with its chief sponsor Iran. The Palestinian cause has tended to be peripheral to Hezbollah's main objectives all along, even though the party rhetorically uses the plight of the Palestinians to boost its resistance profile and legitimacy. The consequences of these developments have been decreasing support for Hezbollah in Lebanese society and a downgrade of its regional prestige. This put Hezbollah in a comparatively weak position in October 2023. Subsequently, the party chose a cautious strategy of military engagement with Israel. It intended to show low-cost solidarity with Hamas while pressuring Israel into a ceasefire in Gaza. Hezbollah's strategy turned out to be a mistake as Israel had used the period since 2006 to prepare meticulously for the next conflict to devastating effect. Today, Hezbollah

J. Daher (✉)
Bonn International Centre for Conflict Studies, Bonn, Germany
e-mail: josephdaher77@gmail.com

© The Author(s) 2025
E. van Veen (ed.), *The Future of the Occupation of the Palestinian Territories after Gaza*,
https://doi.org/10.1007/978-3-031-93798-9_7

is "down, but not out". The movement will focus on rebuilding, re-legitimising and revitalising itself over the next years. The Palestinian cause will have to wait.

Keywords Hezbollah · Dahiyeh · South Lebanon · Nasrallah · Axis of resistance · Sheeba farms · Taif agreement

INTRODUCTION

The Israeli military campaign against the Palestinians in the occupied Gaza Strip, which followed the Hamas attack on Israel on 7 October 2023, gradually expanded into a military confrontation involving the wider region, especially Lebanon.[1] Clashes between Hezbollah and the Israeli army recurred with variable frequency starting on 8 October 2023, and turned into direct conflict in September 2024, including an Israeli ground invasion of southern Lebanon. A ceasefire between Hezbollah and Israel was finally reached on 27 November 2024. It is against this background that the Chapter analyses the evolution of Hezbollah's perspective on Israel, its general posture against it and Hezbollah's specific reactions to the Israeli war on Gaza, including a reflection on the movement's strategic limitations and challenges. The Chapter starts by discussing Hezbollah's historic struggle against Israel since the movement's establishment and examines how this struggle has evolved over the past decades. Next, the chapter examines Hezbollah's political standing and military capacities in the struggle against Israel today, as well as its challenges regarding the present war. Finally, the chapter concludes with reflections on how Hezbollah is likely to relate to the Israeli occupation of Palestine in the future.

---

[1] The Palestinian Islamic movement Hamas launched an attack on the 7th of October in the southern territories of the State of Israel, leading to the death of 1,139 persons, including 695 Israeli civilians, 373 members of the security forces and 71 foreigners. It should be noted that Israeli forces also killed a number of Israeli civilians on this day, including by tank shells fired at houses where Israelis were detained.

Hezbollah's Establishment and Its Fight Against the Israeli Occupation of Lebanon

The establishment and development of Hezbollah is historically connected with different elements of the Israeli invasion of Lebanon in 1982 and Israel's subsequent occupation of the country until 2000 as well as political dynamics in, and regional designs of, the Islamic Republic of Iran (IRI). The party was established as an Islamic political group, based in Shi'a-populated areas in Lebanon, with an emphasis on armed resistance against Israel. The first military operations carried out by Hezbollah prior to its official establishment in 1985 were suicide attacks on Western embassies and targets, as well as kidnappings of Westerners. However between 1985 and the late 2000s, the expansion of Hezbollah's armed apparatus and its military activities has targeted Israel. At the same time, the party's resistance narrative enabled it to widen its social base among Lebanon's Shi'a population. In 2000, Hezbollah routed Israel from the south of Lebanon, ending an occupation that began in 1978. Despite rocket exchanges from both sides of the border since, the Lebanese Shia party has maintained control over this area. Israel launched another war against Lebanon in 2006 that resulted in over 1200 casualties, including 270 Hezbollah fighters and 158 Israelis—mostly soldiers (Human Rights Watch 2007). Despite the dead count "favoring" Israel, it was unable to achieve its objective of significantly weakening Hezbollah politically or militarily. The movement considered this a political success and propagated its victory widely and effectively to increase its popularity in Lebanon and the wider Middle East.

An important part of Hezbollah's legitimacy in its early days was the military struggle it waged against the Israeli occupation of Lebanon. Hezbollah's first manifesto of 1985 outlined the party's rejection of Israel on the grounds that it had occupied Muslim land and had an expansionist agenda. It also expressed Hezbollah's opposition to Western nations, particularly the United States, due to their support for Israel (Hezbollah's Open Letter to the Downtrodden of Lebanon and the World 1985). After the end of the Israeli occupation of southern Lebanon in 2000, however, Hezbollah shifted its narrative by arguing that its military capabilities did not exist to liberate Palestine from the "Zionist enemy", as it had claimed since its creation, but rather to protect Lebanon from renewed Israeli aggression. In 2008, Dr. Ali Fayyad, at the time head of the Consultative Centre for Studies and Documentation (a Hezbollah research centre) and a Hezbollah MP in parliament since 2009, said in regard to Palestine that "We (Hezbollah) support the Liberation of Palestine, but we do not want to take their place to free their lands. Hezbollah is firstly a national liberation movement against the threats and the violence of Israel and to free the Lebanese territories and prisoners" (Fayyad 2008). Ghaleb Abou Zeinab (2008), a Hezbollah member and political advisor of Hassan Nasrallah at this time, affirmed that "Our arms are the liberation of Lebanese lands and the defence of the state and not for Palestine". This evolution of both narrative and strategy was also reflected in Hezbollah's manifesto of 2009. The section regarding "Resistance" limits the movement's role to liberate Lebanese occupied lands and defend the sovereignty of the country against Israeli threats. There was no mention of the liberation of Palestine.

This evolution of Hezbollah's discourse continued at the beginning of the uprising in Syria in 2011 to justify the group's increasing military involvement on the side of the Syrian regime. The war in Syria necessitated a substantial increase in recruitment and produced a growing number of young fighters with significant battlefield experience. Hezbollah MP Hassan Fadlallah (2015) explained that protecting Lebanon from external threats was the main objective of the Resistance. In addition to Israel threatening Lebanon, he also cited "takfiri" groups that want to establish their own emirates, such as Islamic State or perhaps even Jabhat al-Nusra. Notably, he argued that Hezbollah's intervention in Syria against these groups after 2011 was conducted to prevent the threat of their expansion into Lebanon. Hezbollah Secretary General Hassan Nasrallah actually spoke of Lebanon's "second liberation" (the first occurred after the withdrawal of Israeli occupation forces in May 2000) when the last jihadi groups, including the Islamic State (IS), withdrew and/or were chased from Lebanese territory, in the Ersal (Bekaa) at the end of August 2017 (al-Manar 2017). This was the result of a Hezbollah-led military campaign in the Bekaa Valley with the support of the Lebanese army. Hezbollah leaders boasted of having secured Lebanon's borders with Syria. Hezbollah's role in Lebanon and Syria after 2011 also illustrates its growing relevance as the fulcrum of Iranian influence in the Middle East. While Hezbollah is a Lebanese actor with partial domestic political autonomy, the party has also come to act as the main actor serving and participating in Iranian regional interests. This role has been essential to the expansion and consolidation of Iran's network of regional allies, consisting of state and non-state actors, and was especially pronounced after the assassination of the head of the Quds-force of the Islamic Revolutionary Guard Corps (IRGC), Qassem Soleimani, in 2020 (Daher 2023a).

In other words, Hezbollah's resistance against Israel, which stood at the core of the party's identity when it was established, has been increasingly subordinated to the national political objectives of the party, its allies and its sponsor Iran.[2] Between 2006 and 2023, the weapons of the "resistance" were increasingly diverted from the struggle against Israel and used inside and outside of Lebanon. Especially in Syria, but also to attack Lebanese political parties (for example against Sunni fighters and citizens in May 2008).[3] Consequentially, Hezbollah's military confrontation with Israel became secondary to the broader political objectives of the party and its regional allies. Rhetorical support for the "axis of resistance" and the armed apparatus of the party have been used by Hezbollah to justify its policies and actions, including its military involvement in Syria. This did not and does not mean that Hezbollah's military component has not been playing a role against Israel's aggression, as it for example has done after October 7th, but it does mean that Hezbollah's forces have been increasingly used for other purposes, especially after the 2006 war.

The "Unity of the Fronts" Strategy, but Reacting in a "Calculated Way"…

The outbreak of the war in October 2023 led Hezbollah to re-focus its military forces and operations against the Israeli army at its southern borders. Prior to October 7, Hezbollah had already started to strengthen its military collaboration with its Palestinian allies and other groups supported by Tehran, including in Iraq and Yemen. This strategy intended

---

[2] Hezbollah has been politically, socially and financially supported by Iran since its official establishment in 1985 and even earlier if one considers activities of groups linked to it. Iran remains its chief financial supporter. However, diversification of funding has long been a necessity for Hezbollah given the increase of sanctions and growth of its activities. Similarly, Hezbollah's military equipment is largely provided by Iran.

[3] In May 2008, the organization took up arms against other Lebanese political factions and even invaded certain neighborhoods in West Beirut as well as regions, like the Chouf. This came after a Lebanese government announcement that it wanted to dismantle Hezbollah's communications network. The violence ended within a week with over 80 deaths and 250 wounded. Hezbollah attained its objectives and the government cancelled its offending decrees of May 6 and 7 respectively (ICG 2008).

to reinforce its deterrent capacity towards Israel, which took the form of the so-called "unity of the fronts" strategy after October 7 that linked Gaza with Lebanon. The day after Hamas' military operation, Hezbollah launched guided rockets and artillery at three Israeli military posts in the Shebaa Farms "in solidarity" with the Palestinian people (Reuters 2023). Next, the party started to target northern Israel and to a lesser extent the occupied Golan, mostly focusing on military targets. For its part, the Israeli army continuously escalated its military actions against Lebanon. It did not limit its bombing to border areas, but increasingly struck the Bekaa Valley and other areas of southern Lebanon. Israeli military operations killed more than 500 Hezbollah fighters in Lebanon and Syria between October 2023 and September 2024, including many senior officers (Blondel and Haddad 2024). By mid-August 2024, Israeli attacks had also killed over a hundred civilians, displaced over 110,000 people, wrought significant destruction on civilian infrastructure and made large areas of farmland in southern Lebanon unsuitable for cultivation. The Israeli army conducted a veritable scorched-earth policy in the Lebanese border regions. In reaction, Hezbollah intensified its attacks against Israeli military targets but stuck to calculated and proportional reactions. This resulted in the displacement of 60,000 Israeli citizens who fled the country's north (UN 2024).

Hezbollah's War Weariness and Its Internal Challenges

The cautious and calculated actions of Hezbollah in its conflict with Israel contrast somewhat with the massive expansion of Hezbollah's military capacities after the 2006 war. Notably, it has a vast arsenal of rockets and missiles today. According to different Israeli research centres and statements (cited in Jones et al. 2024), Hezbollah has now more than 120,000 missiles, including several hundred Fateh-110s, capable of hitting a target within a radius of 300 kilometres with high precision in addition to tens of thousands of older Zelzal missiles with a range of more than 120 kilometres. The expansion of the party's military capacity has not coincided with a growth in its popular support, however. In fact quite the opposite has happened. This has been one major reason for the party's cautious responses to Israeli attacks. More precisely, Hezbollah has become increasingly politically and socially isolated outside Lebanon's Shia population (Daher 2023b). A survey conducted in July 2024 showed that support for Hezbollah outside the Shia community was one of the lowest in its history with only 30% of the Lebanese population trusting the party (Roche and Robbins 2024). A key driver of this development has been the party's involvement in a number of sectarian clashes with different religious communities in Lebanon over the past few years. The most important one occurred in 2021, following a protest by members from Hezbollah and its ally Amal against Judge Tarek Bitar, who was in charge of the investigation into the explosion at the port of Beirut on August 4, 2020. Street fighting broke out in the neighbouring Tayouné district of southern Beirut. These clashes pitted Shi'a fighters from Hezbollah and Amal against fighters stationed in Christian neighbourhoods, most probably members of the Lebanese Forces, a Christian far-right movement. This street battle left seven people dead and thirty-two wounded, raising fears of a new civil war. Within Lebanon, sectarian political parties opposed to Hezbollah, but also wider sectors of the population, view Hezbollah as the main obstacle to achieving justice for the 2020 August Beirut port explosion. Even the party's former political allies, such as the Free Patriotic Movement, have been increasingly critical of it. The broad-based popular support that Hezbollah enjoyed in 2006 was absent in 2024. Hezbollah's military intervention to support the Syrian regime to crush the popular uprising also undermined its popularity on both a national and regional level. In the same vein, Hezbollah's opposition to the Lebanese uprising of October 2019, and the rallying of its supporters and members to intimidate demonstrators in different localities and to even attack them in downtown Beirut as well as in the city of Nabatiyeh in southern Lebanon, also reduced the prestige of the party.

Until the summer of 2024, however, the party had been able to prevent more sectarian tensions from developing in Lebanon, even after the bombing that killed twelve children in Majdal Shams, a town on the Syrian Golan Heights occupied by Israel and inhabited by a Syrian Druze population. The majority of this population refuses Israeli citizenship and suffers from discrimination by the Israeli state. Hezbollah denied any responsibility or involvement in the attack for which Israel blamed it. According to weapons experts' statement on the Associated Press's website (Frankel and El-Deeb 2024), evidence suggests a rocket from Lebanon, potentially fired accidentally, was responsible for the casualties. Israel's Iron Dome missile defence mechanism detected the launch, but did not intercept it. Regardless of the cause of the deaths, Israeli officials instrumentalized this event to target the southern suburbs of Beirut and stoke sectarian tensions within Lebanon. Hezbollah, in turn, used the incident to initiate a modest rapprochement with sectors of the Lebanese Sunni population since its vast majority is supportive of the Palestinians. Jamiya al-Islamiya—the Muslim Brotherhood in Lebanon—even participated in military actions against Israeli forces at the Lebanese border under Hezbollah's umbrella. In addition, more and more Sunni Sheikhs openly support the "resistance" in their Friday sermons, including senior figures from Dar al-Fatwa (Fawaz 2024), which is the official body overseeing the religious affairs of Lebanon's Sunnis. It used to vehemently oppose Hezbollah.

A second reason for the cautious nature of Hezbollah's engagement with Israel after October 7 was that the country has been facing a deep socioeconomic crisis since October 2019. According to the World Bank (2024a), the share of individuals in Lebanon living under the Lebanon Household Survey poverty line more than tripled between 2012 and 2022—from 12 to 44%. For large sectors of the population, a new war would be devastating. Moreover, Hezbollah wanted to avoid destruction of its own infrastructures that were (re)built after the 2006 war. Finally, Hezbollah's main supporter, Iran, sought to avoid a regional war despite the assassination of Palestinian leader Haniyeh on its territory and numerous other Israeli attacks against Iranian assets across the region. Between October 2023 and mid-August 2024, Israel killed over twenty senior officials of the Islamic Revolutionary Guard Corps. But, much like Hezbollah, Tehran moderated its responses. Iranian's strategic aims, particularly since October 7, have been to improve its political standing in the region so as to be in the best possible position for any future negotiation with the United States and to safeguard its political and security interests.

Hezbollah's Most Important Challenge Since Its Foundation

Hezbollah's plan of pressuring Israel to agree to a ceasefire in Gaza via skirmishes on and over the Lebanese/Israeli border was challenged by Israel initiating an air and ground war against Lebanon in mid-September 2024 with US support. Israeli intelligence first exploded thousands of communications devices used by Hezbollah members, both civilians and soldiers, which killed nearly 40 people and wounded several thousands, upon which its Air Force initiated a massive bombing campaign that also assassinated the party's senior military and political leaders including Secretary General Hassan Nasrallah. It also killed over a thousand civilians and forcibly displaced over a million Lebanese citizens. The Israeli army subsequently commenced a ground invasion of southern Lebanon. Hezbollah clearly underestimated the intensity, duration and military superiority of the Israeli attack. Persisting with the strategy of "unity of the fronts" became more and more difficult in the face of mounting losses and destruction. The party's priority shifted from linking the fronts to protecting its internal structures and chain of command, filling the vacuum at the top by electing a new secretary general, replacing its political and military leadership and preserving its military capabilities.

This shift in priorities partly explains the rhetorical evolution of Hezbollah regarding its objective since October 7. Deputy Secretary General Naim Qassem as well as MPs Hussein Hajj Hassan and Amin Sherri stated after the assassination of Hassan Nasrallah that their priority was to end the Israeli aggression against Lebanon and to support a ceasefire regardless of the status of the fighting in Gaza (Hijazi 2024). Similarly, during his tour in the Gulf, Iranian foreign minister Abbas Araghchi confirmed the separation between the Lebanese and Gaza fronts, saying "there must be a ceasefire in Gaza and Lebanon, but the idea that stopping the fighting in Lebanon is a necessity and a priority is also correct" (Rabih 2024). The Israeli leadership disregarded these statements and continued its war against Lebanon. Israeli politicians—from Prime Minister Benjamin Netanyahu to Israeli army spokesperson Avichay Adraee—instead used incendiary statements to provoke sectarian tensions among the Lebanese to trigger internal strife or even civil war. Similarly, Israel purposefully bombed areas that welcomed internally displaced people (IDP) from majority-inhabited Shi'a areas to encourage sectarian tensions. One example is the Israeli strike on the village of Aito in October 2024 that killed over 20 IDPs. The village is located in the district of Zghorta and inhabited mostly by Christians (al-Jazeera 2024).

A ceasefire between Hezbollah and Israel was eventually concluded on 27 November 2024. The ceasefire agreement provided for a 60-day period (end of January 2025) for the Israeli army to withdraw from southern Lebanon and Hezbollah fighters to withdraw to the north of the Litani River while the Lebanese army and UN peacekeepers were to deploy in these regions instead. The ceasefire, however, did not prevent the Israeli army from continuing to carry out strikes and incursions, as well as to delay its withdrawal from a range of villages in the South to destroy remaining infrastructure and to kill a number of civilians. These actions served as message to Hezbollah that Israel will continue its actions despite the end of the war to prevent the Lebanese movement to reconstitute its military capacities in these areas. At the conclusion of the ceasefire, the total number of deaths in Lebanon after October 2023 amounted to over 4,000 individuals, of which 84% occurred after mid-September 2024, as well as 16,000 injured. A million people were forcibly displaced due to the Israeli offensive (UN 2025) while the World Bank (2024b) estimates the cost of physical damage and economic losses in Lebanon at US$8.5 billion.

However, Hezbollah is not out and remains the most important political actor in Lebanon. It also retains strong military capacities and a large network of institutions. One of the main strengths of the movement has been to build a robust, organised and disciplined organisation in the shadows of the more overt and cult-like veneration of former Secretary General Hassan Nasrallah. Notably, Hezbollah retains a vast arsenal of rockets and missiles. By the end of September 2024, Hezbollah used various mid-range Fadi missiles for the first time since October 7 to strike military sites on the outskirts of Haifa and Tel Aviv. Furthermore, during the Israeli army's initial attempts to infiltrate Lebanese territories, Hezbollah's soldiers destroyed a few Merkava tanks, as well as injuring and killing a score of Israeli soldiers.[4] Alongside its armed forces, Hezbollah still has a large network of institutions that provide essential services. Although this network has been partially undermined by the war and purposefully targeted by the Israeli Air Force, it continues to service a slice of the growing needs of Lebanon's population—Shi'a in particular. Nevertheless, Hezbollah will struggle to provide its popular base with essential services, compensation and financial aid, or to undertake the reconstruction of homes and infrastructure as it did in 2006 due to the scale of destruction. In spite of this, Deputy Secretary General Naim Qassem concluded his third televised speech by mentioning the promise of former Secretary General Hassan Nasrallah: "You will return to your homes, which we will rebuild to be more beautiful than they were, and we have already begun preparations for this" (English al-Manar 2024).

---

[4] Between 30 September 2024 (the start of the Israeli ground offensive) and early December 2024, the number of Israeli soldiers killed stood at 56.

On balance, Hezbollah's popular base is probably secure for now—especially in the absence of an inclusive political alternative, the resolution of Lebanon's rolling economic crisis and continued Iranian support. It is likely that Tehran will contribute financially to assist the party with postwar reconstruction. After all, a fatally weakened Hezbollah puts Iran's regional strategy of protection by deterrence in question and undermines its regional network of armed actors. However, a weakened Iranian regime would undermine signicantly Hezbollah in its ability to maintain its military, political and social structures.

Conclusion

Israel's objectives in Lebanon were not limited to the return of Israeli IDPs to the north of the country or to the withdrawal of all Hezbollah's military forces operating south of the Litani River, as mandated by UN resolution 1701 (2006). Instead, Israel sought to fatally weaken Hezbollah, both military and politically, and through it, the entire "Axis of Resistance". Israeli Prime Minister Netanyahu's call for a "new Middle East" reflects Israeli-American ambitions for a new regional order that is dominated by Washington and its allies. Going forward, Hezbollah's engagement with Israel will greatly depend on future battlefield outcomes and the ability of Israel to keep securing US support in pursuit of its objectives. Future Israeli actions against Iran and the evolution of the relations between Iran and the United States will also impact Hezbollah's stance, including on the Palestinian issue. At the same time, the party's ability to broaden its support base in Lebanon by means of leveraging the Palestinian issue is restricted because of its political strategy of maintaining its autonomy, retaining a key role in Lebanon's political economy and remaining allied with Iran. Many Lebanese view Hezbollah as responsible for the Israeli army's destruction of swathes of Lebanon as a result of its support for Hamas after 7 October 2023. This perception matters because it is isolating the party in Lebanese society. Moreover, the overthrow of the Syrian regime in December 2024 further weakened for Hezbollah. It was a major blow to the party, in particular because Syria served as strategic rear base for funding and weapon transfers from Iran and as a logistical centre for the party, including weapons production facilities. In conclusion, it is fair to say that Hezbollah finds itself in its greatest predicament since its foundation. The situation is unlikely to improve soon given the blows Israel has inflicted and the party's isolation within Lebanon. At the same time, the party will not disappear because it has a strong, disciplined and organised political and militant structure and benefits from the continued assistance of Iran. In parallel, the absence of an inclusive and democratic political alternative within Lebanon, a deep economic crisis and a dysfunctional state also work in the party's favour.

Conflict of Interest The author has no conflict of interests to declare that are relevant to the content of this chapter.

Bibliography

al-Jazeera (2024), "Israeli strike kills 21 in northern Lebanon as Hezbollah steps up attacks", 14 October, https://www.aljazeera.com/news/2024/10/14/isr aeli-strike-kills-18-in-northern-lebanon-as-hezbollah-steps-up-attacks

Al-Manar (2017), "Sayyed Nasrallah: Aug 28 is the Second Liberation Day, ISIL Submitted to Hezbollah", 29 August, https://english.almanar.com.lb/336789

Blondel, Gabriel and Jaimee Haddad (2024), "À combien peut-on estimer les pertes humaines du Hezbollah dans la guerre contre Israël?" *Orient le Jour*, 30 December, https://www.lorientlejour.com/article/1441373/a-combien-peut-on-estimer-les-pertes-humaines-du-hezbollah-dans-la-guerre-contre-isr ael-.html

Daher, Josepj (2023a), "The Growth of Hezbollah: The Nexus of Iran's Influence", *ISPI*, 22 March, https://www.ispionline.it/en/publication/the-gro wth-of-hezbollah-the-nexus-of-irans-influence-121909

Daher, Joseph (2023b), "Hezbollah Is Increasingly Isolated in the Middle East", *Jacobin*, 22 October, https://jacobin.com/2023/10/hezbollah-israel-palest ine-lebanon-iran-history

English al-Manar (2024), "Sheikh Qassem: Hezbollah Will Hold Reins of Israeli Beast and Return It to Barn", 15 October, https://english.almanar.com.lb/2232639

Fadlallah, Hassan (2015), *Hezbollah and the Lebanese State – Perspective and Trajectory* (in Arabic), Beirut: Sharika al-matbu'ât lil-tawzi' lil-nashr sh.m.l

Fawaz, Mohammad (2024), "The Jamaa al-Islamiyya Charts Its Own Course", *Carnegie*, 29 July, https://carnegieendowment.org/middle-east/diwan/2024/07/the-jamaa-al-islamiyya-charts-its-own-course?lang=en

Frankel, Julian and El-Deeb, Sarah (2024), "A cratered field, a mangled fence. Clues emerge from strike that killed 12 children in Golan Heights" *Associated Press*, 30 July, https://apnews.com/article/israel-golan-heights-soccer-rocket-hezbollah-explained-97d4377713a209cf130b7b0f3476e1c4

Hezbollah's Open Letter to the Downtrodden of Lebanon and the World 1985 (in Arabic), cited in Hezbollah's Open Letter to the Downtrodden of Lebanon and the World cited in As-Safir, No. 94, 1985, pp. 59–71

Hijazi, Salah (2024), "Does Hezbollah want to free itself from Iran's unity of fronts?", Orient le Jour, 8 October, https://today.lorientlejour.com/article/1430437/does-hezbollah-want-to-free-itself-from-irans-unity-of-fronts.html?_gl=1*ryz8u2*_gcl_au*MTEyMDQ1OTAzNC4xNzI4MDI5OTMy

Human Rights Watch (2007), "Why They Died Civilian Casualties in Lebanon during the 2006 War", 7 September, https://www.hrw.org/report/2007/09/05/why-they-died/civilian-casualties-lebanon-during-2006-war"

International Crisis Group (ICG) (2008), "Lebanon: Hizbollah's Weapons Turn Inward", https://www.crisisgroup.org/sites/default/files/b23-lebanon-hizbollah-s-weapons-turn-inward.pdf

Jones, Seth G., Byman, Daniel, Palmer, Alexander and McCabe, Riley (2024), "The Coming Conflict with Hezbollah", Center for Strategic and International Studies, March, https://csis-website-prod.s3.amazonaws.com/s3fs-public/2024-03/240321_Jones_Coming_Hezbollah.pdf?VersionId=m9pMWQNUFJr2g8opcaOpfJoNxQn8PMbf

Rabih, Mounir (2024), "War in Lebanon: Diplomatic efforts launched, Israel doesn't want to hear anything", 11 October, https://today.lorientlejour.com/article/1430900/war-in-lebanon-diplomatic-efforts-launched-israel-doesnt-want-to-hear-anything.html

Reuters (2023), "Israel, Hezbollah exchange artillery, rocket fire", 8 October, https://www.reuters.com/world/middle-east/israel-strikes-lebanon-after-hezbollah-hits-shebaa-farms-2023-10-08/

Reuters (2024), "G7 foreign ministers urge efforts to avoid inflaming Middle East tensions", 4 August, https://www.reuters.com/world/middle-east/g7-foreign-ministers-urge-efforts-avoid-inflaming-middle-east-tensions-2024-08-04/

Roche, Mary Clare and Robbins, Michael (2024), "What the Lebanese People Really Think of Hezbollah", Foreign Affairs, 12 July, https://www.foreignaffairs.com/lebanon/what-lebanese-people-really-think-hezbollah?check_logged_in=1

United Nations (2024), "Middle East Facing Dangerous Rise in Violence as Israeli Forces Fire on Peacekeepers in Lebanon, UN Political Affairs and Peace Operations Chiefs Warn Security Council", 10 October, https://press.un.org/en/2024/sc15850.doc.htm

United Nations (2025), "Lebanon: Appeal for $371.4 million to boost life-saving support", 5 January, https://news.un.org/en/story/2025/01/1158786

World Bank (2024a), "Lebanon Poverty and Equity Assessment 2024: Weathering a Protracted Crisis", 23 May, http://documents.worldbank.org/curated/en/099052224104516741/P1766511325da10a71ab6b1ae97816dd20c

World Bank (2024b), "New World Bank Report Assesses Impact of Conflict on Lebanon's Economy and Key Sectors", 14 November, https://www.worldbank.org/en/news/press-release/2024/11/14/new-world-bank-report-assesses-impact-of-conflict-on-lebanon-s-economy-and-key-sectors

INTERVIEWS

Abou Zeinab, Ghaleb (2008) political advisor of Hassan Nasrallah and Hezbollah member, Interview September, Beirut

Fayyad, Ali (2008) Hezbollah MP and former director of the Consultative Centre for Studies and Documentation (CCSD), Interview August, Beirut

Open Access This chapter is licensed under the terms of the Creative Commons Attribution 4.0 International License (http://creativecommons.org/licenses/by/4.0/), which permits use, sharing, adaptation, distribution and reproduction in any medium or format, as long as you give appropriate credit to the original author(s) and the source, provide a link to the Creative Commons license and indicate if changes were made.

The images or other third party material in this chapter are included in the chapter's Creative Commons license, unless indicated otherwise in a credit line to the material. If material is not included in the chapter's Creative Commons license and your intended use is not permitted by statutory regulation or exceeds the permitted use, you will need to obtain permission directly from the copyright holder.

CHAPTER 8

Egypt as Israel's New Ally

Maged Mandour

Abstract After El-Sisi came to power in 2013, Egypt's ruling elites have generally accepted Israel's occupation of the Palestinian territories, including their partial annexation. This position is the result of the simple calculation that Israeli energy supplies, security cooperation with Israel and credit with the US and the Arab states on the Persian Gulf are much more crucial to regime maintenance than greater support for the Palestinians, or a more confrontational policy towards Israel. Apart from slowly increasing Egypt's dependence on Israel, this policy has carried significant costs since 7 October 2023. While Cairo managed to resist the ethnic cleansing of Gaza's Palestinians into the Sinai, it has otherwise been an event taker. As such, it will be confronted with a humanitarian catastrophe on its doorstep, and a possible permanent Israeli military occupation of parts of Gaza in the near future. As long as short-term interests of Egypt's military regime prevail—survival and power consolidation—it will sacrifice Palestinian interests to good relations with Israel.

M. Mandour (✉)
Zurich, Switzerland
e-mail: maged.mandour@cantab.net

© The Author(s) 2025
E. van Veen (ed.), *The Future of the Occupation of the Palestinian Territories after Gaza*,
https://doi.org/10.1007/978-3-031-93798-9_8

Keywords El-Sisi · Sinai · Hamas · Gaza blockade · Military regime · Strategic alliance with Israel · Security cooperation · Gas

INTRODUCTION

Since the creation of the State of Israel in 1948, successive Egyptian regimes have had a complex and evolving relationship with the country as well as with the various Palestinian factions. The regime of Field Marshal Abdel Fatah El-Sisi has proved to be no different from this historical norm even though under his rule Egyptian foreign policy has become subordinated to domestic considerations. That is to say, Cairo's foreign policy prioritizes regime maintenance and the accumulation of political (Rutherford 2018) and economic power (Sayigh 2019) by the military to an unprecedented degree at the expense of traditional foreign policy objectives. These domestic priorities drove the regime to develop and cement a deep strategic alliance with Israel. In the view of some, it even amounts to a situation of negative dependence. This development came at the expense of Cairo's traditional role as mediator between Israelis and Palestinians. In essence, Egypt tacitly accepted the occupation and Israel's pre-7 October 2023 policy that was geared at managing the conflict without resolving it. This, in turn, facilitated Israel's step-by-step colonization of Palestinian lands in the West Bank and the continuation of its blockade of Gaza without having to face real pressure from the largest Arab state. Egypt even participated in the blockade of Gaza after 2007. The flipside of the coin is the relationship between Sisi and Hamas, which oscillated from outright hostility to accommodation and security cooperation in the same period. For example, Egypt labelled Hamas as a terrorist organization responsible for attacks inside the country at the start of Sisi's tenure. Again, domestic considerations drove most such dynamics.

The Hamas attack of 7 October 2023, however, laid bare Egypt's weakened regional position, its vulnerability to Israeli policies and actions, and its inability to contain Hamas from launching the attack while being similarly unable to halt the subsequent Israeli military campaign unfolding right across its border. Apart from holding the line against forced expulsion of Palestinians from Gaza into the Sinai, which would amount to ethnic cleansing, the Sisi regime has been unable/unwilling to exert any real pressure on Israel to halt the war and neither has it been able to provide aid to Gaza to prevent a possible mass influx of refugees. Indeed, Egypt has been missing in action. It has no effective policy regarding Gaza or the occupation except for symbolic diplomatic protests against Israeli massacres and violations of the bilateral treaty.

The Egyptian—Israeli Alliance Under Sisi

The coup of the summer of 2013 that brought Sisi to power saw a transformative deepening of ties between Egypt's military regime and Israel that would eventually produce an uneven relationship in which Israel gained the upper hand. The first signs of this alliance became apparent in August 2013, a mere month after the coup, when it surfaced that AIPAC was lobbying the Obama Administration to not suspend 1.3 billion USD in military aid to Sisi's regime (Hudson 2013). AIPAC lobbying was followed by a "blunt" conversation between Israeli officials and the Obama administration in October 2013, during which the former openly requested that military aid to Egypt be continued after the coup that ousted the late President Morsi (Times of Israel 2013). The pressure was partially successfully as only part of the aid ended up being cut (roughly 260 million USD in cash and the delivery of some military hardware, including Apache helicopters). This suspension would moreover prove to be temporary and full aid was restored in March 2015 when Cairo faced an insurgency by Islamic State (IS) militants in Sinai that it struggled to suppress (*The Guardian* 2015).

Israeli support for the Egyptian regime was not limited to lobbying on its behalf in Washington, but also involved direct security cooperation to combat Sinai insurgents. For example, media reports revealed in February 2018 that Israel conducted over 100 airstrikes in 2017–2018 on Egyptian soil in support of the regime's counter-insurgency campaign (Marcus 2018). Such reports were denied by the Egyptian regime at the time (Times of Israel 2018). Its denial, however, does not change the fact the security cooperation between Israel and the regime reached unprecedented levels. This was reflected in a statement made by an Israeli defence official in January 2017, who confirmed a new policy of allowing Cairo to quickly boost the number of troops it has in the Sinai, as well as allowing the Egyptian military to transport and use heavy military equipment to combat the insurgency. These developments violated the Camp David accords and are hence subject to Israeli approval, which it granted. Israel's new policy contrasts starkly with its traditional "caution" when dealing with similar requests in the past, as confirmed by Israeli defence officials (The Times of Israel 2017a). Close security cooperation between the regime and Israel was not limited to the Sinai, but included repression of political dissent inside Egypt as well. More specifically, this involved the sale of Israeli spyware, which was used for surveillance of Ahmed El-Tantawi, a prominent Egyptian dissident and ex-parliamentarian, among others, which came to light in September 2023 (Benjakob 2023).

Close security cooperation was followed by the establishment of deeper economic ties, mostly with regard to gas deliveries. In February 2018, a deal was announced for the import of Israeli natural gas via the Egyptian company Dolphinus Holdings to the amount of 15 billion USD (Cohen und Rabinovitch 2018). The imported gas would be liquefied in Egypt, and then re-exported. Even though this deal was marked as a private deal with no government involvement, an investigation by Hossam Bahgat revealed that Dolphinus is majority owned by the Egyptian General Intelligence Services (GIS) via a series of shell corporations located in tax havens. This will enable the GIS to claim 80% of company profits without paying taxes while shielding the GIS from any public scrutiny (Bahgat 2018). The regime's ambitions to be a regional energy hub required a partnership with Israel and it is in this context that the deal underlined a new level of cooperation due to its size and strategic relevance.

These developments are illustrative of Egypt's policy before 7 October 2023, which revolved around tacit acceptance of occupation while paying lip service to Palestinian rights. Besides a public call by Sisi in 2016 to support a French initiative to revive the peace process—he promised Israel "warmer ties" if the Palestinian issue was resolved (Reuters 2016)—Cairo exerted no concrete pressure to end the occupation, or even halt settlement expansion. There is even evidence that previous taboos became acceptable. For example, when President Trump decided to recognize an undivided Jerusalem as capital of Israel, a recording of conversations between an Egyptian intelligence officer and a prominent Egyptian talk show host leaked in January 2018 in which the officer instructs the talk show host to downplay the move, equating Jerusalem with Ramallah, to create public acceptance (Al jazeera 2018). The intelligence officer argued that the Palestinians have no choice but to accept and that an intifada would be a boon for Hamas and other Islamists, which is not in the interest of Egyptian national security. It is important to keep in mind that after the coup against Morsi, the GIS became a major player in the Egyptian media market, controlling much of its production, including talk shows. This informal intervention, however, ran counter to Egypt's official position. After all, Egypt drafted a UN Security Council Resolution in December 2017 that called for Trump's unilateral recognition of Jerusalem as the undivided capital of Israel to be countermanded (Times of Israel 2017c). Unsurprisingly, the resolution was vetoed by the United States (France 24 2017). The leaked tapes provided a rare glimpse into the complex and contradictory positions of official and unofficial Egyptian policy, as well as underlining close connections between Egyptian security officials and their Israeli counterparts.

Hence, the Egyptian position did not challenge Israel before 7 October 2023. Even though the official position advocated for a Palestinian state within the 1967 borders, the de facto policy was premised on full acceptance of the status quo, including Israel's policy of managing the conflict in the context of continued occupation and gradual annexation. Indeed, there is good reason to think that the Israeli assessment that the Palestinians were powerless to resist was shared by their Egyptian counterparts. The dominant calculus in Cairo was that Israel was too valuable an ally to justify more support for the Palestinians.

Egyptian Responses to 7 October 2023

The Hamas attack of 7 October 2023, however, disrupted these calculations and created palpable tension between the newfound allies while also revealing the weakness of the Sisi regime vis-à-vis Israel. The first signs of tension appeared a mere two weeks into the war. On 19 October, Sisi openly rejected Israel's suggestion of ethnic cleansing by moving the Palestinians into the Sinai (Abdallah et al. 2024). The official reason is the fear that the Sinai would become a base of operation against Israel, which would drag Egypt into a direct confrontation and require the regime to repress Palestinian armed attacks—which would be highly unpopular among large parts of the Egyptian public. The unofficial reason, which is usually not mentioned, is that anything short of strong Egyptian protest would revive a conspiracy theory used to overthrow Morsi in 2013, namely his alleged plan to sell the Sinai to the Palestinians for 8 billion USD (Abou El Ghet 2014). The theory at the time suggested this would provide a territorial base for a Palestinian state on Egyptian soil. Either way, any hint of facilitating a mass exodus of Palestinians to Egypt would cause massive damage to the regime's legitimacy among its own base. Having such a red line, however, did not mean that the regime was now willing to confront Israel. In fact, it stood by while Israel created the conditions for ethnic cleansing.

The most notable illustration of this stance has been the regime's reluctance to take unilateral action to break the blockade and alleviate the famine in Gaza. This became apparent early in the war when Israel bombed the Palestinian side of the Rafah crossing multiple times (Al Jazeera 2023). This led to closure of the crossing and a muted Egyptian response, but no concrete effort to break the siege. In November 2023, the crossing was re-opened with the flow of aid being around 120 trucks a day via the Rafah and Kareem Shalom crossings (Magid 2023), which amounted to a significant reduction compared with the average of 500 trucks per day before the war. Trucks also had to go through Israeli inspection, which created considerable bottlenecks (Keath 2024). The Egyptian authorities complied with the process and did not try to take steps to ensure faster aid delivery in greater volumes. In May 2024, when Israel occupied the Palestinian side of the Rafah crossing, it was closed again (Al Jazeera 2024b). Egypt and Israel engaged in a war of words, blaming each other for the renewed closure (Preskey 2024). In June 2024, the Egyptian foreign ministry stated that the crossing would only be opened once the Israelis had left the Palestinian side of the crossing (Reuters 2024). This position amounts to a de facto acceptance of the continued Israeli blockade of Gaza—this time in full. Egypt's impotence was on full display.

Another Egyptian redline that was ignored was the Israeli offensive against the border town of Rafah. Cairo feared this could trigger a mass Palestinian exodus across the border. Foreign minister Sameh Shoukry stated this position firmly in March (Gobran 2024) and supported it by threats that Egypt would suspend the Camp David accords if it was not considered. Yet, Israel's military operation against Hamas in Rafah went ahead anyway (Politico 2024) and did not trigger a notable reaction from Egypt. Israeli provocations continued afterwards, for example its occupation of the Philadelphia corridor, a demilitarized buffer zone between Gaza and Egypt (Sio 2024). This allowed Israeli forces to tighten the blockade of Gaza and severe its last connections with Egypt. Once again this evoked only a muted response. The only credible step the regime took was its move to join the South African case at the International Court of Justice, in which Israel stands accused of genocide (Al Jazeera 2024a). At the time of writing, however, Egypt had not yet actually joined the case (ICJ 2024). Complicating matters is Egypt's energy dependence on

Israel, which became apparent in June 2024, when there was a dip in gas supply due to maintenance at the Israeli gas field "Tamar". The supply reduction occurred during a burgeoning energy crisis that saw power cuts of at least two hours a day and widespread industrial shutdowns due to a lack of gas (MEES 2024), which produced significant embarrassment for the regime.

In brief, apart from putting a clear redline in place of categorically refusing to entertain any Israeli notion of cleansing the Palestinians of Gaza into the Sinai, the Egyptian regime has applied zero pressure on Israel to halt its war on Gaza. Instead, it has long accepted the occupation as a matter of fact, valuing Israeli support much more than championing Palestinian rights. In so doing, it has greatly reduced its ability to act as mediator between Israel and the Palestinians in a way that could lead to a substantive political process. This policy has also led to a considerable loss of Egyptian regional influence and increased Egyptian vulnerability towards Israel. The Egyptian regime has become incapable of resisting Israeli policies in the occupied territories.

About Sisi and Hamas

The flipside of Egypt's position regarding occupation is the relationship between Sisi and Hamas. This relationship has featured significant ebbs and flows with time, starting with outright hostility and ending with accommodation and close security cooperation. During the early years of the Sisi regime, Hamas was portrayed as a national enemy, an extension of the banned Muslim Brotherhood, which paved the way for a tighter blockade of Gaza. For example, one of the accusations levelled against the ousted President Morsi was his alleged collaboration with Hamas to orchestrate mass prison breaks during the 2011 protests (Al Jazeera 2013). The regime even accused Hamas of carrying out attacks on Egyptian territory, accusing the group of assassinating the Egyptian attorney general in March 2016 (BBC 2016). This campaign of words was accompanied by a tightening of the blockade of Gaza. For example, in March 2014, the regime destroyed 1,370 smuggling tunnels (The Times of Israel 2014). In September 2015, the regime also used seawater to destroy another set of smuggling tunnels, which collapsed an estimated 95% of them (Omer 2015).

Such tightening of screws, however, did not last for long once it became apparent that cooperation with Hamas was essential to combat the insurgency in the Sinai. A high-level Hamas delegation visited Cairo in March 2016 for talks to improve the poor relationship between Egypt and the movement (Abu Amer 2016). This was followed by another visit by the late Ismail Haniyeh after he was elected head of the political bureau of the group in September 2017 (DW 2017). Haniyeh visit was preceded by a formal severing of ties between Hamas and the Egyptian Muslim Brotherhood. Despite this being a formality since their association was never institutionalized and Hamas always followed an independent policy based on its national context (Al-Mughrabi und Finn 2017), it did enable the Sisi regime to re-engage with Hamas. Ties improved rapidly afterwards, which was reflected in direct security cooperation between the two parties in suppressing Islamic State militants in the Sinai. For example, Hamas arrested 200 Salafi Jihadis in early 2017 in close cooperation with the Egyptians (El-Behiary 2017). This was followed by a pledge in February 2018 that Hamas would tighten its control over the border, even supporting a large-scale Egyptian military operation in Sinai (DW 2018). Cooperation reached its apex in March 2020 with an agreement between Hamas and Cairo to build a border wall equipped with advanced surveillance technology to halt smuggling and to combat IS militants on both sides of the border (I24 2020). The thawing of relations even gives rise to Egyptian efforts to negotiate the return of Mahmoud Dahlan, a rival of President Abbas, to Gaza, in 2017 (Al Jazeera 2017). Leaks showed that the Egyptians had stopped considering Abbas an effective political player for some time already at this point (Wirtschafter und Soliman 2017).

Rapprochement enabled an easing of the blockade of Gaza. Egypt allowed large quantities of diesel to enter Gaza in the summer of 2017 to ease constant blackouts (The Times of Israel 2017b). This move also reduced the financial pressure that Abbas had been putting on Hamas at the time. Cairo continued this approach, for example pledging 500 million USD in support of the reconstruction of Gaza after the 2021 fighting between Israel and Hamas left 450 buildings destroyed, including 9 hospitals (Reuters 2021). The ceasefire was also brokered by Egypt, which even earned Sisi praise from Biden (France24 2021). In October of the same year, the Egyptians went further and promised to increase trade between Gaza and Egypt while installing electronic surveillance equipment at the Rafah crossing after reaching agreement with the Israeli Prime Minister Naftali Bennett (Middle East Monitor 2021).

Hence, in the period leading up to 7 October 2023, relations between Hamas and the Sisi regime were at a high point, especially compared to the period 2013–2016. Indeed, it was the same logic of regime maintenance that drove Cairo's cooperation with Hamas in combating the Sinai insurgency—both parties saw this as direct threat to their rule—just as it did for Egypt's cooperation with Israel. Yet, Egypt's incentives for Hamas—easing the blockade—did not influence the group's calculus regarding its 7 October 2023 attack. Simply put, Egyptian acceptance of the occupation and its dependency on Israel meant it was unable to pressure Israel to re-start the peace process or offer any meaningful concession to the Palestinians. Egyptian efforts to end the rift between Hamas and Fatah were not serious either, as Cairo implicitly accepted the Israeli policy of cementing the division between the two factions. In the end, the improvement in relations between Hamas and Sisi was mostly tactical in nature and did not offer Hamas better longer-term prospects. From this perspective, Egyptian policy indirectly contributed to the 7 October 2023 attacks.

Sisi and Occupation Post-Gaza

The attacks of 7 October 2023 placed the Egyptian regime in a difficult position and exposed the frailty of its policy. Current Egyptian policy revolves around hollow rhetorical condemnation of Israeli massacres as Cairo has little ability to influence events and neither does it seem able to influence post-war scenarios in any meaningful way. Hence, the war will probably produce an even weaker Egyptian position, especially if Hamas is removed from power in Gaza and relations between Egypt and the movement will count for less than before. When the Israeli military campaign in Gaza terminates, the Egyptian regime will have no choice but to accept continued occupation of the West Bank and possibly direct IDF military control over Gaza as long as its red line of mass Palestinian expulsion out of Gaza is not transgressed. Cairo's scope for action is limited as the regime faces a deepening debt crisis that requires continued support from its western and Gulf allies if it is not to become an existential threat to Egypt's ruling military-political elite. Put in simple terms, unless there is international and regional consensus that concrete steps are needed to end occupation, the Egyptian regime is unlikely to take unilateral action that might anger allies whose support is necessary to stave off financial collapse. The regime's priorities are survival and power consolidation.

These goals are better served by working with Israel and accepting the occupation than confronting it. This dynamic creates an opportunistic and tactical foreign policy that is focused on regime preservation in the short term, but without consideration of longer-term national security interests. Its tactical nature implies that such a policy can shift, but this will require international and regional realignment against the occupation.

Conflict of Interest The author has no conflict of interests to declare that are relevant to the content of this chapter.

Bibliography

Abdallah, Nayera, Nadine Awadalla, and Mohamed Wali. 2024. *Reuters*. 19 October. Accessed August 6, 2024. https://www.reuters.com/world/egypt-rejects-any-displacement-palestinians-into-sinai-says-sisi-2023-10-18/#:~:text=%22Egypt%20rejects%20any%20attempt%20to,the%20region%2C%22%20he%20said.

Abou El Ghet, Abadel Rahman. 2014. *Al Jazeera*. 6 September. Accessed August 15, 2024. https://www.aljazeera.net/news/2014/9/6/%D8%A8%D9%8A%D8%B9-%D8%B3%D9%8A%D9%86%D8%A7%D8%A1-%D9%81%D8%B5%D9%84-%D8%A2%D8%AE%D8%B1-%D9%85%D9%86-%D8%AA%D8%A8%D8%A7%D8%AF%D9%84-%D8%A7%D9%84%D8%AA%D8%AE%D9%88%D9%8A%D9%86-%D8%A8%D9%85%D8%B5%D8%B1.

Abu Amer, Adnan. 2016. *Al-Monitor*. 24 March. Accessed August 19, 2024. https://www.al-monitor.com/originals/2016/03/hamas-visit-egypt-renew-ties.html.

Al Jazeera. 2013. *Al Jazeera*. 26 July. Accessed August 19, 2024. https://www.aljazeera.com/news/2013/7/26/morsi-accused-of-plotting-with-hamas.

———. 2017. *Al Jazeera*. 9 July. Accessed August 19, 2024. https://www.aljazeera.com/news/2017/7/9/egypt-and-palestine-discuss-hamas-cairo-rapprochement.

———. 2018. *Al Jazeera*. 18 January. Accessed August 24, 2024. https://www.aljazeera.com/news/2018/1/7/egypt-hosts-told-to-convince-viewers-over-jerusalem.

———. 2023. *Al Jazeera*. 11 October. Accessed August 6, 2024. https://www.aljazeera.com/news/2023/10/10/alarm-as-israel-again-hits-rafah-border-crossing-between-gaza-and-egypt.

———. 2024a. "Al Jazeera." *Al Jazeera*. 12 May. Accessed August 7, 2024. https://www.aljazeera.com/news/2024/5/12/egypt-says-it-will-join-south-africas-genocide-case-against-israel-at-icj#:~:text=Egypt%20says%20it%20will%20formally,war%20on%20the%20Gaza%20Strip.

———. 2024b. *Al Jazeera.* 7 May. Accessed August 7, 2024. https://www.alj azeera.com/news/2024/5/7/israel-takes-control-of-rafah-crossing-gazas-lif eline-whats-going-on.
Al-Mughrabi, Nidal, and Tom Finn. 2017. *Reuters.* 1 May. Accessed August 19, 2024. https://www.reuters.com/article/world/hamas-softens-stance-on-israel-drops-muslim-brotherhood-link-idUSKBN17X1N9/.
Bahgat, Hossam. 2018. *Mada Masr.* 23 October. Accessed August 7, 2024. https://www.madamasr.com/en/2018/10/23/feature/politics/whos-buy ing-israeli-gas-a-company-owned-by-the-general-intelligence-service/.
BBC. 2016. *BBC.* 7 March. Accessed August 19, 2024. https://www.bbc.com/arabic/middleeast/2016/03/160306_egypt_court.
———. 2019. *BBC.* 17 June. Accessed August 19, 2024. https://www.bbc.com/news/world-middle-east-24772806.
Benjakob, Omer. 2023. *Haaretz.* 5 October. https://www.haaretz.com/israel-news/security-aviation/2023-10-05/ty-article/.premium/investigation-how-israeli-spyware-was-sold-to-egypt-and-pitched-to-qatar-and-saudi-arabia/000 0018a-ff33-d037-a9ae-ffffdb00000.
Cohen, Tova, and Ari Rabinovitch. 2018. *Reuters.* 20 February. Accessed August 7, 2024. https://www.reuters.com/article/us-israel-egypt-natgas/egy ptian-firm-to-buy-15-billion-in-israeli-natural-gas-idUSKCN1G31BK/.
DW. 2017. *DW.* 9 September. Accessed August 19, 2024. https://www.dw.com/ar/%D9%87%D9%86%D9%8A%D8%A9-%D9%81%D9%8A-%D8%A3%D9%88%D9%84-%D8%B2%D9%8A%D8%A7%D8%B1%D8%A9-%D9%84%D9%85%D8%B5%D8%B1-%D9%85%D9%86%D8%B0-%D8%AA%D9%88%D9%84%D9%8A%D9%87-%D9%82%D9%8A%D8%A7%D8%AF%D8%A9-%D8%AD%D8%B1%D9%83%D8%A9-%D8%AD%D9%85.
———. 2018. *DW.* 11 February. Accessed August 19, 2024. https://www.dw.com/ar/%D8%B5%D8%AD%D9%8A%D9%81%D8%A9-%D8%AD%D9%85%D8%A7%D8%B3-%D8%AA%D8%AA%D8%A8%D8%B9%D9%87%D8%AF-%D9%84%D9%85%D8%B5%D8%B1-%D8%A8%D8%A5%D8%AD%D9%83%D8%A7%D9%85-%D8%A7%D9%84%D8%B3%D9%8A%D8%B7%D8%B1%D8%A9-%D8%B9%D9%84%D9%89-%D8%A7%D9%84%D8%AD%D8.
El-Behiary, Mohamed. 2017. *Al masry alyoum.* 1 July. Accessed August 19, 2024. https://www.almasryalyoum.com/news/details/1068918.
France 24. 2017. *France 24.* 17 December. Accessed August 6, 2024. https://www.france24.com/en/20171218-us-vetoes-un-resolution-withdrawal-trump-jerusalem-decision.
———. 2021. *France24.* 21 May. Accessed August 19, 2024. https://www.france24.com/en/diplomacy/20210520-us-uk-hail-egypt-brokered-gaza-cea sefire.
Gobran, Mohamed. 2024. *Arab News.* 28 March. Accessed August 7, 2024. https://www.arabnews.com/node/2484531/middle-east.

Hudson, John. 2013. *Foreign Policy.* 19 August. Accessed August 7, 2024. https://foreignpolicy.com/2013/08/19/egypts-rulers-have-a-new-fri end-in-dc-the-israel-lobby/.
I24. 2020. *I24.* 15 March. Accessed August 19, 2024. https://www.i24news. tv/ar/%D8%A3%D8%AE%D8%A8%D8%A7%D8%B1/middle-east/158426 1059-%D8%AE%D8%A7%D8%B5-%D8%A7%D9%84%D8%AA%D8%B9%D8% A7%D9%88%D9%86-%D8%A7%D9%84%D8%A3%D9%85%D9%86%D9%8A-% D8%A8%D9%8A%D9%86-%D8%AD%D9%85%D8%A7%D8%B3-%D9%88% D9%85%D8%B5%D8%B1-%D9%8A%.
ICJ. 2024. "ICJ." *ICJ.* Accessed August 7, 2024. https://www.icj-cij.org/cas e/192.
Keath, LEE. 2024. *AP News.* 6 January. Accessed August 6, 2024. https://apn ews.com/article/israel-gaza-rafah-aid-us-senators-2bc2a3c5e5f8af8e2d3f0b72 42c1a885.
Magid, Jacob. 2023. *Times of Israel.* 15 December. Accessed August 6, 2024. https://www.timesofisrael.com/in-first-since-war-cabinet-approves-reo pening-of-israeli-crossing-to-gaza-for-aid/.
Marcus, Jonathan. 2018. *BBC.* 5 February. Accessed August 7, 2024. https:// www.bbc.com/news/world-middle-east-42950490.
MEES. 2024. *MEES.* 7 June. Accessed August 7, 2024. https://www.mees. com/2024/6/7/economics-finance/israel-tamar-outage-causes-egypt-gas-power-chaos/02142570-24cc-11ef-a290-99dfc8ef9357.
Middle East Monitor. 2021. *Middle East Monitor.* 7 October. Accessed August 19, 2024. https://www.middleeastmonitor.com/20211007-egypt-to-increase-trade-with-gaza-2/.
Omer, Mohammed. 2015. *Middle East Eye.* 27 September. Accessed August 19, 2024. https://www.middleeasteye.net/fr/news/egypt-floods-gazas-tun nels-seawater-351883398.
Politico. 2024. *Politico.* 2 February. Accessed August 7, 2024. https://www.pol itico.com/news/2024/02/11/egypt-threatens-to-suspend-camp-david-acc ords-if-israel-pushes-into-gaza-border-town-00140838.
Preskey, Natasha. 2024. *BBC.* 15 May . Accessed August 6, 2024. https://www. bbc.com/news/world-middle-east-69012303.
Reuters. 2016. *Reuters.* 17 May. Accessed August 7, 2024. https://www.reu ters.com/article/us-israel-palestinians-egypt/egypts-sisi-lends-backing-to-isr ael-palestinian-peace-efforts-idUSKCN0Y81FQ/.
———. 2021. *Reuters.* 18 May. Accessed August 19, 2024. https://www.reu ters.com/world/middle-east/egypt-allocate-500-mln-gaza-rebuilding-effort-presidency-2021-05-18/.
———. 2024. *Reuters.* 3 June. Accessed August 7, 2024. https://www.reuters. com/world/rafah-border-crossing-cant-reopen-unless-israeli-forces-quit-gaza-side-egypt-2024-06-03/.

Rutherford, Bruce K. 2018. Egypt's New Authoritarianism under Sisi. *Middle East Journal* 185–208.
Sayigh, Yezid. 2019. *Owners of the Republic*. Carnegie Endowment for International Peace.
Scolding, Emma, and Sara Seif Eddin. Mada Masr. *Mada Masr.* 6 2024. Accessed August 7, 2024. https://www.madamasr.com/en/2024/06/06/news/u/egypts-gas-supply-dips-due-to-temporary-closure-at-israels-tamar-field/.
Sio, Mohamed. 2024. *AA*. 7 June. Accessed August 7, 2024. https://www.aa.com.tr/en/middle-east/israeli-troops-take-complete-control-of-philadelphi-corridor-fully-isolating-gaza-witnesses/3243367.
The Guardian. 2015. *The Guardian*. 15 March. https://www.theguardian.com/us-news/2015/mar/31/obama-restores-us-military-aid-to-egypt.
The Times of Israel. 2014. *The Times of Israel*. 12 March. Accessed August 19, 2024. https://www.timesofisrael.com/egypt-destroys-1370-gaza-smuggling-tunnels/.
———. 2017a. *The Times of Israel*. 11 January . Accessed August 7, 2024. https://www.timesofisrael.com/israeli-official-confirms-strong-cooperation-with-egypt-in-sinai/.
———. 2017b. *The Times of Israel*. 17 September . Accessed August 19, 2024. https://www.timesofisrael.com/hamas-ponies-up-for-fuel-from-egypt-seeking-to-boost-power-in-gaza/.
Times of Israel. 2013. *Times of Israel*. 15 October . Accessed August 7, 2024. https://www.timesofisrael.com/israel-bluntly-told-the-us-not-to-cut-aid-to-egypt/?fb_comment_id=352282031583933_1717520#fb5674d5416f6c.
———. 2017c. *Times of Israel*. 16 December. Accessed August 6, 2024. https://www.timesofisrael.com/un-security-council-said-considering-resolution-to-annul-us-jerusalem-decision/.
———. 2018. *Times of Israel*. 4 February. Accessed August 7, 2024. https://www.timesofisrael.com/egypt-army-denies-israel-carried-out-secret-airstrike-campaign-in-sinai/.
Wirtschafter, Jacob, and Mohammed Soliman. 2017. *MEI*. 7 March. Accessed August 19, 2024. https://www.mei.edu/publications/egypt-hamas-continue-flirtation-what-end.

Open Access This chapter is licensed under the terms of the Creative Commons Attribution 4.0 International License (http://creativecommons.org/licenses/by/4.0/), which permits use, sharing, adaptation, distribution and reproduction in any medium or format, as long as you give appropriate credit to the original author(s) and the source, provide a link to the Creative Commons license and indicate if changes were made.

The images or other third party material in this chapter are included in the chapter's Creative Commons license, unless indicated otherwise in a credit line to the material. If material is not included in the chapter's Creative Commons license and your intended use is not permitted by statutory regulation or exceeds the permitted use, you will need to obtain permission directly from the copyright holder.

CHAPTER 9

Jordan Between a Rock and a Hard Place

Hasan M. Jaber

Abstract Jordan's deep ties with the Palestinian population of the West Bank and East Jerusalem were forged after the Nakba in 1948, during the 'unity of the two Banks' period from 1950 to 1967 and after the six-day war of 1967. The Nakba and the six-day war caused large-scale Palestinian displacement. With time, these refugees were integrated into Jordanian society. During the seventeen years of the 'unity of the Banks' period, the West Bank was incorporated into Jordan with all West Bank Palestinians being granted Jordanian citizenship. In part as a result of these deep social and political ties, Jordan's government has remained a staunch supporter of a two-state solution even though its ability to advocate forcefully for this result is constrained by its peace treaty with Israel of 1994 and—in particular—its strategic alignment with the U.S., including its economic and military aid. Overall, the Hashemite monarchy seeks to balance maintaining Jordanian national identity and its international relations with advocacy for Palestinian rights. It has sought to walk this

H. M. Jaber (✉)
University of Jordan, Amman, Jordan
e-mail: h.jaber@politicsociety.org

Politics and Society Institute, Amman, Jordan

© The Author(s) 2025
E. van Veen (ed.), *The Future of the Occupation of the Palestinian Territories after Gaza*,
https://doi.org/10.1007/978-3-031-93798-9_9

tightrope in part by emphasising its custodianship of Islam's and Christianity's holy sites in Jerusalem. Jordan's policy regarding occupation will come under increasing strain in the near future from Trump-II and the Israeli extreme right, which has already caused domestic debate about the desired level of Jordanian involvement.

Keywords Arab-Israeli Wars · Oslo Accords · Unity of the two Banks · Jericho conference · Battle of Al-Karameh · PLO · Wadi Araba

INTRODUCTION

The history of Jordan after World War I is deeply entwined with colonial dynamics. The Arab Revolution that Al Sharif Hussein Bin Ali led against the Ottoman Empire to achieve Arab self-determination and the Sykes-Picot Agreement of 1916 offer good starting points for analysis. The former manifested a desire for self-rule and independence that clashed with the imperial and colonial designs of British and French influence in the Middle East of the latter (Rogan 2011). On top of this came the 1917 letter of the British Foreign Secretary Arthur Balfour to Lord Rothschild that promised 'the establishment of a national home for the Jewish people'. A unilateral and colonial act par excellence, even though it stipulated that such establishment 'should not prejudice the civil and religious rights of other population groups'. It became known as the Balfour Declaration and catalysed significant Jewish immigration to Palestine, which gradually exacerbated tensions between Zionist settlers and the existing Arab population over the next decades (Gelvin 2014; Khalidi 2007). In the years following, Britain excluded the Emirate of Transjordan from its mandate for Palestine. The Balfour Declaration was subsequently limited to Palestine and the Emirate became the modern state of Jordan in 1946 (Fromkin 1989; Anderson 2005). Both the mandate and its division were ratified by the League of Nations in 1923. At this point in time, Arab 'nationalism' emphasised regional unity and self-determination rather than the specific establishment of a Palestinian state, as resistance concentrated on countering Zionist immigration and British colonialism (Kamrava 2005).

Although the West Bank was excluded from Transjordan at its creation in 1921, it was incorporated into it in 1950. King Abdullah I viewed it as a vital measure towards stability and Arab unity after the 1948 war and as a response to the ambitions of the West Bank's political elites and people as expressed during the Jericho conference (Abu-Odeh 1999). The ensuing seventeen-year period of the 'unity of the two Banks' enabled deep integration between the West and East Bank of political and economic life (Salibi 1993). It lasted until the six-day war of 1967 when Israel occupied the West Bank (Smith 2021). In 1988, King Hussein formally announced Jordan's disengagement from the West Bank by accepting the leading role of the Palestinian Liberation Organisation (PLO) and signalling his strategic support for a two-state solution in the Israeli-Palestinian conflict (Abu-Odeh 1999). Due to the longstanding ties that had developed, however, Jordan retained important direct stakes in the Palestinian cause. For instance, the sizeable Palestinian demographic in Jordan, comprised mostly of refugees and their descendants, ties stability in the West Bank to stability in Jordan due to the many social, political, and economic connections (Abu-Odeh 1999; Rogan 2011).

From a geopolitical aspect, Jordan views the realisation of Palestinian statehood as vital for regional stability as well. The recent Israeli military actions in Gaza, which highlighted the precariousness of Palestinian rights and the fragility of the regional power equilibrium, underscore the urgent need for a resolution to the Israeli-Palestinian conflict in Jordan's view, in particular due to the risks of greater radicalisation, more Palestinian displacement, and threats to Amman's historic role as custodian of both Islam's and Christianity's holy sites in Jerusalem (Abu Oudeh 2023). This chapter examines Jordan's strategic balancing act between domestic stability, regional stability, and advocacy for Palestinian rights in the context of the Israeli occupation of the Palestinian territories. The tension between its historical ties with the West Bank and its reliance on U.S. aid means that Jordan faces growing pressures on its advocacy given recent geopolitical and conflict developments.

THE MANDATE OF PALESTINE
AND THE EMIRATE OF TRANSJORDAN

The Emirate of Transjordan was established in 1921 under the British Mandate for Palestine by means of a distinct administrative entity. While the British initially intended this division to be temporary, it became permanent as a result of British military intervention to halt the territorial ambitions of neighbouring powers towards the Emirate, a cost-based approach to running the British parts of the Middle East and the governance of Emir Abdullah I in Transjordan (Fromkin 1989; Rogan 2011). As Arab populations dominated both areas under British rule, the Hashemite leadership of Transjordan maintained and cultivated strong relationships with Arab/Palestinian elites based on shared cultural, historical, and familial ties (Salibi 1993). The relationships, established between 1920 and the end of World War II, were pivotal during and after the 1948 Arab-Israeli War. The Jordanian Arab Legion played a crucial role in defending what became the West Bank and East Jerusalem against Israeli advances. Following the cessation of hostilities, Jordan assumed control over both areas, which was formalised in 1950 through the unification of the West Bank with the East Bank. In turn, this was intended to consolidate control and integrate the territories into the newly established Hashemite Kingdom of Jordan (1946). Unification was largely supported by the local populations and the Jericho Conference of 1 December 1948 played a substantial role in this process (Smith 2017; Shlaim 2008). Palestinian delegates included local leaders like the mayors of Hebron, Bethlehem, and Ramallah, military governors and other prominent figures. The conference produced four resolutions regarding the future of the West Bank:

> A declaration of unity between Transjordan and Arab Palestine,
> Recognition of King Abdullah as sovereign of the unified territories,
> Gratitude to Arab states for their efforts in Palestine's liberation,
> A decision to communicate the resolutions to King Abdullah promptly.

These resolutions met with strong opposition from the Arab League that viewed them as violations of the Palestinian right to self-determination. Nevertheless, Jordan integrated the West Bank into its governance structures, formally unifying the territories in 1950 and extending Jordanian citizenship to all Palestinians in the West Bank in early 1949. These developments solidified Jordan's political role but also sparked regional tensions with several Arab states, such as Egypt and Saudi Arabia (Tell 2013; Robins 2004; U.S. Department of State 1948). They viewed unification as an act of annexation and Hashemite expansionism (Laurens 2002). Formal international recognition remained limited to Britain and Pakistan (Fischbach 2012). Unification marked a significant milestone for Jordan, however, as it absorbed a substantial Palestinian population as citizens, which altered the Kingdom's demographic and political dynamics. Between 1950 and 1967, the Hashemite monarchy's policy of granting Jordanian citizenship to Palestinians in the West Bank facilitated deep political, economic, and social integration as it encouraged Palestinians to engage in Jordanian politics and access public services, effectively creating a shared identity and multi-layered interdependencies (Schwedler 2022).

After the unity of the two Banks ended in 1967, Jordan maintained its connections with the West Bank through the familial, economic, and social ties that had been established during its rule (Fischbach 2012). The endurance of this policy until today underlines Jordan's commitment to Palestinian rights. However, not all was plain sailing due to the fact that the PLO built up its bases for armed resistance against Israel's occupation just across the river Jordan on the East Bank after 1967. In a bid to eliminate the PLO, Israel attacked some of these bases, which led to the battle of Al-Karameh on 21 March 1968. The Jordanian Armed Forces ultimately repulsed Israel's forces with involvement from Palestinian fighters. The PLO and Fatah successfully portrayed the battle as a symbolic victory, which significantly boosted their popular legitimacy and their recruitment in the months that followed. (Morris 1999). While both primarily drew their leadership and fighters from among Palestinian refugees, they also included East Bank Jordanians who were ideologically aligned with the Palestinian liberation struggle—viewing it as an Arab cause tied to broader nationalist and anti-colonial aspirations. Such cross-national participation highlighted the shared identity and interconnectedness of the West and East Banks (Abu-Odeh 1999). However, the growing political and military footprint of the PLO and Fatah in Jordan gradually created a kind of state-within-a-state. Strains between both ultimately led to the conflict of September 1970, which resulted in the PLO being banished to Beirut and left profound scars on Jordanian-Palestinian relations (Al Tahir 2018). Violent clashes between the Jordanian Armed Forces and Palestinian groups highlighted internal divisions in Jordan that necessitated the restoration of national cohesion once they were over, but which also forced a rethink of Amman's responsibilities as a sovereign state versus its role in the Palestinian issue (Robins 2004; Shlaim 2008).

Subsequently, the Arab League Summit of 1974 in Rabat officially recognised the PLO as the sole legitimate representative of the Palestinian people, which solidified its regional and international legitimacy.

This decision was instrumental in advancing the Palestinian cause leading, among other things, to the PLO's recognition as observer entity by the United Nations. In addition, the PLO declared the establishment of an independent Palestinian state within the 1967 borders during the Palestinian National Council meeting in Algiers of 1988. This step shifted PLO strategy towards diplomacy, efforts to obtain international recognition and, ultimately, the Oslo Accords (Khalidi 2006). In a strategic shift, Jordan formally ceded sovereignty over the West Bank to the PLO in the same year. This enabled the PLO to assume leadership in negotiations for Palestinian self-determination (Abu-Odeh 1999). By relinquishing its territorial claims, Jordan transformed its ties to the Palestinian inhabitants of the West Bank from being their hypothetical sovereign into one of stewardship, mediation, and advocacy that encompassed both its custodianship of Jerusalem's Islamic holy sites and its role as a proponent of a two-state solution with full respect for Palestinian rights (Tell 2013). It also enabled Jordan to re-consolidate its own sovereignty and internal cohesion on the basis of a more clearly delineated Jordanian identity.

JORDAN AND THE OSLO ACCORDS

The permanent nature of Israel's occupation and mounting tensions in the Palestinian territories caused the first *intifada* of December 1987. It coincided with growing social unrest in Jordan that was caused by severe economic challenges and structural adjustment policies imposed by international lenders. Demonstrations in cities like Ma'an highlighted public discontent with austerity measures, including the removal of subsidies, and called for political reforms. These domestic pressures were compounded by the Gulf War of 1990–1991, during which Jordan's neutral stance, and especially its refusal to host American forces against Iraq, strained relations with key allies. This mix of developments pushed Jordan to participate in the peace process beginning with the Madrid Peace Conference of 1991. A significant obstacle during these peace talks was Israel's refusal to directly negotiate with the PLO, which it categorised as a terrorist organisation. A joint Jordanian-Palestinian delegation was established to surmount this problem, reflecting Jordan's recognition of the PLO as the primary advocate of Palestinian aspirations (Shlaim 2008). However, in the meantime, Israel and the PLO secretly negotiated the Oslo Accords, which were ultimately concluded between 1993 and 1995 without Jordanian involvement. When these secret negotiations were revealed, they came as a surprise to the Jordanian government given its involvement in the Madrid proceedings. Nevertheless, Jordan took a positive view towards the Accords as it aimed for an independent state of Palestine.

In between the Oslo Accords, Jordan signed the Wadi Araba peace treaty with Israel in 1994 (Robins 2004). This treaty formalised Jordan's special role in the management of Jerusalem's Islamic and Christian holy sites (article 9) that forms a crucial element of the identity of the Hashemite monarchy and an important component of its legitimacy. The treaty also secured substantial international economic and military assistance, particularly from the United States. The Madrid proceedings, Oslo Accords, and Wadi Araba peace treaty had two broad effects that are important to understand from a Jordanian national security perspective. First, ceding the West Bank to the PLO in 1988 and making peace with Israel in 1994 enabled Amman to protect itself from any further Israeli ambitions towards Jordan. Second, these landmark events enabled Jordan to remain engaged in the Palestinian issue through its custodianship of Jerusalem's holy sites—an important component of Hashemite religious and national legitimacy. At the same time, this role contributed to reinforcing the perceived strength of the social contract between the monarchy and the Jordanian public. These landmark events moreover underlined that Jordan's internal stability and legitimacy mainly derive from its domestic cohesion rather than its regional religious role (Hussein Al-Sarayreh, personal communication, 2025).

However, concerns soon arose regarding the sustainability of the Oslo Accords, particularly with regard to their asymmetric recognition and lack of robust guarantees. These apprehensions were exacerbated by repeated delays and deliberate marginalisation of the accords by Israel's political right-wing. Ultimately, the peace process stagnated due to relentless Israeli settlement expansion, the second Intifada, and the shift to the right in Israel with the assassination of Yitzhak Rabin and the rise of Benjamin Netanyahu. While this raised significant challenges to Jordan's security and stability, Amman remained a vocal proponent of Palestinian statehood. In doing so, it is, on the one hand, driven by a need to maintain domestic stability, which demands strong advocacy. On the other hand, it is driven by the need to maintain good relations with its international partners, in particular the United States as principal partner that can tolerate advocacy but not overtly supportive action, and that also requires Amman to cooperate with Israel. As a consequence, Jordan has often acted as intermediary between Israel and the Palestinian Authority by hosting talks.

DIFFERENT DIMENSIONS OF JORDANIAN INVOLVEMENT IN THE WEST BANK

Jordan's West Bank legacy creates an overlap between its domestic and foreign policies with regard to Palestinians and the Palestinian territories. This sets Jordan apart from Egypt, Lebanon, and Syria. Even after the administrative disengagement of 1988, Jordan has viewed stability in the West Bank as integral to its security. Understanding the different push- and pull factors that influence Jordanian policies and actions towards the West Bank beyond the politics—discussed above—also requires consideration of social and military issues. Socially, Jordan faces the complex task of balancing its commitment to Palestinian rights with the need to maintain social cohesion among its diverse population. Balance between the two is essential to prevent socioeconomic disparities and tensions between different demographic groups. It makes domestic cohesion a national security interest since fissures spell social conflict and potentially unrest and violence. Inevitably, Jordanian government policies have led to protests when these policies have been perceived as favouring U.S. or even Israeli interests (Abu-Odeh 1999). It is therefore relevant to note that Trump-I style policies that encourage Israeli annexation will not just undermine the prospects of Palestinian statehood but also endanger social stability in Jordan by reigniting opposition. Emphasising and reinforcing its commitment to its custodianship over Jerusalem's Islamic and Christian holy sites is one way by which Jordan seeks to maintain domestic peace and good international relations. The stabilising function of this commitment was underlined during a focus group session of the Politics and Society Institute with activists from Jerusalem that the author attended (also: Abu-Odeh 1999; Robins 2004).

Militarily, Jordan prioritises border security and efforts to mitigate spillover effects of Israel's occupation of the West Bank. This prioritisation stems from Jordan's twin obligations: on the one hand, its commitment to the internationally binding peace treaty with Israel; on the other hand, the need to be seen in action if and when Palestinians are forcibly displaced to Jordan. This tension is exacerbated by growing public discontent with Israel's inhumane policies against Palestinians after 7 October 2023. So far, joint security operations with the United States have been pivotal in ensuring that Jordan's borders remain secure from external threats, but efforts to infiltrate Jordan's borders have increased in the recent past. At the same time, the Israeli far-right's disregard for negative political and security consequences in Jordan heightens the likelihood of tensions escalating. Jordan's military relationship with the United States is a cornerstone of regional stability. It comes with substantial military and development aid. For instance, the United States provided Jordan with over $22 billion in assistance between 2010 and 2020. After 2021, Jordan received c. $1.65 billion in annual economic and military aid (Schwedler 2022). This support is crucial for Jordan's military forces as it enables their modernisation and allows the Kingdom to protect its borders and to counter terrorism. Yet this aid also constrains the Kingdom's ability to oppose U.S. policies that conflict with its own national priorities, particularly regarding the occupation of the Palestinian territories. Trump's initial 'Deal of the Century' of 2020 cast these limitations into starker relief. Despite Jordan's outright rejection of the plan due to the threat it posed to Palestinian statehood and the concerns it raised about further Palestinian displacement into Jordan, Amman had to be prudent in how it raised its critique in Washington on the basis of King Abdullah II's policy of 'three no's': no to displacement, no to Jordan as alternative homeland, and no to compromise on Jordan's custodianship regarding the holy sites of Jerusalem or the status of East Jerusalem as capital of the Palestinian state. Jordan's population could afford to be less mindful of international relations and protested vehemently against the plan (Shar'aan 2020; Hasan Al Momani, personal communication, 2025). With this in mind, the return of Donald Trump to the presidency threatens the delicate balance between Jordanian custodianship of Jerusalem's Islamic and Christian holy sites, its advocacy for Palestinian rights, and the maintenance of its strategic partnership with the United States. Ultimately, Jordan's role as a stabilising factor in the region is vital to U.S. interests, but not as vital as U.S. support for Israel.

JORDANIAN POLICY AFTER 7 OCTOBER 2023

Following the 'Al-Aqsa Flood' operation of Hamas, Gaza has faced devastating military aggression. This war targets a region already described as the world's largest open-air prison due to the blockade imposed since 2007. After 7 October 2023, Jordan initially engaged in shuttle diplomacy in a bid to de-escalate the situation. The Jordanian government also condemned the ongoing aggression with its official rhetoric towards Israel becoming increasingly hawkish (Ababneh 2023). Simultaneously, public outrage within Jordan has surged and widespread expressions of solidarity with Palestinians have underlined once more how deep socio-political ties run between Jordan and the Palestinian cause. However, growing public anger challenges the government to balance public sentiment with its diplomatic relations and initiatives. Protests in front of the Israeli embassy in Amman are now standard, for example, as are widespread calls for more decisive action in support of the Palestinian cause. On the humanitarian front, Jordan has expanded its relief efforts in Gaza and the West Bank. For example, Jordanian field hospitals in the West Bank have provided critical medical support. From a Jordanian perspective, 7 October 2023 and thereafter underscores its longstanding warning regarding the repercussions of denying Palestinian rights to self-determination and the risks associated with Israel's hardline policies. Jordan attributes the current crisis to Israel's persistent refusal to resolve the Palestinian issue in a just manner. However, Amman has had to hew closely to core Jordanian national interests in its response to unfolding events in Gaza and on the West Bank.

The first such interest is Amman's custodianship of Jerusalem's holy sites. It views any Israeli move against this status as a fundamental challenge to its national identity and the legitimate role of Jordan. The rise of extremist elements within the Israeli government, along with provocative incursions into some of the holy sites, has already raised the alarm (Jones and Sharif 2023; Sharnoff 2024). Further displacement of Palestinians from their land represents another critical national security interest, just as it does to Egypt in respect of Gaza. Historically, Jordan has borne the brunt of Israel's ethnic cleansing, which has fundamentally altered its demography and strained its resources. Like their Egyptian counterparts, Jordanian officials have unequivocally stated that displacement is a 'red line' that amounts to a declaration of war (International Crisis Group 2023).

STRATEGIC CHALLENGES

As Muasher (2025) highlights, the lack of progress on the two-state solution raises existential risks for Jordan. The re-election of Donald Trump and the resurgence of the far-right settlement agenda have cast these risks in starker relief of late (Rabai'a 2025). While the primary risk is forced population transfer, relevant subsidiary risks include the systematic erosion of the Palestinian Authority's governance, economic strangulation of the Palestinian territories, and aggressive settlement expansion that destabilise the West Bank. Addressing these risks requires a multi-track response. To begin with, Jordan will need to intensify its bilateral coordination with the Palestinian Authority to develop robust political and security strategies that strengthen Palestinian resilience and address shared threats. In addition, Jordan must upgrade its diplomacy to mobilise Arab and global efforts to counter annexation. By leveraging Jordan's established diplomatic networks, the recent Saudi stance against normalisation without a Palestinian state and its bipartisan relations in Washington, Amman can resist unilateral Israeli actions (Rabai'a 2025). Finally, Jordan will have to renew its own national dialogue to forge consensus on a path forward that draws lessons from Jordan's historical response to crises such as the 1989 National Covenant, Muasher (2025).

Different Strands of Thought on Future Jordanian Engagement with Occupation

The hardline policies of the current Israeli government, bolstered by unconditional U.S. support and the absence of substantial international pressure, have significantly curtailed Jordan's capacity to counter Israeli actions. In fact, Jordan's leadership has expressed increasing frustration at the lack of credible international partners to restrain Israeli policies or advance a viable peace process. This frustration has been evident in Jordan's diplomatic advocacy in the region that advocates for stronger collective measures against Israel (Al Rantawi 2024; Ozcelik 2024). In parallel, however, there is a domestic debate going on within Jordan's political and intellectual elites about what approach to take to occupation.

The first strand of thought amounts to a rights-based approach that prioritises support for Palestinian rights and the establishment of an independent Palestinian state with East Jerusalem as its capital, even at the cost of straining international partnerships. This perspective draws on Jordan's moral, historical, and strategic commitments to the Palestinian cause, which are embedded in the Kingdom's national identity and form part of the legitimacy of the Hashemite monarchy. The strategic importance of Jordan's custodianship of Jerusalem's Islamic and Christian holy sites is also central to its regional influence (Mohammad Abu Rumman, personal communication, 2025). Proponents argue that this role is not just symbolic, but contributes significantly to regional stability and security. However, this view, championed by King Abdullah II, aligns Jordan's foreign policy with the two-state solution as a path to regional stability and security. The King has consistently used international platforms such as the United Nations General Assembly to condemn Israeli settlement expansions and advocate for Palestinian statehood, framing these positions both as moral imperatives and strategic necessities to avoid further waves of refugees or regional destabilisation.

A second strand of thought prioritises Jordan's internal stability and economic development over a high(er) level of involvement in the Palestinian issue. Advocates of this approach adopt a *realpolitik* view, arguing that Jordan should recalibrate its post-October 7th hawkish stance in light of its limited means and the significant constraints on its ability to influence regional dynamics. Scholars like Al Momani (2024) highlight that Jordan's relation with the U.S. for economic stability makes it imperative to avoid alienating traditional Western allies. From this perspective, Jordan should adopt a more pragmatic approach that prioritises domestic stability and positions the Palestinian issue within a broader framework of national interests rather than risk being perceived as a single-issue state. Adding to this view is the re-election of Donald Trump and his strongly pro-Israel team that increases the risk of further Palestinian displacement to Jordan and highlights Amman's limitations in managing regional escalations without broader international or regional support.

A third line of thought centres on the prospect of Jordan re-incorporating the West Bank. This concept is advocated by the likes of former politician Jawad Anani. In his 2024 article, Anani calls for a re-examination of the historical ties between the two banks, proposing a confederal arrangement as a possible solution to the Israeli-Palestinian conflict. He argues that this confederation could allow for local governance in both Jordan and Palestine while preserving a unified framework under the Hashemite monarchy. Such an approach would require regional and international backing, in particular guarantees from global powers and financial support for the reconstruction of Gaza as well as the West Bank. Advocates believe this could restore Jordan's historical role on the West Bank, challenge Israeli territorial claims, and ensure a dignified existence for Palestinians (Anani 2024). However, critics point to significant challenges that include reversing the Arab League's 1974 decision that recognises the PLO as the sole legitimate representative of the Palestinian people, geopolitical risks associated with the prospect of opposing Israel, the unresolved status of Gaza, and the substantial financial, demographic, and security implications for Jordan.

Concluding Reflection

While these perspectives reflect Jordan's internal debate regarding its positioning towards Israeli occupation, Jordan's advocacy for a two-state solution remains firmly in place for the moment, anchored as it is in international law and United Nations resolutions. This makes the establishment of an independent Palestinian state along the 1967 borders, with East Jerusalem as its capital and in line with the Arab Peace Initiative of 2002, a constant feature of Jordanian policy (Jaber 2025). The rise of Israel's extreme right and the return of Trump-era dynamics pose significant challenges to Jordanian policy, however. In the near future, the Kingdom once more faces its permanent challenge of navigating the delicate equilibrium between advocating for Palestinian rights, preserving its custodianship of Jerusalem's holy sites, maintaining good relations with key international partners as well as ensuring domestic stability and cohesion—but under greater pressure.

Conflict of Interest The author has no conflict of interest to declare relevant to this chapter's content.

Bibliography

Ababneh, S. (2023). Jordanian public opinion and the Gaza crisis. *Middle East Journal*.

Abu Rumman, M. (2024). The relations with the Palestinians from the perspective of Jordanian national security. *Jordanian Politics & Society Magazine*, *1*(1), 96–105.

Abu-Odeh, A. (1999). *Jordanians, Palestinians, and the Hashemite Kingdom in the Middle East peace process*. United States Institute of Peace Press.

Abu Oudeh, A. (2023). *The Two-State Solution and Its Dual Significance for the Palestinian People and the Hashemite Kingdom of Jordan* (2nd ed.). Friedrich-Ebert-Stiftung.

Al Momani, H. M. (2024). Jordanian diplomacy and the war on Gaza amid shifting dynamics. *Jordanian Politics & Society Magazine*, *1*(1), 84–94.

Al Rantawi, O. (2024). Jordan and the war on Gaza: The Israeli threat is existential. Institute for Palestine Studies.

Al Tahir, M. (2018). The Adnan Abou Awda diaries: What was left unsaid. *Siyasat Arabiya, 33,* 139–146. Arab Center for Research and Policy Studies.
Al-Tamimi, N. (2023). Jordan's regional diplomacy amid the Gaza conflict. *Carnegie Middle East Center.* Retrieved from https://carnegie-mec.org
Amnesty International. (2023). *Humanitarian challenges in Gaza and the West Bank.* Retrieved from https://www.amnesty.org
Anani, J. (2024, July 25). *The future of Jordanian-Palestinian relations.* Al-Araby Al-Jadeed.
Anderson, B. S. (2005). *Nationalist voices in Jordan: The street and the state.* University of Texas Press.
Brand, L. A. (1995a). Palestinians and Jordanians: A crisis of identity. *Journal of Palestine Studies,* 24(4), 46–61. https://doi.org/10.2307/2538196
Brand, L. A. (1995b). *Palestinians in the Arab world: Institution building and the search for the state.* Columbia University Press.
Brynen, R. (1992). Dynamics of Palestinian political development. *Journal of Palestine Studies,* 22(3), 30–44.
Fischbach, M. R. (2012). *State, society, and land in Jordan.* Brill.
Fromkin, D. (1989). *A peace to end all peace: The fall of the Ottoman empire and the creation of the modern Middle East.* Henry Holt and Company.
Gelvin, J. L. (2014). *The Israel-Palestine conflict: One hundred years of war* (3rd ed.). Cambridge University Press.
Harel, A. (2023). Escalation in Gaza and its regional implications. *Haaretz.* Retrieved from https://www.haaretz.com
International Crisis Group. (2023). *Preventing further displacement in the Palestinian territories.* Retrieved from https://www.crisisgroup.org
Jaber, H. (2025). Debating Jordan's Strategy Approach: Documenting Security or Embracing Flexibility? Jordanian Politics & Society Magazine, (2), 96–113.
Jones, T., & Sharif, A. (2023). Jerusalem's holy sites and Jordanian custodianship are under threat. *Foreign Affairs.* Retrieved from https://www.foreignaffairs.com
Kamrava, M. (2005). *The modern Middle East: A political history since the First World War.* University of California Press.
Khalidi, R. (2006). *The iron cage: The story of the Palestinian struggle for statehood.* Beacon Press.
Khalidi, R. (2007). The Palestinians and 1948: The underlying causes of failure. In E. L. Rogan & A. Shlaim (Eds.), *The War for Palestine: Rewriting the History of 1948* (pp. 12–36). Cambridge University Press.
Laurens, H. (2002). *La question de Palestine: 1947–1967.* Fayard.
Lucas, R. E. (2005). *Institutions and the politics of survival in Jordan: Domestic responses to external challenges, 1988–2001.* State University of New York Press.
Lynch, M. (1999). *State interests and public spheres: The international politics of Jordan's identity.* Columbia University Press.

Lynch, M. (2023). The fragility of peace in the Middle East post-October seventh. *Brookings Institution*. Retrieved from https://www.brookings.edu
Milton-Edwards, B., & Hinchcliffe, P. (2009). *Jordan: A Hashemite legacy* (2nd ed.). Routledge.
Muasher, M. (2025). The Jordanian challenge under Trump. *Jordanian Politics & Society Magazine*, 2, 34–38.
Morris, Benny. 1999. *Righteous Victims: A History of the Zionist-Arab Conflict, 1881-1999*. 1st ed. New York: Knopf.
Ozcelik, B. (2024, November 26). Why Jordan's role as a 'buffer state' is being tested. The Royal United Services Institute for Defence and Security Studies (RUSI).
Robins, P. (2004). *A history of Jordan*. Cambridge University Press.
Rabai'a, I. (2025, January 20). Interactions within the West Bank: Mutual national security of Jordan and Palestine. *Jordanian Politics & Society Magazine*, (2), 124–131. Politics and Society Institute.
Rogan, E. (2011). *The Arabs: A history*. Penguin Books.
Salibi, K. (1993). *The modern history of Jordan*. I.B. Tauris.
Schwedler, J. (2022). *Jordan: Stability and the politics of containment*. Stanford University Press.
Shar'aan, M. (2020, February 2). Three Jordanian Nos in the face of the triple threat in the U.S. peace plan. *Al Jazeera*.
Sharnoff, M. (2024). Arab challenges to Jordan's custodianship of holy sites in Jerusalem. *Journal of South Asian and Middle Eastern Studies, 47*(3), 57–78.
Shlaim, A. (2008). *Lion of Jordan: The life of King Hussein in war and peace*. Allen Lane.
Smith, C. D. (2017). *Palestine and the Arab-Israeli conflict: A history with documents* (9th ed.). Bedford/St. Martin's.
Smith, M. J. (2021). *Pan-Arabism: Origins and outcomes of postcolonial unions*.
U.S. Department of State. (1948, December 4). Foreign Relations of the United States, 1948, The Near East, South Asia, and Africa, Volume V, Part 2 (Document 809). Telegram from Mr. Wells Stabler to the Acting Secretary of State. https://history.state.gov/historicaldocuments/frus1948v05p2/d809
Tell, T. (2013). *The social and economic origins of monarchy in Jordan*. Palgrave Macmillan.
Wilson, M. C. (1987). *King Abdullah, Britain and the making of Jordan*. Cambridge University Press.
World Bank. (2023). *Jordan economic monitor*. Retrieved from https://www.worldbank.org
Yom, S. L. (2015). *The impossible state: Islam, politics, and modernity's moral predicament*. Oxford University Press.
Zureik, E., & Shibli, R. (2011). *Palestinian refugees: Identity, space, and place in the Levant*. Routledge.

Open Access This chapter is licensed under the terms of the Creative Commons Attribution 4.0 International License (http://creativecommons.org/licenses/by/4.0/), which permits use, sharing, adaptation, distribution and reproduction in any medium or format, as long as you give appropriate credit to the original author(s) and the source, provide a link to the Creative Commons license and indicate if changes were made.

The images or other third party material in this chapter are included in the chapter's Creative Commons license, unless indicated otherwise in a credit line to the material. If material is not included in the chapter's Creative Commons license and your intended use is not permitted by statutory regulation or exceeds the permitted use, you will need to obtain permission directly from the copyright holder.

PART III

Regional Powers

CHAPTER 10

Enduring Resistance from Tehran

Hamidreza Azizi

Abstract Iran has been a key supporter of militant Islamist Palestinian movements against Israeli occupation. Despite recent setbacks regarding Hezbollah, the fall of Assad in Syria, the election of Trump and the Israeli/US assault on Iran itself, Tehran is likely to continue supporting Palestinian factions and promote resistance against Israel more broadly. This is because the Israeli-Palestinian conflict forms the bedrock of the "persona" of the Islamic Republic as leader of resistance against "global arrogance." Moreover, in the long-term Iranian leaders believe that the war in Gaza dealt severe strategic blows to Israel, such as damaging its international standing. Iran has been able to strengthen its regional relations instead. Tehran will try using growing opposition to Israel among Global South countries to find new partners and break free from US/Europe imposed isolation. To counter the short-term risk of conflict escalation with Israel and to compensate for weakened deterrence, Iran may revise key aspects of its military doctrine, including a potential shift toward weaponizing its nuclear program. There should, however, be no mistaking of Iran's strategic intention toward the Palestinian issue. While

H. Azizi (✉)
German Institute for International and Security Affairs (SWP), Berlin, Germany
e-mail: hamidreza.azizi@swp-berlin.org

it desires the end of the war in Gaza, Tehran does not seek the end of the broader Israeli-Palestinian conflict. It is as firmly opposed to a two-state solution as Israel's extreme right.

Keywords Iran · Axis of resistance · Forward defense · Hezbollah · Unity of the fronts · Revolutionary ideology · Hamas · Palestinian Islamic Jihad

Introduction

Iran's approach to the Israeli occupation of the Palestinian Territories is deeply rooted in its Islamist revolutionary ideology and geopolitical ambitions. Since the 1979 Islamic Revolution, Iran has consistently positioned itself as a staunch opponent of Israel, perceiving Israel's occupation not only as affront to the Muslim world but also as a manifestation of Western imperialism in the region. This dual perception of religious insult and imperial dominance underscores Iran's enduring commitment to opposing Israel and its allies. Iran's role in the Israeli-Palestinian conflict extends beyond rhetoric as Tehran materially supports Palestinian armed factions, particularly Hamas and Palestinian Islamic Jihad (PIJ), with funds, weapons, logistics, and military advice. This support is a critical component of Iran's broader strategy to challenge Israel, counterbalance Western influence in the region, and expand Iran's regional influence through the "Axis of Resistance"—a network of non-state and hybrid armed actors united in opposition to Israel and its allies. This essay explores the political and philosophical underpinnings of Iran's perspective on the Israeli occupation of the Palestinian territories, assesses its strategic interests and red lines, examines Tehran's capabilities and role in the conflict, and considers what its engagement with the occupation might look like in the future. By understanding Iran's motivations and strategies, deeper insights can be gained into the broader regional conflict of which the Palestinian issue has become part, as well as its implications for regional peace and stability.

Iran's Religious, Socio-political and Ideological Views on Occupation

Iran's primary interest in the Palestinian issue stems from its desire to assert itself as a leader of the Muslim world, particularly in the Middle East. By positioning itself as the most ardent supporter of the Palestinian cause, Iran seeks to galvanize Muslim populations and movements under its leadership against Israel and its Western allies (Parchami 2022). This strategy aligns with Iran's broader objective of expanding its influence across the region, challenging the dominance of rivals like Saudi Arabia, and countering the influence of Western powers. In this context, Iran views the Israeli-Palestinian conflict as a proxy battleground for its broader struggle against Western, especially American, influence in the Middle East (Sternfeld 2024). Supporting Palestinian resistance against Israeli occupation allows Iran to challenge the US-led regional order, undermine American allies, and promote an alternative power arrangement.

Central to this strategy is the Axis of Resistance, a regional network of armed groups that Iran maintains and strengthens to deter Israeli military actions, disrupt American interests, and secure its regional ambitions (Azizi et al. 2020). The Palestinian territories, especially Gaza, serve as a critical front in this network. Hence, Iran makes every effort to ensure the survival of its Palestinian allies, such as Hamas and the Palestinian Islamic Jihad (PIJ), against Israeli military pressure. These groups are seen as integral components of the Axis of Resistance, whose dismantling or significant weakening would risk a domino effect that could undermine the entire structure and, ultimately, jeopardize Iran's own security. This concern was the primary reason behind Iran and its Axis partners' decision to escalate on multiple fronts against Israel after the start of the Israeli military campaign in Gaza in October 2023 (Azizi 2023).

The Palestinian cause also plays a significant role in Iran's domestic politics (Azizi and van Veen 2023). Although the majority of Iranian society today is disillusioned with the Islamic Republic's ideological ambitions and propaganda, maintaining a pro-Palestinian stance helps to satisfy the conservative religious support base of the regime. Although the mass killing of civilians in Gaza has increased sympathy for the Palestinian cause among broader segments of Iran's population beyond its political classes, this does not amount to greater support for the Iranian regime's stance on the Israeli-Palestinian conflict. In fact, the risk of continuous direct war between Iran and Israel has prompted renewed public questioning of the Islamic Republic's involvement in the Palestinian issue.

In addition to these strategic considerations, Iran also has an ideological redline concerning the status of Jerusalem, particularly the Al-Aqsa Mosque (The Office of the Supreme Leader 2007). Tehran views any Israeli effort to further assert control over Jerusalem, such as expanding settlements or altering the status quo at religious sites, as an escalation. In response to such moves, should they occur, Iran is likely to increase its support for Palestinian groups and encourage more aggressive forms of resistance against Israel. Finally, it is important to consider that Iran's understanding of "occupation" extends beyond Gaza and the West Bank to what it refers to as "the entire Palestinian land, from the river to the sea" (Khamenei.ir 2024). Iran's refusal to recognize Israel means that, even in the event of a settlement between Palestinian factions and Israel, Tehran will continue to promote its narrative of armed resistance and challenge Israel's right to exist. Iranian leaders appear to believe that militant actions, along with domestic and international political pressures, could ultimately cause Israel's decline.

Ideational and Material Capabilities

Iran's main ideological tool regarding Palestine is its discourse of resistance against Israel and the United States, of which Tehran positions itself as leader and sponsor. The Iranian government's narrative portrays itself as the vanguard of resistance against "global arrogance" (*estekbar-e-jahani*), with the Palestinian cause serving as a central pillar of this worldview (Khamenei.ir 2009). This discourse has been a potent instrument in Iran's foreign policy, enabling it to forge and sustain alliances with various non-state actors and sympathetic governments across the Muslim world. Its narrative features a significant religious dimension that is tied to Iran's claims of safeguarding the interests of the Islamic world. In the context of Palestine, the importance of Al-Quds (Jerusalem) as the first *Qibla* (direction for prayer) of Muslims and one of Islam's holiest sites is emphasized (Khamenei.ir 2022). This frame provides an ideological justification for Iran's involvement in the Palestinian issue while also mobilizing armed groups on an Islamist basis but in support of Iran's broader (geo-)strategic objectives. Iran has developed extensive media networks to spread its ideological narrative throughout the region. Channels such as Al-Alam (Arabic), Press TV (English), and Al-Kawthar (Arabic) function as platforms to disseminate Iranian perspectives on regional conflicts, highlight Palestinian plight, and broadcast messages supportive of the Axis of Resistance (Malik 2021). These media outlets also counter narratives from Western and pro-Western Arab media by offering an alternative viewpoint that frequently emphasizes resistance and opposition to Israel and the West. However, their impact on Arab and Islamic public opinion has been somewhat limited compared to outlets like Qatar's Al Jazeera or Saudi Arabia's Al-Arabiya.

In terms of material capabilities, Iran's most significant means of projecting power lies in its support for armed groups across the region. These groups act as force multipliers and force projectors as they enable Iran to exert influence in regional conflicts without direct military engagement of its own. Additionally, Iran's development of missile and drone capabilities has established a somewhat asymmetrical mechanism of deterrence with Israel and the United States, as well as empowering Tehran's partners within the Axis of Resistance (Azizi 2021). Through the direct provision of missiles and drones, as well as the transfer of technology to produce these locally, Iran has enabled its partners—ranging from Hezbollah to the Houthis and Iraqi armed groups—to become serious security risks for Israel.[1] The impact of this approach has been particularly evident during the ongoing war in Gaza in which groups such as Hamas and Hezbollah conducted numerous missile and drone attacks against Israel. For over a year, Hezbollah's attacks on northern Israel forced more than 60,000 residents to flee their homes. Beyond military support, Iran's financial backing of its allies has also been significant, allowing these groups to arm themselves, grow, and challenge Israel. For instance, Iran reportedly provided Hezbollah with $700 million annually. Increasing US sanctions after 2018 did not reduce Iran's willingness and capacity to offer such support (Karam 2018). However, the fall of Bashar al-Assad's regime and the loss of Iran's direct access to Hezbollah, combined with internal developments in Lebanon following the ceasefire with Israel that bolstered Hezbollah's rivals, do present significant obstacles to Iran's efforts to effectively support and rebuild Hezbollah.

---

[1] Despite the significant weakening of Hezbollah following the events of 7 October 2023, Iran remains optimistic about its strategy of bringing multi-front military pressure to bear against Israel. This optimism is fueled by Israel's inability to eliminate Hamas and the rise of the Houthis as a prominent force opposing Israeli interests.

Nonetheless, Iran is expected to maintain and even expand its backing for the Houthis and Iraqi militias as it explores new ways to support Hezbollah.

Iran's Role in the Conflict Over the Past Years

Iran's most significant role in the Israeli occupation of the Palestinian territories is its position as the principal patron of Palestinian armed groups, particularly Hamas and Palestinian Islamic Jihad (PIJ). These groups are heavily dependent on Iranian financial, military, and logistical support to sustain their operations against Israel. Iran's financial backing is essential for maintaining the long-term viability of these organizations, especially in the face of economic hardships caused by blockades and international pressures (Clarke 2023). In addition to financial support, Iran supplies Palestinian factions with weapons, including rockets, small arms, and other military equipment (Hinz 2021). Moreover, Iran shares technological expertise, enabling these groups to develop their own weapons, such as the locally produced rockets that Hamas has used in its conflicts with Israel. The Islamic Revolutionary Guard Corps (IRGC), either directly or through Hezbollah, plays a key role in training fighters from Hamas, PIJ, and other Palestinian groups (Levitt and Margolin 2023). This training covers guerrilla warfare tactics, intelligence operations, and the use of advanced weaponry.

The "joint operations room" of the Axis of Resistance, first established during the fight against ISIS in Iraq and Syria after 2014 and developed further after the assassination of general Qasem Soleimani in 2020, enhanced Iran's ability to coordinate support for Palestinian militias and the broader fight against Israel (The Times of Israel 2021). This joint operations room was structured into three operational echelons (Azizi 2023). The foundational tier comprised the Palestinian territories, where Iranian-backed Palestinian factions, particularly Hamas and Islamic Jihad, would operate. The second tier included Hezbollah, which was responsible for liaising with the Palestinian factions and co-managing the entire structure. The third tier incorporated Iranian-backed armed groups in Syria, Iraq, and Yemen. This operational framework was a reflection of the concept of the "unity of the fronts," referring to a coordinated campaign to combat Israel by emphasizing Iran's multi-front response capability (Vazirian 2023). The concept envisions four primary fronts: the Gaza Strip (southern front), the West Bank (central front near major

Israeli cities), southern Lebanon (northern front) run by Hezbollah, and the Golan Heights (eastern and northeastern front), also managed by Hezbollah. However, the Gaza war has significantly weakened the Axis of Resistance, especially the loss of Syria and the diminished strength of Hezbollah. In turn, this has reduced the functionality and significance of the joint operations room and the notion of unity of the fronts. It is nevertheless likely that Iran and its regional partners will reevaluate and reorganize this network, including coordination strategies, so it can re-emerge more strongly.

Beyond its military and logistical support, Iran plays a prominent role as diplomatic and ideological supporter of the Palestinian cause on the international stage. Iran consistently raises the issue of Palestinian rights in international forums such as the United Nations, the Organization of Islamic Cooperation (OIC), and non-aligned gatherings. This amounts to what is referred to in Iran's official narrative as "resistance diplomacy" (Iranian Ministry of Foreign Affairs 2023). As the core of the Axis of Resistance and as the only capable state actor in this network, Iran assumes the role of promoting the interests of the entire network and not just those of Tehran itself. Its diplomatic activism has been particularly evident after October 7 with Iranian diplomats acting as de facto spokesmen for the Axis of Resistance in international forums as part of a broader strategy to challenge Israel's legitimacy and mobilize global opinion against occupation while also supporting Iran's regional ambitions in the process (Azizi and van Veen 2024b). At the same time, Iran's absence from the diplomatic efforts that led to the Gaza ceasefire in January 2024 underscored the limitations of Tehran's influence on regional diplomacy, in contrast with the roles played by Qatar and Egypt.

Levers of Influence and Points of Vulnerability

In line with its strategic vision, capabilities, and current role in the Israeli-Palestinian conflict, Iran possesses significant levers of influence but also faces considerable vulnerabilities that have become more apparent over time. Although Palestinian groups, especially Hamas and PIJ, as well as all other groups within the Axis of Resistance are united by a shared anti-Israeli vision and their common interest in opposing Israel and the United States, none can be considered a proxy (Saad 2024). Their informal alignment serves as a critical lever for Iran to influence the trajectory of the Israeli-Palestinian conflict but the absence of central command and control can also produce surprises. For example, Iran reportedly did not have prior knowledge of Hamas's plan to carry out the October 7 attack against Israel, particularly with regards to details and timing even though it is clear that this attack would not have been possible without years of military, logistical and training support from Iran (Cohen et al. 2023). It did, however, have far-reaching consequences for the regional balance of power.

To begin with, a year of attrition has significantly eroded Hamas' and Hezbollah's capabilities. Both organizations have adapted to an extent by shifting tactics (Hamas to guerilla, Hezbollah by partial withdrawal and accepting a ceasefire), which enable them to continue their struggle in the longer term (Ezzeddine 2024). Despite their resilience, Iran's ability in the near future to supply them with weapons and other materials has been significantly reduced by the fall of Assad and the loss of Iran's "land bridge" between Iraq and Lebanon (Al-Nidawi 2017). On a more positive note for Tehran, the war in Gaza has offered it additional opportunities for political and diplomatic maneuvering in the region. The never-ending nature of the fight against Hamas and the widespread public outcry over Israel's actions in Gaza have made it challenging for Arab leaders to openly pursue formal cooperation with Israel. This has brought expansion of the Abraham Accords to a halt, which previously threatened to further isolate Iran. At the same time, Tehran seized the opportunity to strengthen its diplomatic ties with Arab states. The gradual improvement of relations between Iran and Saudi Arabia, along with ongoing talks with Egypt and Jordan, has helped Iran to enhance its regional influence and push back against the formation of an anti-Iran alliance. Donald Trump's return to the White House is likely to produce a stronger push by Washington to bring Saudi Arabia into the Abraham Accords, which would be facilitated by a ceasefire in Gaza that actually lasts. But even in the event of formal normalization of relations between Saudi Arabia and Israel, Riyadh is unlikely to join a military coalition against Tehran.

Nevertheless, the Gaza war has also exposed the limitations and vulnerabilities of Iran's strategy. Since the end of the Iran-Iraq War in 1988, one of Iran's main justifications for developing and supporting the Axis of Resistance has been to use it as a tool for "forward defense," engaging with threats at locations far from Iran's territorial borders before they can pose a direct threat to Iran's national security (Vatanka 2021). This network was also intended to provide Iran with plausible deniability, allowing it to avoid direct involvement in conflicts when necessary (Steinberg 2021). However, Israel's increasing threat perception of the Axis of Resistance has led to operations that target Iranian interests and even its territory directly. A clear example of this occurred in April 2024, when an Israeli attack on the Iranian consulate in Damascus killed senior IRGC commanders. In response, Iran launched hundreds of missiles and drones at Israel, a move that nearly escalated into a direct war (Azizi and van Veen 2024a). Additionally, the assassination of Haniyeh on Tehran's soil highlighted the fact that, despite all its efforts, the Axis of Resistance has not been able to provide adequate deterrence against Israel. This became even more apparent during Israel's unprecedented attack on a number of Iranian military sites in October 2024.

The possibility of a continuous direct military confrontation with Israel after its strike against Iran in June 2025, or even a broader regional war, presents a significant risk for Iran. Such a conflict could severely strain Iran's resources and expose it to strikes against its critical infrastructure. This risk is further heightened by Israel's advanced military capabilities and its alliance with the United States. Consequently, the dilemma facing Iran's leadership after the end of the Gaza war will be how to balance its ongoing support for the Axis of Resistance, including Palestinian factions, with the strategic necessity of (re-)establishing deterrence to avoid direct conflict with adversaries that command superior military capabilities.

Strategic Perspectives for Future Action

Despite the risks and limitations just outlined, in particular the limited deterrent value of the Axis of Resistance, Tehran is likely to continue its comprehensive support for Palestinian factions and its broader promotion of resistance against Israel. Its persistence can primarily be explained by two factors. First, Iran's ideological commitment to support anti-Israeli resistance is enduring as it emerges from, and is interwoven with, the contemporary "persona" of the Islamic Republic as an aspirant leader of global resistance against oppression, particularly in the Israeli-Palestinian conflict. Second, despite a significant tactical weakening of Hamas' military capabilities at the hands of the IDF, Iranian leaders believe that the war in Gaza has dealt severe strategic blows to Israel, not in the least damaging its international standing with Israel facing increasing isolation on the world stage (Van Veen 2024). Plus, while the Axis of Resistance did not provide the level of deterrence Iran had counted on, it still serves as a valuable alternative regional power structure (Soury and Khajehsarvi 2022). As a bloc, it can capitalize on the current geopolitical environment to establish a new regional equation that could ultimately benefit Iran and enhance its international standing, particularly with the newfound role for the Houthis as gatekeepers of the Red Sea. Iran's ultimate goal is to transform the Axis of Resistance into a unified military-political bloc that advances the shared geopolitical and ideological objectives of its members. Despite the significant weakening of the Axis during the Gaza war, Iranian leaders remain hopeful that Israel's unprecedented violence in Gaza, along with its occupation of parts of Lebanon and Syria, will reignite the core notion of "resistance" among the region's populations. This, they believe, could ultimately lead to the restoration and even expansion of a unified military-political network opposing Israel.

With this in mind, Iranian officials have been trying to use the growing opposition to Israel among Global South countries to find new partners and to break free from its isolation imposed by the United States and Europe. These diplomatic efforts are likely to continue after the guns in Gaza fall silent. Simultaneously, to compensate for its weakened deterrence, Iran is likely to consider revising its military doctrine, including the potential development of a nuclear weapon (Vaez 2024). This scenario would become particularly acute if another war were to erupt between Iran and Israel plus the United States. Furthermore, Iran is likely to maintain its opposition to any two-state solution to the Israeli-Palestinian conflict. This stance is rooted in its fundamental rejection of Israel's existence and refusal to recognize a Jewish state. Iran will likely attempt to align more radical Palestinian factions with its position since the core ideological justification for Tehran's regional strategy has always been its support for Palestinian armed resistance. A political solution that renders such resistance irrelevant would significantly undermine Iran's long-term designs to expand its regional influence. Despite concerns about the normalization of Arab–Israeli relations, particularly between Saudi Arabia and Israel, Tehran will also use any next normalization steps to bolster its standing among Palestinian groups, rhetorically positioning itself as their only true supporter (Reuters 2023b). However, Iran's success in this regard will depend on the failure of the two-state solution. Ironically, as the late Iranian Foreign Minister Hossein Amir-Abdollahian said in December 2023, "The only issue on which Iran and Israel agree is their opposition to the two-state solution!" (Reuters 2023b).

Conclusion

Over the past four decades, Iran has been one of the main supporters of militant Islamist Palestinian movements in their struggle against Israeli occupation. Paradoxically, Tehran benefits from the longevity of Israeli occupation to sustain its ideological discourse and expand its regional influence. While Iran desires the end of the war in Gaza, it does not seek the end of the broader Israeli-Palestinian conflict. From the perspective of Iranian leaders, the optimal outcome of the Gaza war is to preserve some of Hamas' military infrastructure while ensuring that other members of the Axis of Resistance, particularly Hezbollah as Iran's main ally, can rehabilitate and restructure afterward. This would allow Iran to maintain its influence and continue to pursue its ideological and strategic goals in the region.

However, the risks of continuing to support the Axis of Resistance have also become apparent for Iran. Even if a broader war involving the United States or a direct confrontation between Tehran and Tel Aviv does not re-occur, Iran's military and regional strategy may eventually be challenged by growing economic difficulties and the increasing threat of domestic instability driven by public discontent. A significant part of this discontent stems from frustration over Iran spending resources abroad to support armed groups while the domestic economy continues to deteriorate. Furthermore, despite Iran's efforts to capitalize on the passive stance of most Arab states regarding the Gaza war, the continuation of normalization of relations between Israel and Arab states would further complicate Iran's position as this threatens to marginalize its influence on the issue of occupation. Ultimately, Iran's engagement in the Israeli-Palestinian conflict reflects a complex interplay of ideology, strategy, and realpolitik.

Conflict of Interest The author has no conflict of interests to declare that are relevant to the content of this chapter.

Bibliography

Al-Nidawi, Omar. 2017. "An Iranian Land Bridge Is Not the End of the World | The Washington Institute." 2017. https://www.washingtoninstitute.org/policy-analysis/iranian-land-bridge-not-end-world.

Azizi, Hamidreza. 2023. "How Iran and Its Allies Hope to Save Hamas." War on the Rocks. November 16, 2023. https://warontherocks.com/2023/11/how-iran-and-its-allies-hope-to-save-hamas/.

Azizi, Hamidreza. 2021. "The Concept of 'Forward Defence': How Has the Syrian Crisis Shaped the Evolution of Iran's Military Strategy? | GCSP." 2021. https://www.gcsp.ch/publications/concept-forward-defence-how-has-syrian-crisis-shaped-evolution-irans-military-strategy.

Azizi, Hamidreza, Vali Golmohammadi, and Amir Hossein Vazirian. 2020. "Trump's 'Maximum Pressure' and Anti-Containment in Iran's Regional Policy." *Digest of Middle East Studies* 29 (2): 150–66. https://doi.org/10.1111/dome.12219.

Azizi, Hamidreza, and van Veen, Erwin. 2023. "Iranian Reactions to 7/10 and the Invasion of Gaza." Clingendael. 2023. https://www.clingendael.org/publication/iranian-reactions-710-and-invasion-gaza.

Azizi, Hamidreza, and van Veen. 2024a. "Playing with Fire: Patterns of Iranian-Israeli Military Confrontation." War on the Rocks. June 25, 2024. https://warontherocks.com/2024/06/playing-with-fire-patterns-of-iranian-israeli-military-confrontation/.

Azizi, Hamidreza, and van Veen, Erwin. 2024b. "Tehran's Perpetual Motion: The Threat of War Abroad and Contested Legitimacy at Home." Clingendael. 2024. https://www.clingendael.org/publication/tehrans-perpetual-motion-threat-war-abroad-and-contested-legitimacy-home.

Beaumont, Peter. 2024. "Israel Is Fighting on Four Fronts – but the Defeat May Come at Home." *The Observer*, April 20, 2024, sec. World news. https://www.theguardian.com/world/2024/apr/20/israel-is-fighting-on-four-fronts-but-the-defeat-may-come-at-home.

Clarke, Colin P. 2023. "Iran and the 'Axis of Resistance' Vastly Improved Hamas's Operational Capabilities - Foreign Policy Research Institute." 2023. https://www.fpri.org/article/2023/10/iran-and-the-axis-of-resistance-vastly-improved-hamass-operational-capabilities/.

Cohen, Zachary, Katie Bo Lillis, Natasha Bertrand, and Jeremy Herb. 2023. "Initial US Intelligence Suggests Iran Was Surprised by the Hamas Attack on Israel | CNN Politics." CNN. October 11, 2023. https://www.cnn.com/2023/10/11/politics/us-intelligence-iran-hamas-doubt/index.html.

Hinz, Fabian. 2021. "Iran Transfers Rockets to Palestinian Groups | Wilson Center." 2021. https://www.wilsoncenter.org/article/irans-rockets-palestinian-groups.

Iranian Ministry of Foreign Affairs. 2023. "*Resistance Diplomacy Conference Held with FM Amirabdollahian in Attendance.*" Last modified October 20, 2024. https://en.mfa.ir/portal/newsview/713456/Resistance-Diplomacy-Conference-held-with-FM-Amirabdollahian-in-attendance.

Karam, Joyce. 2018. "Iran Pays Hezbollah $700 Million a Year, US Official Says." The National. 2018. https://www.thenationalnews.com/world/the-americas/iran-pays-hezbollah-700-million-a-year-us-official-says-1.737347.

Khamenei.ir. 2009. "The Supreme Leader's View of Global Arrogance." Text. www.khamenei.ir. September 10, 2009. https://farsi.khamenei.ir/speech-content?id=101179.

Khamenei.ir. 2022. "Everything is signaling a new equation in Palestine's future." Text. www.khamenei.ir. http://english.khamenei.ir/news/8960/Everything-is-signaling-a-new-equation-in-Palestine-s-future.

Khamenei.ir. 2024. "Divine Promise of Palestine's Liberation 'from the River to the Sea' Will Be Fulfilled." Text. www. khamenei.ir. http://english.khamenei.ir/news/10800/Divine-promise-of-Palestine-s-liberation-from-the-river-to-the.

Levitt, Matthew, and Margolin, Devorah. 2023. "The Road to October 7: Hamas' Long Game, Clarified." Combating Terrorism Center at West Point. November 28, 2023. https://ctc.westpoint.edu/the-road-to-october-7-hamas-long-game-clarified/.

Malik, Hamdi. 2021. "Understanding Iran's Vast Media Network in Arab Countries | The Washington Institute." 2021. https://www.washingtoninstitute.org/policy-analysis/understanding-irans-vast-media-network-arab-countries.

Nancy Ezzeddine نانسي عزالدين [@NancyEzzeddine]. 2024. "Hezbollah's Field Brigades Have Adopted a Decentralized Communication Structure, with Each Brigade Operating Semi-Independently Using Unique Networks and Protocols. This Flexibility Has Allowed for Quick Tactical Adjustments on the Ground but Has Also Led to Isolated (Mostly." Tweet. *Twitter*. https://x.com/NancyEzzeddine/status/1843585305527328935.

Parchami, Ali. 2022. "An Iranian Worldview: The Strategic Culture of the Islamic Republic." *Journal of Advanced Military Studies* 2022 (special): 9–23. https://doi.org/10.21140/mcuj.2022SIstratcul001.

Reuters. 2023a. "Iranian Foreign Minister Says Neither Iran nor Israel Believe in a Two State Solution | Reuters." 2023. https://www.reuters.com/world/middle-east/iranian-foreign-minister-says-neither-iran-nor-israel-believe-two-state-solution-2023 12 11/.

Reuters. 2023b. "Iran's Khamenei Says Normalising Israel Ties Is a Losing Bet - State Media," October 3, 2023, sec. Middle East. https://www.reuters.com/world/middle-east/irans-khamenei-says-normalising-ties-with-israel-is-betting-losing-horse-state-2023-10-03/.

Saad, Amal. 2024. "Iran's Proxies Aren't Really Proxies." TIME. February 7, 2024. https://time.com/6692282/iran-doesnt-have-proxies/.
Soury, Fatemeh, and Gholamreza Khajehsarvi. 2022. "Iran, the Axis of Resistance and the Formation of the Regional Order of West Asia." *Quarterly Journal of Environmental Studies Strategic of the Islamic Republic of Iran* 6 (2): 39–64.
Steinberg, Guido. 2021. "The 'Axis of Resistance.'" Stiftung Wissenschaft und Politik (SWP). Accessed October 21, 2024. https://www.swp-berlin.org/publikation/irans-expansion-in-the-middle-east-is-hitting-a-wall.
Sternfeld, Lior. 2024. "The Realignment of the Middle East - Foreign Policy Research Institute." 2024. https://www.fpri.org/article/2024/03/the-realignment-of-the-middle-east/.
The Office of the Supreme Leader. 2007. "Muslims Must Move against Desecration of Al-Aqsa Mosque." 2007. https://www.leader.ir/en/content/3593/Muslims-must-move-against-desecration-of-al-Aqsa-mosque.
The Times of Israel. 2021. "Iran, Hamas and Hezbollah Coordinated Gaza Fighting in Joint War Room—Report | The Times of Israel." 2021. https://www.timesofisrael.com/iran-hamas-and-hezbollah-coordinated-gaza-fighting-in-joint-war-room-report/.
Vaez, Ali. 2024. "Why the War in Gaza Makes a Nuclear Iran More Likely." *Foreign Affairs*, January 25, 2024. https://www.foreignaffairs.com/israel/why-war-gaza-makes-nuclear-iran-more-likely.
Vatanka, Alex. 2021. "Soleimani Ascendant: The Origins of Iran's 'Forward Defense' Strategy." Whither the IRGC of the 2020s? New America. https://www.jstor.org/stable/resrep28480.5.
Vazirian, Amir Hossein. 2023. "Iran's Unification of the Arenas Campaign against Israel: Foundations and Prospects." Middle East Institute. 2023. https://www.mei.edu/publications/irans-unification-arenas-campaign-against-israel-foundations-and-prospects.
Van Veen, Erwin. 2024. "Israel against Iran: Regional Conflict Scenarios in 2024." Clingendael. 2024. https://www.clingendael.org/publication/israel-against-iran-regional-conflict-scenarios-2024.

Open Access This chapter is licensed under the terms of the Creative Commons Attribution 4.0 International License (http://creativecommons.org/licenses/by/4.0/), which permits use, sharing, adaptation, distribution and reproduction in any medium or format, as long as you give appropriate credit to the original author(s) and the source, provide a link to the Creative Commons license and indicate if changes were made.

The images or other third party material in this chapter are included in the chapter's Creative Commons license, unless indicated otherwise in a credit line to the material. If material is not included in the chapter's Creative Commons license and your intended use is not permitted by statutory regulation or exceeds the permitted use, you will need to obtain permission directly from the copyright holder.

CHAPTER 11

The Rocky Road of Israeli-Saudi Normalization

Paul Aarts

Abstract Saudi Arabia has long maintained informal ties with Israel in various domains while also pushing for a negotiated solution to the Palestinian issue. As the latter has fallen on deaf ears of various Israeli governments, Riyadh has basically accepted Israel's occupation of the Palestinian territories in the sense of not resisting it. After the Abraham Accords of 2020, Mohammed bin Salman started to negotiate a normalization agreement with Israel via the U.S. that intends to deliver a range of American-sponsored security benefits to the Kingdom in exchange for full diplomatic relations. The destruction of Gaza halted the completion of this process. However, this is not because Mohammed bin Salman or the Saudi ruling elites care greatly about the Palestinian cause, but because doing so would be domestically unpopular and risk Saudi Arabia's standing in the Arab as well as Islamic worlds. As Riyadh has at best mounted an ineffective form of 'conference diplomacy' to protest the carnage in Gaza, which is devoid of tangible pressure on Israel, it is quite

P. Aarts (✉)
University of Amsterdam, Amsterdam, Netherlands
e-mail: p.w.h.aarts@uva.nl

© The Author(s) 2025
E. van Veen (ed.), *The Future of the Occupation of the Palestinian Territories after Gaza*,
https://doi.org/10.1007/978-3-031-93798-9_11

possible that normalization talks resume as soon as headlines fade or a cease-fire agreement proves to be lasting, and a watery compromise on the future of the Palestinian issue is agreed.

Keywords Normalization · Mohammed bin Salman · Intelligence cooperation · Defense treaty · Iran · Abraham Accords

Introduction

After '10/7', relations between Israel and Saudi Arabia shifted from increasingly cordial to more of a wait-and-see attitude. While Crown Prince Mohammed bin Salman had announced in late September 2023 that 'every day we move closer to normalization' (Aitken 2023), his tone changed in the following months. Riyadh gradually adopted a more cautious approach, illustrated by the crown prince's description of Israeli behavior in the Gaza Strip as a 'collective genocide'. (ECFR 2024; ICG, 2024; Cook 2024). Nevertheless, even after the carnage in Gaza halted talks between Washington and Riyadh, negotiators indicated several times that a deal may be imminent, highlighting just how temporary the pause in talks might turn out to be. In the course of 2024, it was even reported that Saudi and U.S. diplomats were 'finalizing the details' of an accord (Keating 2024). Such an accord would combine a bilateral security, nuclear, and weapons deal between Riyadh and Washington with normalization of relations between Saudi Arabia and Israeli, probably followed by more intense intelligence and security cooperation. It can be expected that any sustained cease-fire in Gaza will further strengthen and accelerate this process.

Opinions vary widely on the likelihood of a 'normalization deal', the idea of which has been kept afloat during the many months of extreme Israeli violence in Gaza. On the one hand, there are voices that tirelessly advocate for seizing the momentum of the Abraham Accords and reaching an agreement as soon as possible. Dennis Ross is the spokesman for this line of thinking (Ross 2024). It is in the same vein that Elie Podeh lists six significant advantages of normalization for Israel (Podeh

2024a).[1] In these circles, there is consensus that it is not so much 'if' but 'when' a deal will be concluded. On the other hand, there is a growing chorus of skeptical voices, ranging from mild criticism to sharp condemnation (Dassa Kaye 2023; Pillar 2024; Pressman 2024; Fantappie and Nasr 2024; Kurtzner and Miller 2023; Al-Sheikh 2024; Wright 2024). A recurring issue in all criticisms is the risk of squandering Palestinian rights for better bilateral ties with Saudi Arabia. Some criticasters assume that, behind closed doors, Mohammed bin Salman has had his cards on Israel for quite some time. Rightly or wrongly, he is thought to assume that his future and Israel's are intimately intertwined (Arab Digest 2023).[2]

Remarkably, the possibility of a defense agreement with the U.S. *without* formal Israeli-Saudi relations is barely scrutinized.

What to make of these mixed views? This chapter sketches the historical background of Saudi-Israeli relations. It also explores Riyadh's position vis-à-vis Palestine before the Gaza war. Next, it undertakes a similar analysis of Saudi policies *after* 7 October 2023. Moreover, the chapter briefly outlines what a triangular deal between the U.S., Saudi Arabia, and Israel might look like from Riyadh's perspective. Finally, it discusses possible trajectories for such a deal in the years ahead.

The 'Secret' History of Israeli-Saudi Relations

Should it ever come to Saudi diplomatic recognition of Israel, it should not be forgotten that this could never have come about without decades of informal and under-the-radar ties between both countries. Contacts go back to the 1930s—that is, they even pre-date the creation of the state of Israel—and include regular dialogue between Ben-Gurion, later Israel's first prime minister, and Fu'ad Hamza, King Abdul Aziz's foreign adviser (Podeh 2018). However, from 1945 onwards, the Kingdom joined the

---

[1] Podeh reminds his readers what Mohammed bin Salman told Jewish leaders in April 2018: 'Over the past 40 years, the Palestinian leadership has repeatedly missed opportunities and rejected all the offers it was given. It's time for the Palestinians to accept proposals and come to the negotiating table—or shut up and stop complaining' (Podeh 2024b). Such statements are suspiciously similar to those made by Prince Bandar bin Sultan in his 2020 Al Arabiya interview, in which even more venomous language was used (Al Arabiya English, October 7, 2020).

[2] It is noteworthy that, after Jamal Khashoggi's murder in 2018, Netanyahu, in one of his White House lobbying efforts to keep Mohammed bin Salman out of trouble, proudly observed 'I saved [MB's] ass' (Hashemi (2020), based on Bob Woodward's *Rage*, 2020).

Arab League's boycott of companies dealing with Zionists in Palestine. After 1948 this would become a full boycott of Israel. It also opposed the U.N. Partition Plan for Palestine in 1947 and has not officially recognized the State of Israel to date.

Yet, Israel and Saudi Arabia were on the same side during the heyday of Nasserism in the 1960s. This was evident during the war in Yemen when Israel as well as Saudi Arabia provided various forms of support to Yemeni royalist militants. King Faisal also refrained from sending troops to Egypt during the six-day war in 1967 and even enabled indirect economic cooperation between Saudi Arabia and Israel by means of the Trans-Arabian pipeline. During the October War of 1973, Saudi troops did not fight, but Riyadh was a full partner in the wartime oil embargo of Israel and the West under the auspices of OAPEC. From the early 1980s, Saudi Arabia was involved in the Arab-Israeli peace process. At the time of the 1991 Gulf War, Israel and Saudi Arabia faced Iraq's Saddam Hussein as their common adversary. Following the war, the first formal public meeting between Saudi and Israeli officials took place during the Madrid peace conference and in the following years Saudi Arabia quietly supported the Oslo process. From the mid-2000s onwards the 'cold war' between Iran and (mainly) Saudi Arabia was in full swing, enabling direct yet secret talks between Israel and Saudi Arabia. It was during the Lebanon War of 2006 that intelligence cooperation between the two countries really took off. On the Saudi side, Prince Bandar bin Sultan (then head of the Saudi National Security Council) was instrumental in forging close relations between the countries' intelligence agencies against a backdrop of shared threat perceptions, such as Iran's mounting regional influence, Tehran's nuclear program, the rise of non-state armed groups and president Obama's declared 'pivot to Asia'. In that same year, the Arab Uprisings created a shared fear of regional democratization with a real possibility of religiously based parties coming to power, first and foremost in Egypt where the Muslim Brotherhood entered office (Hamid 2022; Hashemi 2020).

All this led to what Jones and Guzansky describe as a 'tacit security regime', which resonated with Israel's 'periphery doctrine' of the 1950s (Jones and Guzansky 2019). This policy concept refers to Israel's clandestine ties with non-Arab minority groups (for example in Iraq and Southern Sudan) but also with non-Arab state actors—most famously Turkey, Ethiopia, and Iran. The doctrine, the brainchild of Israel's first Prime Minister David Ben-Gurion, was meant to prevent and/or weaken any united Arab front. In some cases, such as the Islamic Republic of Iran, it lasted till the late 1980s/early 1990s (Parsi 2007). During the 2010s, Saudi-Israeli relations developed in fields like intelligence, agriculture, cyber technology, medicine and the economy to the point that both countries fell short of mutual diplomatic recognition, but maintained many of the features of 'normal relations' (Podeh 2018: 579, Haniehc 2017). In 2020, Netanyahu and Mossad chief Yossi Cohen visited Saudi Arabia and met with Mohammed bin Salman. In April 2024, Riyadh provided intelligence on Iran's impending military attack, which marked a major contribution to Israel's largely successful repulse of the assault.

Saudi Arabia and the Question of Palestine Before '10/7'

The centrality of 'Palestine' to Middle Eastern politics and Saudi Arabia's view of it has gone through three phases with time: (1) from 1948 until the 2011 uprisings Palestine was a significant factor in Saudi foreign policy that aspired to contribute to a positive conflict resolution for the various Palestinian populations; (2) from 2011 to 2023, it was absent in the regional geopolitical equation and less of a Saudi priority while (3) after October 7 it returned to regional and Saudi foreign politics with a vengeance, but mostly as a negative factor—i.e., impeding or blocking the realization of other Saudi priorities (Valbjørn et al. 2024).

Although Pan-Arabism declined in the 1970s at state level, Palestine continued to play a prominent role in how Arab regimes related to Israel. Saudi Arabia is a case in point. After the 1973–1974 oil embargo, Riyadh launched an eight-point peace plan in 1981, including implicit recognition of Israel, in a bid to initiate negotiations about the Palestinian issue. Unfortunately, Crown Prince Fahd did not make any impression on the Israeli government. In February 2002, shortly after '9/11' and the outbreak of the Second Intifada, Crown Prince Abdullah made a second attempt. His plan, based on full normalization of relations with Israel in exchange for full Israeli withdrawal from the occupied territories, gained prominence through the Arab League as the 'Arab Peace Initiative' (Kostiner 2005; Shtayyeh 2024). Israeli Prime Minister Sharon did not even bother to respond, however. Nevertheless, Palestine remained a central symbol and reference point for Saudi foreign policy (Valbjørn et al. 2024).

The Palestinian issue shifted to the background after the Arab Uprisings of 2011 as other conflicts took center stage. Popular mobilizations against autocratic regimes that resulted in the ousting of the leaders of Tunisia, Egypt, Libya, and Yemen were foremost on the mind of the Saudi royal family since they posed a direct threat to its rule. Both Saudi Arabia and the United Arab Emirates soon embarked on a counter-revolutionary course that sought to undermine newly minted revolutionary regimes. At the same time, regional politics is increasingly sectarianized (Allinson 2022; Hashemi and Postel 2017; Potter 2013; Matthiesen 2013). Iran's intervention in Syria gave this phenomenon a major boost by transforming what began as a political uprising against Assad into a conflict with pronounced sectarian dimensions. The intervention involved political, financial, and military support for the Assad regime, which is dominated by the Alawite sect, an offshoot of Shia Islam. Tehran's policies increased Sunni-Shia tensions as many Sunni-majority opposition groups framed their rebellion as a fight against Shia dominance, which was exacerbated by Iran's explicit alignment with the regime in Damascus.

The politics of sectarian framing were also quite evident in the case of Yemen where Saudi Arabia emphasized the connection of the Houthis with Iran to garner regional and international support. Specifically, by portraying the Houthis as 'Shia' insurgents backed by Iran, Riyadh was able to frame its intervention as countering Iranian influence, which in turn resonated with Western concerns about Iran's regional ambitions via the 'axis of resistance'. However, the Houthis are predominantly Zaydi Shia Muslims, which is rather distinct from the Twelver Shia Islam practiced in Iran. Zaydi theology is historically closer to Sunni Islam in some respects.[3]

The near total neglect of the occupation of the Palestinian territories had become evident in the early 2020s when Bahrain, the UAE, Morocco, and Sudan signed the Abraham Accords. Saudi Arabia was not (yet) ready at the time, although negotiations were ongoing and the Crown Prince showed guarded optimism about a deal. In March 2022, he crossed the Rubicon by declaring: 'We don't look at Israel as an enemy, we look at it as a potential ally' (France 24, 2022). While the Saudi regime hardly paid any attention to the Palestinians, support for their cause remained undiminished among the Saudi population. Hamas's attack on 7 October

---

[3] During the first Arab 'Cold War' between Egypt and Saudi Arabia in the 1950s and 1960s, the kingdom backed the Shia Zaydi imamate against revolutionary Yemeni republicans.

2023 and the subsequent Israeli assault on Gaza had a transformational impact, however. The Palestinian issue returned to the heart of regional and Saudi politics with Arab popular sympathy for the Palestinain cause now extending across the Global South (Valbjørn et al. 2024).

Saudi Arabia and the Question of Palestine After 7 October

How did the Saudi government react to 7 October 2023 and what about Saudi public opinion? Although there is no need to go as far as Cook by claiming that Saudi Arabia has been 'mysteriously absent in the Israel-Hamas war', it can safely be said that Riyadh's disapproval of Israel's war in Gaza has remained 'tepid' (Cook 2023; Belkaid 2024). What Riyadh did in recent months was to draw on its convening power in the Arab and Islamic worlds. Conference after conference was held via the Organization of Islamic Cooperation (OIC) and the Arab League. All these summits were accompanied by grandiose tirades and pontificating final statements, but also silent inaction. There was not even a call for international sanctions on Israel like those that Russia faced after its invasion of Ukraine, or a radical re-examination of the normalization process (Belkaid 2024; Rabbani 2024; Coates Ulrichsen 2023).

Domestically, the Saudi government did take action, but not in favor of the Palestinians. For instance, the government-sponsored a social media campaign against the Palestinians, using slogans such as 'Palestinians sold their lands', 'Palestinians hate us', 'Palestine is not my cause' through to 'Israel is not my enemy' (Nasser 2024). The notorious Saud Al Qahtani, former Royal Court advisor on social media affairs and suspected of direct involvement in Saudi journalist Jamal Khashoggi's murder, used his 'army of electronic flies' to promote pro-Israel accounts (O'Toole 2022). Other well-known pro-MbS media figures, such as Saud Al Shammari, spoke flippantly on Israeli TV about the atrocities in Gaza. In an attempt to suppress pro-Palestinian dissent, Saudi security forces worked overtime. Although the government did not forbid consumer boycotts of Western brands perceived to support Israel, most public expressions of pro-Palestinian sentiment, be it a tweet, post, or video, became banned and could be cause for immediate arrest (Arab Digest 2023; Keating

2024).[4] Israeli spyware (including Pegasus) is used extensively to monitor dissidents.

It is not only through social media that the Saudi government seeks to justify its policies of rhetorical condemnation of and silent inaction toward Israel. The Saudi religious establishment—which has been fully subservient to the regime for several years now—has been used for the same purpose. This happens in numerous ways via the Muslim World League and through sermons by the imams of the Grand Mosque in Mecca, for example, who has emphasized positive relations with Jews in the past. Many an imam quoted from the Quran to explain that Palestine is also the homeland of Jews. Alternatively, they lay all the blame for the tragedy in Gaza at the doorstep of Hamas and even the Muslim Brotherhood (Zalayat 2024).[5] Just like at the time of the Oslo Accords, when Saudi Arabia quietly supported peace negotiations, Saudi religious authorities can refer to the fatwa of Sheikh Abd al-Aziz bin Baz, former Grand Mufti of Saudi Arabia, who legitimized a peace treaty with Israel based on the legal precedent of the Treaty of Hudaybiyya (628). In that treaty, Prophet Mohammed entered into a ten-year truce with Mecca, which was under control of the polytheistic Quraysh tribal leadership at the time (Podeh 2018).

Indeed, there is hardly any open opposition in Saudi Arabia to the normalization diplomacy that MBS has continued to pursue.[6] Nevertheless, pro-Palestinian sentiments prevail among broad swathes of the Saudi population. Regular polls have been conducted on this topic by the Washington Institute for Near East Policy since the Abraham Accords of 2020. The latest poll dates from November to December 2023. The trend

---

[4] This government policy may explain Saudi interlocutors' reluctance to express independent opinions on the matter of normalization. With a few exceptions, in his communications with colleagues, the writer of this article was confronted with either total silence or 'his master's voice' kind of utterances.

[5] It is well known that many Arab leaders are secretly as keen to be rid of Hamas as the Israelis are. Former Saudi spy chief, Turki al-Faisal, is less restrained in this matter and regularly shows his disgust for Hamas.

[6] Opposition to regime policies comes in different forms. Regarding normalization, three trends can be discerned: the religious dimension, using Islamic arguments to reject peace with Israel; second, the liberal opposition in exile, which warns that ties with Israel may empower the regime and increase human rights violations; and thirdly a pro-Palestinian dimension that disagrees normalization would favor the Palestinian cause (Zalayat 2024).

in public responses is clear: from mild skepticism about Saudi government policy toward Israel before '10/7' to outspoken criticism of Saudi government policy afterward. In the latest poll, 96 percent of Saudis voiced the sentiment that Arab countries should cut all ties with Israel in protest of the war in Gaza (Nereim 2023; Cleveland and Pollock 2023).[7] This is broadly in line with the results of another public opinion poll, held in 16 Arab countries and conducted by the Arab Center Washington D.C. in cooperation with The Arab Center for Research and Policy Studies (ACRPS). In that poll, 95 percent of Saudis opined that the Palestinian question concerns *all* Arabs and not just Palestinians (Arab Center, 2024). Aware of these views, fully cognizant of Saudi Arabia's prominent position in the Arab world and mindful of its leading role in the Islamic world as custodian of the Two Holy Mosques, what kind of normalization policies could the Saudi elites pursue in the context of occupation, annexation, and Gaza?

Turbid Texts

The Saudi 'ceaseless quest for security' (Safran 1985), which is reinforced by the perception of the U.S. 'leaving' the Middle East, makes the intended agreement between Riyadh and Washington the primary prize of any three-way normalization deal for the Kingdom (Pillar 2024; Coates Ulrichsen, 2024; Wight 2024). It would be modeled on the defense pacts Washington has with non-NATO countries like Japan and South Korea. In addition, the deal would include American assistance to help Saudi Arabia build a civilian nuclear reactor and give it access to more advanced weaponry. While it will be possible to agree on additional armaments for the Saudi armed forces as long as Israel's qualitative edge is not endangered, the other elements might face greater barriers in U.S. Congress.[8] However, since the election of Donald Trump, the Republicans hold a majority in Congress and it is likely that everything will be done to get

---

[7] As Zayalat rightly adds, 'Although the timing of the poll may have influenced the response, it should be noted that even before the war, 87 percent of Saudis believed that Israel could eventually be defeated, and only five percent agreed that world Jewry should be respected and that relations with them should be improved' (Zayalt 2024: 5).

[8] For a solid appraisal of Saudi Arabia's nuclear ambitions, including pathways to an atomic weapon, see Julian Reich, 'The Nuclear Kingdom: Assessing Saudi Arabia's Nuclear Behavior'.

to an agreement during the first half of Trump's second presidency, i.e., before the U.S. midterm elections in 2026 when Republicans might lose control of Congress once more (Miller 2023; Barel 2024; Byman et al. 2024; Herrera 2023; Ibish 2023, 2024).[9] However strong the Trump's 'signature aspiration' might be, success is far from assured as Saudi Arabia is not popular in the U.S.

Against the backdrop of an increasingly multipolar regional system, it should likewise be questioned that a U.S.-Saudi security deal would actually succeed in detaching Saudi Arabia from China and Russia, as envisaged by Washington (Darwich et al. 2024; Valbjørn et al. 2024; Gause 2024; Young 2024; Xiaotong 2024). For the purposes of this Chapter, however, it is more relevant to shed light on Saudi Arabia's maneuvering space regarding recognition of Israel. As noted, Saudi officials adopted tougher language in their criticism of Israeli actions after 7 October 2023. Riyadh sounds increasingly assertive in crafting formulas on the 'Significant Palestinian Component' (Ibish 2024). At its core, this would involve an Israeli commitment to a 'practical pathway'—sometimes also phrased as 'credible' or 'irreversible'—that leads to the establishment of a Palestinian state. Apart from the fact that Israel—Netanyahu or virtually any political alternative to him—wants nothing to do with this, it is unclear what such a pathway means in operational terms. Even statements by the Saudi foreign ministry that indicate normalization can only take place after 'an independent Palestinian state is recognized … and all Israeli occupation forces withdraw from Gaza' leaves room for interpretation (ICG, 2024). As the International Crisis Group notes: 'It is difficult to gauge how firm this demand is, and whether in the Saudi view other [Western] countries could recognize a Palestinian state before it exists on the ground, but for now the formula provides a lever in negotiations, especially with the U.S.' (ICG, 2024). Moreover, putting real pressure on Israel would require a completely different set of actions that go far beyond bold statements (Belkaid 2024). Lastly, as Pressman points out, there is a notable difference with the 2002 Arab Peace Initiative. The official Saudi position back then was that diplomatic relations with Israel could only be established *after the establishment* of a Palestinian state. This antecedent makes the current wording used by Washington

---

[9] A so-called plan B, according to which Saudi Arabia would be able to refrain from recognizing Israel and still get the much-wanted agreements with the U.S., is a non-starter (Saab 2024; Barel 2024).

and Riyadh look muddy and has more of a window-dressing feeling to it than that it sounds as a demand for serious concessions. Unlike in 2002, today's approach gives leverage away (i.e., Saudi recognition) because, once granted, it can no longer be used to press Israel to make meaningful concessions vis-à-vis Palestine (Pressman 2024).

A Lack of Credibility

There is little reason to doubt that the quest for Saudi-Israeli normalization will continue under a Trump presidency, the more so if a cease-fire agreement between Israel and Hamas would last. It might even become the principal goal of U.S. planning for the post-war period. Though American officials are aware that the facts on the ground have shifted, they still cling on to their pre-October 7 vision and remain bullish about the prospect of some kind of arrangement. It would advance broader U.S. interests in the Middle East. More precisely, it would advance further economic (and political) integration of Israel with the Gulf States in a manner favorable to U.S. interests. As convincingly argued by Adam Hanieh, U.S. strategy in the Middle East has become to rest upon two core pillars: Israel on one side, and the Gulf monarchies (Saudi Arabia in the first place), on the other. Since the 1990s, a variety of mechanisms have been employed to enable Israel's economic integration into the wider Middle East—such as deepening of economic liberalization, the introduction of so-called Qualifying Industrial Zones (QIZs), and the promotion of a Middle East Free Trade Area (MEFTA). 'The central axis of these inter-regional dynamics remains the connection between Israel and the Gulf states' (Hanieh 2024). If realized, Saudi-Israeli normalization would be the culmination of this process. The Abraham Accords (2020–2021), resulting in the establishment of formal diplomatic relations between several Arab countries and Israel, were another major step in that undertaking.

But, as indicated above, the road to normalization is not without obstacles. Some are more difficult to overcome than others. For the time being, the war in Gaza has blocked any transformative breakthrough toward a triangular deal that can seal the normalization process. More importantly, while Saudi emphasis on the Palestinian aspect of such a deal—which has been partly designed to serve as an optical compensation for Riyadh's inaction during the war—is greater than before, Israel's rejection of a two-state formula seems insurmountable. Yet, surprises cannot be ruled out, especially after a cease-fire agreement was reached in late January 2025 (but subsequently broken by Israel in March 2025). President Trump could use his leverage and ambition to cut deals to knock heads together in both Israel and Saudi Arabia, for example, based on a formula of 'creative fudging and constructive ambiguity' (Ibish 2024), most probably underpinned by an open-ended process toward a Palestinian 'state'. Much like in the 'Peace to Prosperity' proposal, originally launched in 2020 and purported to be a model for two states, this time the Palestinians would be under greater pressure to agree. In this formula, Israel would be allowed to annex over 30 percent of the occupied West Bank in return for the recognition of Palestinian statehood. This design of a two-state 'solution' could provide the Saudis with the much-needed pretense for normalization with Israel. Such a deal then would help Riyadh to obtain a ratified security agreement with Washington, while saving its reputation in the Arab world. The Palestinians would lose out.

Another scenario, though less likely, is that somewhere down the road the Saudis may assess their relationship with the Islamic Republic of Iran differently than they have up to this point. They might conclude at some point that the threat from Tehran is greater than that of pro-Palestinian Arab sentiment and consequently drop their advocacy of a Palestinian state based on that assessment. Like in the previous scenario, the Palestinians would be thrown under the bus. In virtually every conceivable scenario the Saudi government's narrative that normalization promotes the Palestinian cause lacks credibility and Mohammed bin Salman will have a hard time convincing his own people. However, in an autocratic context like Saudi Arabia with a crown prince as headstrong as he is ambitious, it is conceivable that some watery compromise might be agreed under pressure of Washington. For Mohammed bin Salman that would probably not be a problem as long as Saudi interests—rather than Palestinian ones—are promoted along with it.

Conflict of Interest The author has no conflict of interests to declare that are relevant to the content of this chapter.

Bibliography

Aitken, Peter. 2023. "Bret Baier Interviews Saudi Prince: Israel Peace, 9/11 Ties, Iran Nuke Fears: 'Cannot See Another Hiroshima'." Fox News, September 20, 2023.
Allinson, Jamie. 2022. *The Age of Counter-Revolution. States and Revolutions in the Middle East*. Cambridge: Cambridge University Press.
Al-Sheikh, Y.L. 2024. "A Middle East Security Pact Won't Free Palestine." Foreign Policy, May 10, 2024.
Arab Center (Washington D.C.). 2024. "Arab Public Opinion About Israel's War on Gaza." February 8, 2024.
Arab Center for Research and Policy Studies. 2024. "Saudi-Israel Normalization Persists Amid Gaza War." The Unit for Political Studies, May 3, 2024.
Arab Digest. 2023. "Popular Support of the Palestinians Is a Problem for MBS." Fair Observer, November 10, 2023.
Barel, Zvi. 2024. "Saudi Arabia and the U.S. Want a Mutual Defense Pact—With or Without Israel." *Haaretz*, May 2, 2024.
Belkaid, Akram. 2024. "The Arab World's Resounding Failure". *Le Monde Diplomatique*, March 2024.
Byman, Daniel, Doreen Horschig, and Elizabeth Kos. 2024. "Will Saudi Arabia Get the Bomb?" *Foreign Affairs*, May 6, 2024.
Cleveland, Catherine, David Pollock. 2023. "New Poll Sheds Light on Saudi Views of Israel-Hamas War." The Washington Institute, December 21, 2023.
Coates Ulrichsen, Kristian. 2023. "GCC States and the War on Gaza: Positions, Perceptions, and Interests." Arab Center for Research and Policy Studies, November 22, 2023.
Coates Ulrichsen, Kristian. 2024. "Difficulties Facing a US-Saudi Agreement." Arab Center Washington D.C.: Policy Analysis, June 25, 2024.
Cook, Steven. 2023. "Saudi Arabia Is Mysteriously Absent in the Israel-Hamas War." *Foreign Policy*, October 26, 2023.
Cook, Steven. 2024. "The Real Reason for Saudi Arabia's Pivot to Iran." *Foreign Policy*, December 2, 2024.
Darwich, May, F. Gregory Gause III, Waleed Hazbun, Curtis Ryan, and Morten Valbjørn. 2022. "International Relations and Regional (In)security." In: Marc Lynch, Julian Schwedler, Sean Yom, eds., *The Political Science of the Middle East. Theory and Research Since the Arab Uprisings*. New York: Oxford University Press, pp. 86-107.
Dassa Kaye, Dalia. 2023. "The Case Against an Israeli-Saudi Deal. America Shouldn't Push for a Hollow Accord". *Foreign Affairs*, August 17, 2023.
ECFR. 2024. "Wars and shadow wars: What are Europe's options in the Middle East?" European Council on Foreign Relations, Annual Council Meeting 2024.

Fantappie, Maria, Vali Nasr. 2024. "The Dangerous Push for Israeli-Saudi Normalization." *Foreign Affairs*, July 11, 2024.
France 24. 2022. "Saudi Crown Prince Says Israel 'Potential Ally'", March 3, 2022.
Gause, Gregory III. 2024. "The Limits of a U.S.-Saudi Security Deal. Don't Expect Riyadh to Take Washington's Side Against China and Russia." Foreign Affairs, August 2, 2024.
Hamid, Shadi. 2022. *The Problem of Democracy. America, the Middle East, and the Rise and Fall of an Idea*. New York: Oxford University Press.
Hanieh, Adam. 2017. "The Qatar Crisis." Jacobin, 26 June 2017.
Hanieh, Adam.. 2024. "Framing Palestine. Israel, the Gulf States, and American Power in the Middle East." Amsterdam: Transnational Institute. June 13, 2024.
Hashemi, Nader, and Danny Postel, eds., 2017. *Sectarianization. Mapping the New Politics of the Middle East*. London: Hurst & Company.
Hashemi, Nader. 2020. "The Chimera of Peace Between Israel and the Arab World: A Critique of the Abraham Accords." *Occasional Paper Series*, Paper No. 10. Denver: Josef Korbel School of International Studies. Center for Middle East Studies, October 2020.
Herrera, Manuel. 2023. "Saudi Arabia's Nuclear Ambitions: Frozen Once Again?" IAI Commentaries. Rome: Instituto Affari Internationale, November 29, 2023.
Ibish, Hussein. 2023. "Obstacles From All Sides Face a U.S.-Saudi Arabia-Israel Grand Bargain." Arab Gulf States Institute in Washington, (blog), August 14, 2023.
Ibish, Hussein. 2024. "For Saudi Arabia, There's a Dealmaking Opportunity With Trump." Arab Gulf States Institute in Washington, November 22, 2024.
International Crisis Group. 2024. "The Danger of Regional War in the Middle East." Commentary. Brussels: ICG. February 27, 2024.
Jones, Clive, Yoel Guzansky. 2019. *Fraternal Enemies. Israel and the Gulf Monarchies*. London: Hurst & Company.
Keating, Joshua. 2024. "The Longshot Plan to End the War in Gaza and Bring Peace to the Middle East." VOX, May 3, 2024.
Kostiner, Joseph. 2005. "Coping With Regional Challenges: A Case Study of Crown Prince Abdullah's Peace Initiative", in Paul Aarts & Gerd Nonneman, eds., *Saudi Arabia in the Balance. Political Economy, Society, Foreign Affairs*. London: Hurst & Co, pp. 352-371.
Kurtzner, Daniel C., Aaron David Miller. 2023. "Getting Israeli-Saudi Rapprochement Right." *Foreign Affairs*, August 21, 2023.
Miller, Aaron David. 2023. "Is Saudi-Israeli Normalization Worth It?" *Foreign Policy*, June 5, 2023.

Matthiesen, Toby. 2013. *Sectarian Gulf. Bahrain, Saudi Arabia, and the Arab Spring That Wasn't.* Stanford: Stanford University Press.
Nasser, Safa. 2024. "The Winds of Normalization: Reshaping Saudi Arabia's Image." Sada. Carnegie Endowment for International Peace, March 12, 2024.
Nereim, Vivian. 2023. "Saudis Overwhelmingly Oppose Ties With Israel, Poll Finds." *The New York Times*, December 22, 2023.
O'Toole, Megan. 2022. Digital authoritarianism: The rise of electronic armies in the Middle East. Middle East Eye (blogpost). https://www.middleeasteye.net/opinion/middle-east-digital-authoritarianism-electronic-armies-rise
Parsi, Trita. 2007. *Treacherous Alliance. The Secret Dealings of Israel, Iran, and the U.S.* New York and London: Yalebooks.
Pillar, Paul. 2024. "Implications of a Security Pact With Saudi Arabia." Quincy Institute for Responsible Statecraft, Quincy Brief #58.
Podeh, Elie, 2018. "Saudi Arabia and Israel: From Secret to Public Engagement, 1948-2018." *Middle East Journal*, 72:4, Autumn 2018: 563-586.
Podeh, Elie, 2024a. "Normalization With Saudi Arabia Looks Unlikely, But We Should Try Anyway." *Jerusalem Post*, February 25, 2024.
Podeh, Elie, 2024b. "Why Israel Can't Miss Yet Another Opportunity to Normalize Ties With Saudi Arabia." *Haaretz*, June 1, 2024.
Potter, Lawrence G., eds., 2013., eds., 2013. *Sectarian Politics in the Gulf.* London: Hurst & Company.
Pressman, Jeremy. 2024. "A Saudi Accord: Implications for Israel-Palestine." Quincy Institute for Responsible Statecraft, Quincy Brief #61. July 22, 2024.
Rabbani, Mouin. 2024. "All Shook Up: Regional Dynamics of the Gaza War', in Jamy Stern-Weiner, ed., *Deluge. Gaza and Israel. From Crisis to Cataclysm.* New York: OR Books, pp. 157-167.
Reich, Julian. 2024. "The Nuclear Kingdom: Assessing Saudi Arabia's Nuclear Behavior." *Georgetown Security Studies Review*, December 18, 2024.
Rosenberg, David E. 2024. "Why Arab States Haven't Broken With Israel." *Foreign Policy*, April 19, 2024.
Ross, Dennis. 2024. "Biden's Middle East Moonshot. The Time Is Right for an Israeli-Saudi Deal That Could Help End the War in Gaza." *Foreign Affairs*, August 7, 2024.
Saab, Bilal Y. 2024 "A U.S.-Saudi Deal Without Israel Is an Illusion", *Foreign Policy*, May 3, 2024.
Safran, Nadav. 1985. *Saudi Arabia. The Ceaseless Quest for Security.* Ithaca, NY: Cornell University Press.
Shtayyeh, Mohammad. 2024. "The Best Way to End Israel's War in Gaza. Reviving the Arab Peace Initiative Would Resolve the Conflict—and Build a New Reality." *Foreign Affairs*, July 4, 2024.
Valbjørn, Morten, André Bank, and May Darwich. 2024. "Forward to the Past? Regional Repercussions of the Gaza War." *Middle East Policy*, 2024: 1-15.

Wight, David M. 2024. "How a Defense Treaty Would Transform the U.S.-Saudi Relationship." DAWN, October 30, 2024.
Wright, David M. 2024. "The U.S.-Saudi Agreement Is a Fool's Errand." *Foreign Policy*, May 29, 2024.
Young, Karen. 2024. "The Myth of the Middle Eastern Economy. How Economic Fragmentation Has Insulated the Region From the War in Gaza." *Foreign Affairs*, July 31, 2024.
Xiaotong, Yang. 2024. "Better offer needed if the US wants to pull Saudi Arabia away from China." Amwaj, November 26, 2024.
Zalayat, Ilan. 2024. "Peace Amid War: Saudi Arabia's Public Opinion Challenge in Promoting Normalization with Israel." Special Publication. Tel Aviv: The Institute for National Security Studies.

Open Access This chapter is licensed under the terms of the Creative Commons Attribution 4.0 International License (http://creativecommons.org/licenses/by/4.0/), which permits use, sharing, adaptation, distribution and reproduction in any medium or format, as long as you give appropriate credit to the original author(s) and the source, provide a link to the Creative Commons license and indicate if changes were made.

The images or other third party material in this chapter are included in the chapter's Creative Commons license, unless indicated otherwise in a credit line to the material. If material is not included in the chapter's Creative Commons license and your intended use is not permitted by statutory regulation or exceeds the permitted use, you will need to obtain permission directly from the copyright holder.

CHAPTER 12

Let's Talk About Peace

Omar Dweik and Erwin van Veen

Abstract Neither the scenario evidence nor the stakeholder analysis included in this volume supports the view that there is an end in sight for the Israeli occupation of Palestine. Instead, the massacre of 7 October 2023 and the wholesale slaughter unfolding in its wake have relegated talk about 'solving the conflict' to the realm of fantasy. If further suffering is to be minimized, a first necessary step is the recreation of conditions that enable conversations about how occupation can be ended. In contrast with the habitual approach, peacebuilding has to proceed peacekeeping and peacemaking. Even this, however, requires solid international intervention, of which the likelihood is low at present. For now, Palestinian survival and resistance depend on steadfastness and resilience. International intervention should have four major components if it is to be effective, according to the analysis contained in this volume: (1) bring pressure to bear on Israel to raise the cost of occupation and its annexation policies. Non-state social and economic actors seem best

---

O. Dweik (✉)
University of Tilburg, Tilburg, Netherlands
e-mail: o.dweik@tilburguniversity.edu

E. van Veen
Clingendael Institute, Wassenaar, Netherlands

© The Author(s) 2025
E. van Veen (Ed.), *The Future of the Occupation of the Palestinian Territories after Gaza*,
https://doi.org/10.1007/978-3-031-93798-9_12

placed to do so; (2) support long-term dialogue, activism and media coverage of conflict framing, mutual grievances and possible solutions; (3) link Arab–Israeli normalization and Iran-Gulf rapprochement with ending occupation; (4) revitalize Palestinian leadership, for example by rejuvenating and re-empowering the PLO.

Keywords Human rights · Ending occupation · BDS · PLO · Palestinian authority · Israeli-Arab normalization · Iran-Arab rapprochement

About Scenarios and Stakeholders

The aim of this book is to explore what the future of occupation might look like after Gaza, so that the international community can base its efforts to bring a just resolution of Israel's unlawful occupation closer on the basis of decent analysis (see ICJ 2024). It does so by means of two methods. To begin with, it sketches scenarios for the future of occupation that take account of the tragedy of 7 October 2023, its destructive aftermath as well as decades-old legacies and practices of occupation. This is not an easy task as 7 October 2023 and the events beyond turned many assumptions about occupation to dust, such as the idea that regional normalization could proceed without resolving the Palestinian issue, the notion that Israel could 'manage' occupation and gradual annexation to advantage, the mantra that a two-state solution remained within reach and the hope that mass killings and forced displacement had become ghosts of the twentieth century.

Even though the future remains uncertain and unpredictable, scenarios invite thinking about what it can look like under different sets of circumstances. It is with this logic in mind that Chapter 2 outlined four occupation scenarios for the years to come: (1) 'colonial-style suffering' (i.e., continuation of occupation as it was prior to 7 October 2023); (2) 'squid game' (Palestinian militant resistance across the West Bank with a measure of international pressure holding Israeli counter-violence in check); (3) 'revisionist Zionism comes true' (relatively peaceful full annexation due to the decimation of Hamas, disarmament of the Palestinian Authority (PA) and the absence of Iran); and (4) 'Gaza on the Jordan river' (full annexation triggering Palestinian militant resistance that meets the same violent Israeli methods used in Gaza, unrestrained by the international community).

The fact that these scenarios are all bleak is based on the increasingly uncompromising views and actions of both Israel's political elites and large parts of its population toward the Palestinians, as discussed in Chapters 1 and 5 (see also Mordechai 2025). Annexation and repression are nowadays considered either as Israeli rights or as route to short-term safety given the searing memory of the massacre of 7 October 2023. The bleakness of the scenarios is also based on the lack of meaningful action by the international community to halt Israeli atrocities as it watched Gaza burn, its residents being slaughtered and its infrastructure destroyed in reprisal for 7 October 2023, which stands in stark contrast with the international community's rightful condemnation of the killing of hundreds of non-combatants by Hamas on that fateful day. Instead, the US and a few Western allies have enabled the carnage in Gaza in a Faustian pact that does Goethe proud (the policies and actions of the United States are extensively analyzed in Chapter 6).[1] Finally, the bleakness of the scenarios is based on the fact that Hamas has been decimated and the Palestinian Authority (PA) is on the ropes, depriving the Palestinians of leaders that can walk the fine line between peaceful and militant resistance (see Chapters 3 and 4 respectively). In short, bleakness results from Israel's explicit agenda of forced displacement, annexation and mass killing; international indifference (or even support for Israel); and the absence of Palestinian leadership that can mount effective resistance to occupation. Even though prominent Palestinian voices such as Khalid Elgindy and Sari Nusseibeh have recently expressed hope regarding the end of conflict and occupation (Elgindy 2025; Kester 2025), neither the scenario evidence nor the stakeholder analysis conducted for this volume support such a view in the practical sense or in the short-term. It will require a good measure of solid international intervention to turn the tide in the near future, of which the likelihood is low.

The second method the book applies is analysis of the interests, past policies and actions, as well as future intentions and capabilities of the main stakeholders of occupation. The volume distinguishes between stakeholders directly involved in occupation (Israel, Hamas, Fatah/Palestinian Authority and the United States), neighbors of Israel

---

[1] See also Garcia Navarro (2025) for a morally revealing account of Secretary of State Blinken's take on the events in Israel and Gaza from 7 October 2023 onwards.

(Hezbollah, Egypt and Jordan) and significant regional actors (Saudi Arabia and Iran). Written by subject matter experts, the essays about each of these stakeholders produce several insights. To begin with, Israel has established even greater conflict dominance in the near term due to the decimation of both Hamas and Hezbollah while also dealing hard blows to Iran and enjoying peak levels of US support (see Chapters 5 and 6). Paired with an unapologetic and accelerating annexationist agenda, this indicates Israel will seek to leverage its military successes into land gains before the bill of unresolved security and governance problems, international isolation and renewed Palestinian resistance comes due in a domestic context that is fragmented, polarized and low on trust.

Another insight amounts to a variation of the saying that 'the Kurds have no friends but the mountains,' emphasizing in other words Palestinian self-reliance as a core element of near term resilience and survival. The stakeholder analysis of Hezbollah (Chapter 7) and Iran (Chapter 10) shows that these actors primarily use the Palestinian cause in support of their own legitimacy and priorities. They will, as a figure of speech, gladly fight Israel to the last Palestinian even though both have also made sacrifices, in particular in support of Hamas. The stakeholder analyses of Egypt (Chapter 8), Jordan (Chapter 9) and Saudi Arabia (Chapter 11) highlight that these countries are neither able nor willing to translate their rhetorical professions of empathy with Palestinian plight and criticism of Israel into meaningful action. Egypt's military regime has become too dependent on Israel to dissent too strongly, Jordan's monarchy is caught between US/Saudi interests and an indignant population while Mohammed bin Salman has paused normalization with Israel mostly to avoid domestic and international-Islamic backlash. It is correct to point out that Egypt has prevented forced displacement of Palestinians from Gaza to the Sinai and that Saudi Arabia has put its normalization trajectory on hold, but this only puts a minimum floor under the occupation enterprise without addressing its continuation or excesses.

A final insight is that both existing formulas for Palestinian resistance against occupation have run out of road. The militancy of Hamas has led to a violent Israeli response of apocalyptic proportions while Fatah's strategy of collaboration with Israel via the Palestinian Authority under President Abbas has merely enabled Israel to take what it can while demanding more. Both formulas are also highly authoritarian, non-accountable and exclude significant parts of the Palestinian community, regional as well as global, including its energies, creativity and influence.

Together, these insights confirm the validity of the scenarios outlined in Chapter 2 and suggest the more violent scenarios are likelier at present than the less violent ones—i.e., 'squid game' and 'Gaza on the Jordan river' rather than 'colonial-style suffering' or 'revisionist Zionism comes true.' More importantly, these insights provide a basis for identifying enabling conditions and associated actions that might bring an end to occupation and the vicious cycles of violence and insecurity that maintain it.[2] However, the massacre of 7 October 2023 and the likely genocide unfolding in its wake (see: Amnesty 2024; Albanese 2024; Mordechai 2025), have relegated talk about 'solving the conflict' to the realm of fantasy. What is needed instead as a first step is the recreation of conditions that enable debate and conversation about how occupation can be ended. In brief, and in contrast with the habitual approach, peacebuilding will have to proceed peacekeeping and peacemaking.[3] Based on the analysis contained in this volume, the next section identifies such enabling conditions and outlines practical actions that the international community can take to help bring these conditions about.

NECESSARY CONDITIONS TO ENABLE CONVERSATIONS ABOUT ENDING OCCUPATION

The starting point for thinking about conditions that can enable conversations about ending occupation lies in the justness of the Palestinian cause in terms of international law. This concerns both 'hard law' in the form of the advisory opinions of the International Court of Justice of 2004 and 2024 on the illegality of the Israeli separation barrier and the unlawfulness of Israel's occupation as a whole, and 'soft law' in the form of

---

[2] A notable point here is that achieving a maximum level of Israeli security by means of full occupation and repression creates a minimal level of Palestinian security. This will create new security threats to Israel that will likely produce a level of security that is lower than accepting a decent (but not maximum) level of security for both Israelis and Palestinians.

[3] Peace-building is the process of transforming social relations to address the grievances which underlie conflicts through platforms of understanding and dialogue, among other measures. Peace-making refers to the dispute-resolution mechanisms aimed at ending hostilities. Finally, peace-keeping involves the monitoring, separation and regulation of the conflict parties so as to evade further cycles of violence (Bickmore and Awad 2023). See: https://www.oise.utoronto.ca/peacebuildingeducation/peace-keeping-peace-making-or-peace-building (Accessed 7 July 2025).

dozens of UN General Assembly and UN Security Council resolutions such as A/ES-10/L.31/Rev.1 of 13 December 2024 and UNSC RES 2234 of 23 December 2016. However, the current power imbalance and geopolitical developments since 1967 make realization of these rights in their fullest form impossible in the near future, and difficult in the long term. The practical implication is that peacebuilding efforts will have to be based on Palestinian rights but must also consider Israeli fears and needs, and take account of geopolitical realities such as the contested status of Iran, the rise of the Arab states on the Persian Gulf and the dire socio-economic conditions in much of the Levant (see Chapter 1). In other words, there will have to be flexibility with regard to *how* rights can be realized. For example, it is hard to see the return of millions of Palestinians to their ancestral homelands within the 1967 boundaries of Israel in the near term. This right might only be satisfied gradually, through a token number of returns, or through a compensation scheme financed in part by the international community and in part by Israel.

Another necessary condition to enable a conversation about ending occupation is to create sustained and tangible international pressure on Israel to level the playing field on which subsequent negotiations can take place. The purpose of such pressure is to make it clear to Israel's political elites and the Israeli people that the continuation of occupation and annexation comes with costs in the form of international isolation, ruptured relations and sanctions. Without such pressure, they have no reason to adjust their occupation and annexation policies that enjoy tacit consent from Israel's center-left and hardcore support from its extreme right (see Chapter 5). There are two main obstacles to realizing this condition: the United States (see Chapter 6) and collective barriers to action. Many countries will be reluctant to risk their relation with the United States, especially under the Trump presidency, by putting political, social and/or economic pressure on Israel (see Chapters 6, 8, 9 and 11). Moreover, a diverse global coalition will be needed to create such pressure since blocs like the European Union and Arab League are too divided. Yet, worldwide consensus is hard to realize.

Considering both obstacles makes it likely that an international solidarity movement of activists, union leaders, journalists, intellectuals and ordinary people moved by injustice has the better chances of propelling a Boycott Divestment and Sanctions-style campaign forward, i.e., dissuade pension funds and other large investors to invest in Israel by an appeal to their corporate social responsibility and, if needed, by naming and shaming; convince banks to break financial ties with Israeli financial institutions; convince consumers and businesses to avoid Israeli products and companies; as well as getting educational institutes to pause ties with Israeli organizations—excepting trilateral pro-peace research projects between Israeli, Palestinian and foreign universities. In addition, national solidarity movements could start legal proceedings under local laws against representatives and agents of the Israeli state that might be guilty of war crimes given the prevailing impunity for such deeds in Israel itself. As long as cases are prosecuted in a transparent manner by independent legal systems that maintain due process, individuals will have nothing to fear if they are as innocent as the Israeli state proclaims.

The flipside of more coercive pressure, as outlined above, is soft pressure that confronts but also convinces. A campaign of long-term financial and diplomatic support for Israeli and Palestinian human rights NGO's, peacebuilding NGOs, labor unions, syndicates and joint pro-peace research projects by Israeli and Palestinian universities can be undertaken by a coalition of European and Arab countries under the banner of putting human rights front and center. It could see countries like Spain, Ireland, Norway and perhaps even France team up with Turkey, Jordan, Qatar and Oman. The purpose of such an undertaking is to create mutual understanding of grievances on both sides, which is not to say that these have equal weight. This is a necessary precondition to foster societal change among important segments of Israeli and Palestinian societies and aims to create openings for peacemaking at the people level. Discourse has a significant impact on the escalation or de-escalation of conflicts after all (Chiluwa 2021). A protracted campaign on social media, traditional media, in universities and through street protests can change the 'tone of voice' in political discourse.

A further necessary condition to enable new conversations about ending occupation is to diplomatically synchronize conversations and actions about further rapprochement between Iran and the Arab states on the Persian Gulf, normalization of Arab–Israeli ties and ending occupation. 7 October 2023 showed that Arab–Israeli normalization is difficult without resolving the Palestinian issue. A key driver of the Hamas attack was the imminence of a Saudi-Israeli deal and Israel's destruction of Gaza has pushed such a deal further into the future (see Chapter 11). Despite its recent beating, Iran retains powerful incentives to spoil any repeat of the Israeli-Saudi normalization process and it will likely find a ready mass of radicalized Palestinians at its disposal to do so (see Chapter 10). Hence,

Israel's integration into the Middle East by normalizing its relations with key Arab states requires resolution of the security conundrum that Iran poses, as well as an end to occupation. Linkage between these issues should be welcomed as it creates the potential of transforming a zero-sum game into a positive-sum game. Iran can have its economic isolation diminished in return for constraints on its nuclear program and the armed groups associated with it; Israel can gain in security by a diminished threat from Iran, realize greater prosperity through regional integration and enjoy an uplift in moral standing by ending occupation; and the Arab states can gain in prosperity by engagement with Israel as well as enjoy an uplift in moral status by facilitating an end to occupation.[4] However, this set of outcomes can only be achieved when a few dedicated countries, including the United States, Iran and Saudi Arabia, take the lead in patiently working toward a package deal, and when both hard and soft pressure is simultaneously brought to bear on Israel. Absent the latter, Israel is likely to try once more to normalize relations with Saudi Arabia under the Trump presidency without resolving the Palestinian issue. But this formula is bound to end in tragedy similar to 7 October 2023, despite the decimation of Hamas and Hezbollah. For example, the Saudi royal family instead of Israeli kibbutzniks could become the next target of spoilers prepared to act with violence.

A final necessary condition for enabling new conversations about ending occupation is the revitalization of Palestinian leadership given the current state of Hamas, Fatah and the Palestinian Authority, in particular their repressive practices toward their own populations. New leadership can subsequently develop modalities of resistance that are in line with international law, reflect the priorities of the Palestinian population and are conducted in a manner that makes greater international support attractive. With much of Hamas' military capabilities eroded and Fatah's reputation tarnished by corruption and collaboration, both parties have incentives to make concessions. Yet, as Chapter 4 indicates, the pivotal moment will be the departure of President Abbas. Once that happens, one possible avenue to realize changes in leadership and leadership style is the revitalization of the PLO by resetting its relation with the Palestinian Authority so that the former becomes the executive decision-maker

---

[4] An important point underpinning this logic is the failure of the US policy to reduce Iran as a security threat by means of economic sanctions.

and the latter an administrative agency, and by incorporating Hamas (or a successor) into the PLO.[5]

The relation between the PLO and PA can be reformed if the PA's international funders insist on it as condition for their financial support and, moreover, re-organize their support in a way that breaks Israel's financial chokehold over the PA.[6] This can be realized through the creation of a trust fund linked to the PLO, underpinned by a multi-year concessional loan by donors that is retroactively repaid based on Israeli tax transfers actually received by the PA. The trust fund has to be managed by a third-party intermediary that is independent of the Israeli banking system, knows how to put meaningful anti-corruption measures in place (e.g., tranche payments being dependent on actioned audit reports) and has limited exposure in the United States. For example, a country like Norway can commission a (semi-)commercial entity. The trust fund should feature a board that includes PLO representatives, Palestinian diaspora representatives and funders. If such a trust fund goes hand in hand with the PA joining the World Bank, more efficient service delivery becomes a possibility.

The inclusion of Hamas into the PLO sounds like an odd argument to make after the 7 October 2023 massacre, and yet Hamas retains substantial support among Palestinians just as Israeli extreme right-wing parties that encourage settler violence do in Israel. But a key difference is that Hamas is in principle engaged in lawful resistance against occupation as long as it respects the laws of war (e.g., not intentionally targeting noncombatant civilians), whereas Israeli violence to maintain occupation is unlawful as per the ICJ advisory opinion of 19 July 2024. Nevertheless, in exchange for joining the PLO, Hamas will have to agree to the integration of its militants into the (reformed) PA security services and publicly rescind remaining rhetoric, principles or statements that call for the destruction of the Israeli state or the Jewish people, as it partially sought to do with its policy document of 2017 (Baconi 2022). This will make it harder for Hamas to operate on its own or to benefit from Iranian support without, however, disabling its ability to resist occupation.

---

[5] Even this route remains precarious, however, due to the low levels of trust among Palestinian youth in both the PA and PLO. It might be that entirely new structures are required that will emerge from the grassroots.

[6] Which is the result of the Israeli practice of withholding PA tax revenues that the Paris Protocol of 1994 obliges it to transfer without conditions. See Chapter 4.

Final Considerations

In his book 'Memoirs of a Jewish extremist,' Yossi Klein Halevi (2014) asks 'How does one live as a Jew in this world after the Holocaust?' From this perspective, one can argue that the creation of the State of Israel as a safe haven for the Jewish people has been both a blessing and a curse. The latter is arguably the result of the inability of Israel's political leaders to come to terms with the Arab/Palestinians population that inhabited the same lands for centuries prior to the founding of modern-day Israel. In a cruel twist of history, forced displacement and expulsion at creation have combined with the ethno-nationalism of occupation that, after 7 October 2023, has even produced an Israeli version of the 'banality of evil' (Pappé 2007; Morris 2011; Arendt 2022; Mordechai 2025).

Against such a dark and complex context, peacebuilding efforts must avoid the mistake of having unattainable expectations. Notions such as a one-state 'solution' (of the repressive or the equal rights variety), a two-state 'solution' or a confederal 'solution' (Dweik 2021) are vistas at present. The core goal of peacebuilding is to create the conditions that allow for an informed, ethical and empathetic discussion about a form of co-existence and governance that can provide basic human, civil and political rights for all those living between the Jordan River and Mediterranean Sea. The alternative is a variation of Thucydides' Melian dialogue in which 'the strong do what they can and the weak suffer what they must.' We have witnessed where that leads.

Conflict of Interest The authors have no conflict of interests to declare that are relevant to the content of this chapter.

References

Albanese, Francesca. 2024. "Anatomy of a Genocide." UN report Human Rights Council A/HRC/55/73. Geneva: UN Special Rapporteur on the situation of human rights in the Palestinian territories occupied since 1967. https://doc uments.un.org/doc/undoc/gen/g24/046/11/pdf/g2404611.pdf.

Amnesty International. 2024. "'You Feel Like You Are Subhuman': Israel's Genocide Against Palestinians in Gaza." MDE 15/8668/2024. London: Amnesty International. https://www.amnesty.org/en/latest/news/2024/12/amnesty-international-concludes-israel-is-committing-genocide-against-palestinians-in-gaza/.

Arendt, Hannah. 2022. *Eichmann in Jerusalem: A Report on the Banality of Evil*. Modern Classics. London: Penguin Books.
Baconi, Tareq. 2022. *Hamas Contained: The Rise and Pacification of Palestinian Resistance*. First paperback printing, 2022. Stanford, California: Stanford University Press.
Bickmore, Kathy and Yomna Awad. 2023. *Peace—Keeping, Peace—Making, or Peace Building*. Toronto: University of Toronto.
Chiluwa, Innocent. 2021. *Discourse and Conflict: Analysing Text and Talk of Conflict, Hate and Peace-building*. Cham: Springer International Publishing.
Dweik, Omar. 2021. *Peace to Unity: A Framework for Peace between Palestine and Israel*. Sparsnäs: Irene Publishing.
Elgindy, Khaled. 2025. "The Case for Hope for Palestinians." *The New York Times*, January 3, 2025, sec. Opinion. https://www.nytimes.com/2025/01/03/opinion/palestinians-israel-gaza.html.
Garcia-Navarro, Lulu. 2025. "Antony Blinken Insists He and Biden Made the Right Calls." *The New York Times*, January 4, 2025, sec. Magazine. https://www.nytimes.com/2025/01/04/magazine/antony-blinken-interview.html.
International Court of Justice. 2024. "Legal Consequences Arising from the Policies and Practices of Israel in the Occupied Palestinian Territory, Including East Jerusalem." Advisory Opinion General List No. 186. The Hague: International Court of Justice. https://www.icj-cij.org/sites/default/files/case-related/186/186-20240719-adv-01-00-en.pdf.
Kester, Sacha. 2025. "Deze Palestijnse onderhandelaar blijft geloven in vrede: 'De behoefte aan een normaal leven is heel krachtig.'" *de Volkskrant*, January 3, 2025, sec. Interview with Sari Nusseibeh. https://www.volkskrant.nl/buitenland/deze-palestijnse-onderhandelaar-blijft-geloven-in-vrede-de-behoefte-aan-een-normaal-leven-is-heel-krachtig~b0fe8453/.
Klein Halevi, Yossi. 2014. *Memoirs of a Jewish Extremist: The Story of a Transformation*. First Harper/Perennial paperback edition. New York: Harper/Perennial.
Mordechai, Lee. 2025. "Bearing Witness to the Israel-Gaza War." 2023–2025. https://witnessing-the-gaza-war.com/.
Morris, Benny. 2011. *Righteous Victims: A History of the Zionist-Arab Conflict, 1881 - 2001*. Westminster: Knopf Doubleday Publishing Group.
Pappé, Ilan. 2007. *The Ethnic Cleansing of Palestine*. Repr. Oxford: Oneworld Publ.

Open Access This chapter is licensed under the terms of the Creative Commons Attribution 4.0 International License (http://creativecommons.org/licenses/by/4.0/), which permits use, sharing, adaptation, distribution and reproduction in any medium or format, as long as you give appropriate credit to the original author(s) and the source, provide a link to the Creative Commons license and indicate if changes were made.

The images or other third party material in this chapter are included in the chapter's Creative Commons license, unless indicated otherwise in a credit line to the material. If material is not included in the chapter's Creative Commons license and your intended use is not permitted by statutory regulation or exceeds the permitted use, you will need to obtain permission directly from the copyright holder.

Index

A
Abbas, Mahmoud, 60–67
Abraham Accords, 95, 154, 164, 168, 170, 173
Abu Obaida, 5, 30
Al-Aqsa Flood, 137
Al Qahtani, 169
Al-Qassam, 46
American Israel Public Affairs Committee, 92
annexation, 21, 28, 29, 31, 33
apartheid, 29, 31, 33
Arab League, 166, 167, 169
Arab Peace Initiative, 167, 172
Arab Uprisings, 166, 167
axis of resistance, 9, 11, 21, 28, 34, 47, 105, 149

B
Balfour Declaration, 130
Barghouti, Marwan, 61
battle of Al-Karameh, the, 133
Beirut port explosion, 107
blockade, 116

Boycott Divestment and Sanctions, 184

C
chimera, 47
civil society organizations, 51, 52
conflict management, 80
custodianship, 134, 136–139, 141

D
Dahlan, Muhammad, 61
decisive plan, 72, 79–81
Dolphinus Holdings, 118

E
Egyptian regime, 123
Emirate of Transjordan, 131
ethnic cleansing, 119
evangelical Christians, 91

F
far-right, 72–74, 77, 78, 80–82

Fatah, 3, 8, 13, 45, 46, 48, 49,
    59–63, 65–67, 181, 182, 186
forced displacement, 48, 49

G
Gaza, 102
genocide, 3, 6
Grand Mosque
    Grand Mufti, 170

H
Hamas, 2–5, 8, 10, 11, 13, 59,
    61–63, 65–68, 121, 149, 153,
    180–182, 185–187
Hamas governance, 45
Hezbollah, 9, 10, 13, 102
hilltop youth, 28

I
intelligence cooperation, 166
International Court of Justice (ICJ),
    6, 20, 22
International Criminal Court, 20
international law, 183, 186
Iran, 9–11, 13, 89, 90, 92, 93, 103
Iron Dome, 90
Islamic State, 90, 93

J
Jericho Conference, 132
Jewish terror, 78
joint operations room, 152
Jordanian Arab Legion, 132
judicial reform, 28, 81

M
Madrid Peace Conference, 134
Majdal Shams, 107

military assistance, 93
Mohammed bin Salman, 164, 165,
    167
municipalities, 50
Muslim Brotherhood, 122

N
Nasrallah, 104, 109
normalization, 164, 167, 169–173,
    180, 182, 185

O
occupation, 180–188
oil embargo, 166, 167
Organization of Islamic Cooperation
    (OIC), 169
Oslo Accords, 7, 46, 52, 58, 72, 75,
    78, 134
outposts, 7, 75, 78

P
Palestinian Islamic Jihad (PIJ), 148
Palestinian Liberation Organisation
    (PLO), 48, 58–60, 65, 68, 131
Palestinian resistance, 182
Palestinian state, 172
Paris Protocol, 79
peacemaking, 183, 188
Peace to Prosperity, 95, 174
polls, 170

Q
Quartet, 62

R
Rafah, 120
reconstruction, 30, 33, 34
relationship, 88–90, 92–94

resistance, 4, 5, 9–11, 150
resistance diplomacy, 153
Revisionist Zionism, 27
revolutionary ideology, 148

S
sanctions, 78–81
scenario planning, 22–25, 27
scenarios, 180, 181, 183
security coordination, 63
security partner, 89, 93
settlements, 73, 75, 77
settlers, 4, 7, 8
settler violence, 73, 75, 77, 78
Sinai, 117
Sisi
  El-Sisi, 116
Smotrich, 72, 74–76, 78–81
social media, 169, 170
soft pressure, 185, 186
stakeholders, 180, 181

statehood, 63, 64
Syria, 104

T
talk show, 118
terrorism, 2, 4
Trump, Donald, 88, 91, 94–96
two-state solution, 8, 12, 156

U
United States, 135–137
unity of the fronts, 106
unity of the two Banks, 131
unliveable, 44, 51
UN resolution 1701, 111

W
Wadi Araba peace treaty, 135
West Bank, 21, 27–34

The manufacturer's authorised representative in the EU is Springer Nature Customer Service Centre GmbH, Europaplatz 3, 69115 Heidelberg, Germany. If you have any concerns regarding our products, please contact ProductSafety@springernature.com

Printed and bound by CPI Group (UK) Ltd, Croydon, CR0 4YY

03/03/2026

02063910-0003